TEACHING THE SILK ROAD

SUNY series in Asian Studies Development

Roger T. Ames and Peter D. Hershock, editors

TEACHING THE SILK ROAD

A Guide for College Teachers

Edited by

Jacqueline M. Moore

and

Rebecca Woodward Wendelken

Published by State University of New York Press, Albany

Printed in the United States of America

For information, contact State University of New York Press, Albany, NY
www.sunypress.edu

Production by Kelli W. LeRoux
Marketing by Michael Campochiaro

Library of Congress Cataloging-in-Publication Data

Teaching the Silk Road: a guide for college teachers/edited by Jacqueline M.
   Moore and Rebecca Woodward Wendelken.
       p. cm.
   ISBN 978-1-4384-3103-1 (hardcover: alk. paper)
   ISBN 978-1-4384-3102-4 (pbk.: alk. paper)
   1. Silk Road—History—Study and teaching (Higher) 2. Asia—
History—Study and teaching (Higher) 3. Trade routes—Asia—Study and
teaching (Higher)   I. Moore, Jacqueline M. II. Wendelken, Rebecca Woodward.

   DS33.1.T43 2010
   950.071'1—dc22   2009033550

10 9 8 7 6 5 4 3 2 1

Contents

Illustrations

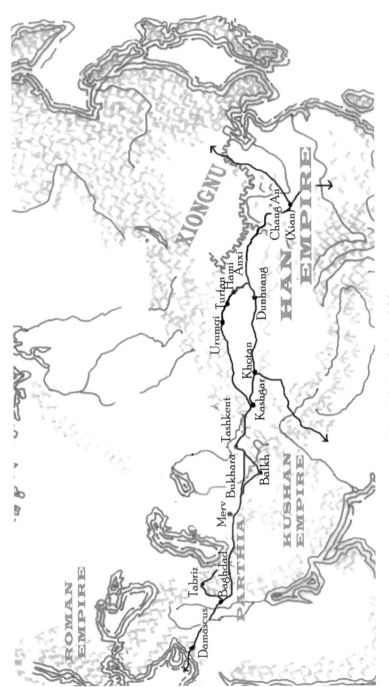

The Silk Road circa 100 C.E..

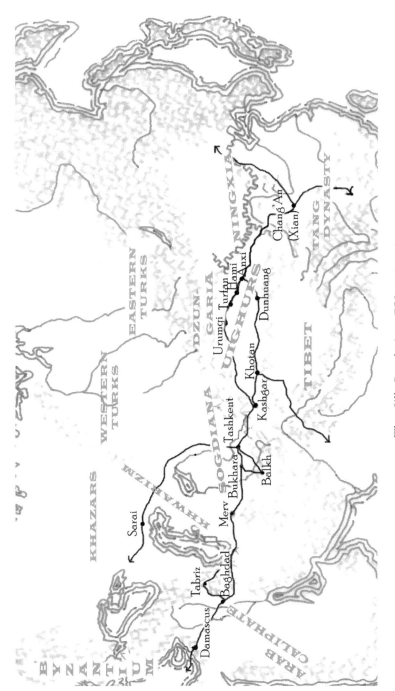

The Silk Road circa 750 C.E..

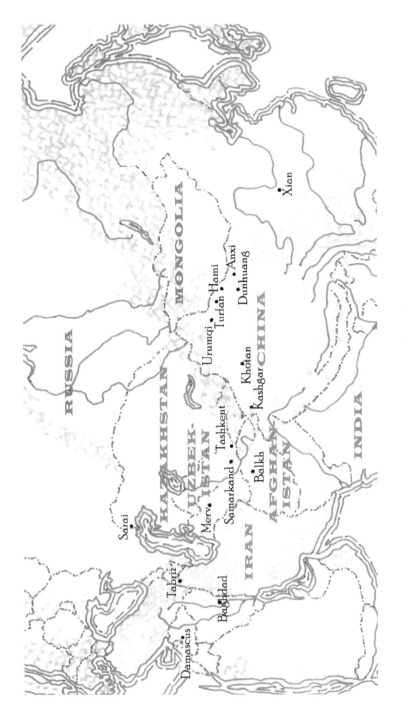

The Silk Road Today.

Introduction

Morris Rossabi

Globalization has become so identified with the late twentieth and early twenty-first centuries that it seems to overshadow earlier eras of international relations. Many in the modern world have associated such contacts with recent times, a view that prevailed in education as well. For example, most so-called World History courses in secondary schools and community colleges placed Europe at the center, considering other civilizations principally when they interacted with the West. A global history perspective would reveal that globalization, in the form of East-West relations that significantly influenced both, far predated the twentieth century.

The World History Association pioneered such a global history approach. Established in the 1980s, it founded the *Journal of World History* as an exemplar of the latest research that links political, cultural, and social interactions among civilizations. Textbooks with an emphasis on global history have proliferated over the past few decades. Many simply provide the history of individual civilizations in separate chapters, but a few have attempted to integrate developments in one part of the world with other regions. Such efforts at global history have gone beyond the previous Eurocentric views.

Study of the Silk Roads, in particular, offers a unique means of conveying the significance of intercultural relations. Although most historians date the origins of the Silk Roads with the Han dynasty mission of Zhang Qian to Central Asia in the second century,BCE, contacts between China and Central Asia no doubt preceded that time, as evidenced by scraps of silk (which only the Chinese then knew how to produce) in Middle Eastern tombs centuries before Zhang's expedition. From the second century BCE, to the sixteenth century CE, Silk Roads commerce persisted, with some notable exceptions. Caravans ceased to travel in significant numbers when China or Iran were weak or faced chaotic conditions and could not protect merchants and other travelers journeying across Eurasia. Even during those turbulent eras, fragile connections were maintained, as individual traders, missionaries, and entertainers continued to travel, despite the hazards.

The Tang (618–907) and Yuan (1260–1368) witnessed the efflorescence of the Silk Roads. Edward Schafer, as early as the publication of his *Golden Peaches of Samarkand* (1963), drew attention to the remarkable exchange of ideas, goods, and techniques during the Tang. Schafer's exhaustive examination of literary texts, encyclopedias, and histories yielded a cornucopia of data confirming the wide range of Tang Silk Roads trade. Commerce and tribute in the forms of animals, birds, drugs, aromatics, jewels, relics, and books reached China. Most of these items were luxuries; few, generally bulky essentials were suited for such long-distance trade because of their heavy weight or burdensome volume. Together with products came tribute of slaves, dwarfs, and exotic-looking individuals, who impressed the Chinese and played minor roles in Chinese history. At the same time, Chinese inventions filtered their way westward. The secrets of silk production, a Chinese monopoly, had been revealed to the Byzantine empire even before the Tang, and Chinese captives introduced paper to Arab armies in Samarkand in the mid-eighth century. Chinese weavers and gold craftsmen survived the Islamic invasions in Bukhara and transmitted Chinese motifs and designs.

The Silk Roads trade constituted a relatively small sector of the Chinese economy, but it had great influence on Chinese culture. The Tang rulers invited Turkic musicians and dancers from Central Asia, the real nexus of the Silk Roads, to perform at court, leading to fads for foreign music, dance, and costume. The Chinese adapted and adopted Middle Eastern musical instruments, borrowings that enriched Chinese music. Central Asian music appears to have influenced Li Bo, one of China's greatest poets. The rhyme and irregular meters of Turkic music characterized some of his poetry, not really a surprise, as he was born along China's northwestern border. His family was "engaged in trade," and his work "shows the marked influence of Central Asian culture."[1] Even stronger evidence of the fascination with foreigners that resulted in substantial impact on Chinese culture is the Tang tricolored ceramic figurines.[2] These exquisite objects, which were often buried with prominent figures (still another indication of how valued they were), frequently depicted Silk Roads travelers. Members of the Chinese elite prized the Central Asian and Middle Eastern merchants, entertainers, and guardian figures portrayed in these ceramics, as evidenced by the number of these ceramics discovered in tombs. Similarly clear indications of the prestige accorded to facilitators or facilities of Silk Roads trade were the tricolored ceramic horses and camels, some of which were quite sizeable. These animals were essential for Eurasian commerce, and it is thus no accident that ceramicists would choose to portray them.

Perhaps the most lasting cultural impact of the Tang Silk Roads was the introduction of foreign religions. Buddhism had first been transmitted to China via the Silk Roads oases during the Han dynasty. In the following centuries, teachers and translators had brought Buddhist texts and translated them into Chinese. The pace of interaction with Buddhists outside of China accelerated during the Tang, as such renowned pilgrims as Xuanzang traveled to India and Central Asia to study with great Buddhist masters and to collect Buddhist artifacts and texts. Travels by these pilgrims naturally contributed to greater Sino-Indian interaction not only in religion but also in trade and cultural and artistic transmission.[3]

However, the Tang also witnessed the arrival of a profusion of Middle Eastern religions. The early Tang court did not try to exclude or discriminate against foreign religions. Zoroastrianism and Manichaeism—Iranian religions—reached China, and believers constructed a few of their temples in Chang'an, the Tang capital. Neither attracted many adherents, but Manichaeism went northward to convert many Uyghur Turks, serving as the foundation for the Uyghur empire (744–840).[4] Nestorian Christianity also arrived via merchants and clergy, but it too did not take hold in China. Like Manichaeism, Nestorianism eventually became popular north of China, particularly among Mongol women. Islam was, by far, the most important foreign religion to attract a Chinese constituency. Muslim communities formed mostly in Northwest and Southeast China, and Arab, Iranian, and Turkic Muslims played important roles in the government and economy of Tang China. However, when the Tang declined, both the court and many in the populace blamed foreigners and their religions for the country's problems. Starting around 845, the court, as well as rebels, targeted and attacked Buddhism and other foreign religions. Most foreigners reacted by avoiding China, leading to four centuries of limited intercultural contact along the Silk Roads. Trade between the Northern Song (960–1126), the succeeding great Chinese dynasty, and its closest neighbors, including oases in modern Northwest China along the Silk Roads, persisted, as did artistic interchanges, specifically in the production of textiles, but the long-distance trade reaching to Iran and the Middle East dissipated. The nearby oases sent horses, jewels, and incense as tribute and brought horses, camels, copper utensils, and bullion for trade while the Chinese provided gifts, as well as trade, of silk, lacquer ware, tea, paper, and porcelain, among other goods.

The rise and expansion of the Mongol empire set the stage for the great renewal of the Silk Roads trade. By carving out the largest contiguous land empire in world history, the Mongols imposed a Pax Mongolica on Eurasia, permitting relatively easy travel from one region to another. Although the various Mongol Khanates in Russia (the Golden Horde), Iran (the Ilkhanate), Central Asia (Chaghadai), and China (Yuan dynasty) were occasionally in conflict with each other, they generally continued to protect trade caravans, leading to considerable East-West contacts. Merchants, missionaries, adventurers, astronomers, interpreters, military commanders, and rulers, among others, traveled along the oases and cities through Eurasia. As in the Tang, trade items consisted of luxuries and thus did not have a tremendous impact on the economies of the great Asian civilizations of that era. To be sure, the oases and individual merchants profited from the Silk Roads trade, but it hardly made a dent on what might be called the Gross Domestic Product of China, Iran, the European states, and others involved in this commerce. Nonetheless, the extensive flow of travelers, goods, ideas, and artifacts contributed to cultural interchanges in such fields as astronomy, medicine, agronomy, and the arts. Iranian astronomers and physicians came to China while Chinese textiles, porcelains, and agricultural texts reached Iran.

Peace and commerce provided opportunities for considerable cultural exchanges and influences, but the significance of such interactions, particularly for China, ought not to be exaggerated. China benefited from the introduction of Iranian astronomical instruments and conceptions and medical precepts, and Chinese motifs and designs appeared in Iranian tiles, illustrated manuscripts, and pottery. However, neither culture was fundamentally altered because of its borrowings from the other. Thus, the Ming dynasty, which compelled the Mongols to withdraw from China, adopted policies to avert any "barbarian" invasions and scarcely differed from most traditional Chinese dynasties. Moreover, the Safavids, who reestablished indigenous rule in Iran in the early sixteenth century after three hundred years of Mongol and Timurid domination, restored Iranian civilization with only traces of Chinese influence. The Russians who eliminated the last vestiges of so-called Tartar rule, also in the early sixteenth century, show little direct influence from the Mongols.

Despite this caveat, the thirteenth and fourteenth centuries produced an astonishing number of travelers and travel accounts. The Franciscans John of Plano Carpini and William of Rubruck voyaged from Europe to the Mongol encampments in East Asia to persuade the "barbarians" to convert to Christianity and to cease further incursions on the West. Their reports offered invaluable information about Mongol customs, beliefs, and practices. Marco Polo provided perhaps the most renowned travel account in world history. The Nestorian Christian Rabban Sauma departed from Dadu (modern Beijing) on a pilgrimage to the Holy Lands and eventually served as an ambassador from the Mongol rulers of Iran to propose an alliance with the Europeans against the major Islamic dynasty in the Middle East. He wrote descriptions of Naples, Rome, Paris, and Bordeaux and of his dialogues with the College of Cardinals. Other travelers who capitalized on the Pax Mongolica to undertake lengthy journeys included Ibn Battuta, a voyager to many regions in Asia and Africa, and Zhou Daguan, the astute recorder of Cambodian society.

Although all of these contacts among China, Central Asia, and the Middle East did not end with the collapse of the Mongol empire, the number of travelers along the Silk Roads diminished. The Ming dynasty imposed restrictions on foreign trade and tribute. Zheng He's expeditions (1405–1432), the greatest naval journeys until Columbus's time, were magnificent sea voyages that reached the east coast of Africa, but they were aberrations and were rapidly halted after the death of their most supportive emperor. Similarly, Chen Cheng's embassies to Herat, Samarkand, and fifteen other oases and states, ended with the demise of the same emperor, and the Ming court dispatched no further official envoys to Central Asia. Silk Roads trade continued on a lesser scale through the early sixteenth century because of the demand for Chinese silk, porcelain, and tea in nearby oases such as Turfan and the more distant empire ruled by Tamerlane's (or Temür's) descendants. Starting in the early sixteenth century, considerable turbulence along the Silk Roads, the emerging competition of the sea route from Europe to East Asia, and Safavid Iran's conversion to Shi'ism and the ensuing conflicts with its neighbors, the mostly Sunni Ottoman Turks and the Central Asian Khanates, impeded and then led to a near cessation of the land-borne East-West caravan trade. Cultural contacts between China and Central Asia and the Middle East also diminished, although Middle Eastern dynasties collected Ming porcelains, now found in the Topkapi museum in Istanbul and the Ardebil shrine in Iran, which influenced motifs and decorations on Turkish and Iranian pottery.

By the seventeenth century, overland trade had shifted to a northerly route, from China via Central Asia and Siberia to Russia, undermining some of the traditional oases and towns through which merchants had traveled. Towns such as Samarkand, Turfan, and Khotan declined in population and influence. Russo-Chinese trade substituted for Central

Asian and Middle Eastern commerce, with Tsarist Russian merchants eager to obtain traditional items such as silk, porcelain, and tea, as well as rhubarb, a new product which they could sell at sizable profits to Europeans who valued its purported medicinal properties. Prospective Russian interpreters, translators, and envoys traveled to Beijing to study Chinese and Manchu, the language of the rulers of China in the Qing dynasty (1644–1911), and a Russian ecclesiastical mission catered to their spiritual needs. Meanwhile, Central Asia, bereft of the profitable Silk Roads trade and enduring religious and political schisms often leading to conflict, became weaker and more vulnerable to the expansionist desires of Qing China and Tsarist Russia. The Qing conquered eastern Central Asia by 1760, and the Russians encroached gradually on western Central Asia, first gaining control over the nomadic Kazakhs and then the major towns and oases by around 1870. As the Qing itself began to decline in the mid-nineteenth century, the British and the Russians sought to play a greater role in eastern Central Asia and to replace the weakening Manchu dynasty.

Growing foreign interest in Central Asia in the late nineteenth and early twentieth centuries led adventurers, archaeologists, and scientists to explore the region. To be sure, trade along the old land routes did not flourish, but as one observer noted, there were "Foreign Devils on the Silk Road." Aurel Stein, Paul Pelliot, Nikolai Przevalski, and Albert von le Coq were a few of these "devils" who braved desert heat and mountain chill to find and explore some of the archeological and artistic treasures of the Silk Roads. They discovered such spectacular sites as Dunhuang, Bezeklik (near Turfan), and Kyzyl and carried away some of the beautiful sculptures and paintings to their native lands, controversial actions which many Chinese considered to have been pillaging of their artistic, not to mention religious, heritage.

In the twentieth century, the main centers of the old Silk Roads trade encountered more turbulence. China underwent two revolutions—the overthrow of the Qing dynasty in 1911 and the communist defeat of Chiang Kai-shek and the Nationalist regime in 1949. Iran was ruled in a dictatorial fashion by the Pahlavi dynasty until a revolution in 1979 brought to power Islamic fundamentalists who currently govern the country. Eastern Central Asia became relatively independent after the Qing dynasty's collapse, but the communist government reestablished control over the region (known as Xinjiang since 1884) in 1949–1950. The region has faced considerable unrest, as more and more Chinese have moved in. Estimates vary, but the Chinese, who constituted about 10 to 15 percent of Xinjiang's total population in 1950, now make up about 45 to 50 percent, leading to tensions between the primarily Turkic and Muslim community and the Chinese settlers. After a decade of intermittent conflicts, the Soviet Union established jurisdiction over western Central Asia by 1928. Soviet leaders suppressed the local people, their culture, and Islam, though they introduced modern educational and health practices. In 1991–92, five Central Asian republics broke away from Russia and founded independent countries.

After four centuries of relative obscurity, with the collapse of the Silk Roads and perceptions of these areas as minor regions, the 1990s witnessed a revival and a renewed view of their significance. This change of attitude was partly based upon the discovery of abundant quantities of virtually untapped mineral and natural resources. Kazakhstan and Azerbaijan, in western Central Asia and the Caucasus, are endowed with considerable petroleum reserves, and Turkmenistan, also in Central Asia, has natural gas deposits. North Xinjiang (or Ili) is the site of the Karamai oil fields. Because all these regions are landlocked, pipelines are essential, and many of the great powers, seeking this oil, have different views about the routes. China has already worked out an agreement for a pipeline to Xinjiang, but the other pipelines are under negotiations, with some states favoring a route through Iran, others through the Caucasus and Turkey and still others, via Russia, to the West. The twenty-first century may witness the substitution of the Oil Routes for the Silk Roads as major economic sectors.

The glorious history of the Silk Roads offers extraordinary pedagogical possibilities. In an article entitled "The Silk Roads: An Educational Resource," published in *Education About Asia* and later in *From Silk to Oil*, a curricular package that my collaborators and I developed for secondary school teachers, we described some of these possibilities. Several of the units we developed for *From Silk to Oil* can be adapted and used for community colleges, but greater detail and different methodologies are required for colleges and universities.

The essays in this work, produced by professors who participated in a National Endowment for the Humanities–funded seminar at the East-West Center of the University of Hawaii, offer just such assistance for instructors who are not necessarily specialists on Asia or intercultural relations or trade. The authors, who have taught Silk Roads units or courses, provide positive and successful strategies for teaching and secondary source research. All suggest bibliographic references for professors and students, furnishing the basic sources without overwhelming instructors with a plethora of texts. Some contribute personal recollections of life or visits along the Silk Roads or broader historical and philosophical discussions related to this romanticized link between East and West.

Pedagogic assistance comprises the bulk of the essays, which offer a variety of approaches to the instructor for a variety of courses and disciplines. The first chapters take a geographic approach to incorporating the Silk Roads into existing courses. Professor Racel furnishes guidance on the incorporation of Silk Roads studies into a one-semester World History course. She shows how study of the Silk Roads can lead to insights not only about global interconnectedness but also about specific regions. Professor Carlson discusses the role of the Silk Roads in European history, focusing on trade products, particularly silk, but also such other commodities as porcelain and even tulips. Discreet study of these goods as they were transmitted from East to West leads to greater understanding of economic interrelationships among civilizations. She shows that it is impossible to study European history in isolation from the rest of the world.

In a tour de force essay on the historical significance of the Silk Roads to Chinese identity, Professor Foster points to a new way of analyzing Chinese civilization. Scholars have often studied Chinese history in isolation, with only limited reference to other cultures and civilization. Professor Foster challenges this paradigm and shows that from earliest times other lands repeatedly influenced China. Starting with the chariot and bronze technology and moving to the introduction of Buddhism and Islam, among other religions, to the arrival of Iranian astronomers and physicians, the so-called Middle Kingdom has interacted with neighbors, as well as far-flung lands, via the Silk Roads. Professor Foster demonstrates the value of studying Chinese history and civilization from a Eurasian, or even global, perspective.

The next chapters turn to ways to incorporate the Silk Roads into disciplines other than history. Two political scientists provide links between the Silk Roads and globalization and other contemporary issues. Professor Parrish associates the Silk Roads with globalization, but he also shows how the modern identities of groups such as the Uyghurs, Mongols, and Tibetans have been shaped by both accurate and imagined connections with reputed forebears, who were often related to the Silk Roads. In addition, he pleads for incorporation of Chinese and other Asian concepts into political theory courses. Like many of the other essayists, Professor Guo emphasizes the interdependence of the world and the scholarly disciplines, an insight inspired by study of the Silk Roads. He then focuses on analysis of the Silk Roads as a means of understanding contemporary China and shows that the myth of a monolithic, isolated, and exclusionary traditional China does not jibe with its involvement with its neighbors and the wider Asian world, via the Silk Roads. He confirms that China and the other Asian civilizations borrowed technologies and ideas from each other, but in each case adapted and adopted these features to blend in with their own societies. Similarly, he trusts that students and policymakers will recognize that the current U.S. model presented to the world as a market economy and democracy may deviate considerably from the original, just as China, Japan, Korea, and Southeast Asia each altered and adopted a different form of Indian Buddhism. He concludes that no single development model will suit the world's diverse cultures and that the U.S. paradigm for democracy may not be appropriate for all.

Professor O'Mara introduces the use of visual culture as a means of understanding cultural interactions among different civilizations. A study of material remains, including sculptures, porcelains, and tomb decorations, reveals the remarkable interchanges among the Eurasian civilizations. Art history can examine the motifs, shapes, and techniques of these art works and can derive insights about the interconnectedness of West Asia and East Asia during specific historical eras. Because of the paucity of written texts describing such contacts, these objects assume even greater importance in documenting the relations of the various civilizations along the Silk Roads. Thus, art history supplies a vital vehicle for a greater understanding of cultural borrowing and adaptation.

Two chapters take a thematic approach to addressing the Silk Roads, providing lenses through which to approach the subject in any class. Professor Bai offers philosophic reflections about contemporary issues of globalization and identity, focusing on the Chinese model. He makes the interesting point that the Chinese traditionally emphasized culture rather than ethnicity in determining identity, which certainly has contemporary repercussions. He also makes an argument for the beneficial nature of nationalism. Professor Ronald Frank offers ways of introducing students to the lifestyles and culture of the pastoral nomads, a vital but little studied group in Silk Roads history. He shows that most students of the Silk Roads have focused their attention on the sedentary peoples who lived in well-defined territories. Yet nomads often transported goods from one part of Eurasia to another, and students can understand a different way of life by studying the herders. Professor Frank demonstrates that most studies view the pastoral nomads through the lens of the sedentary civilizations. Thus, a true Silk Roads perspective needs as far as possible to examine the nomads' history and their contributions to Eurasian trade from their own viewpoint, albeit the few sources that reflect the herders' perceptions limit historians. Nonetheless, Professor Frank offers some useful interpretations about the pastoral nomads' role along the Silk Roads.

The next four chapters focus on alternative pedagogical strategies and the nuts and bolts of teaching courses on the Silk Roads. Professor Diamant developed a service-learning program that emphasized the Silk Roads' association with current concerns about globalization. He drew out such themes from Silk Roads history as identity, assimilation, and intercultural borrowing and applied them to a modern world that requires peace and understanding among ethnic and national groups. He combined travel to the region with service requirements for students, hoping to instill the values of true globalization and intercultural understanding. Professor Frost capitalized on travel as a means of helping students develop insights about the Silk Roads. She led a tour to Northwest China, one of the cradles of the Silk Roads. The students' experiences, combined with reading of important texts, challenged their perceptions about identity. They observed a China in which imams played significant roles, the food was more Middle Eastern than Chinese, and even the craftsmen produced items, such as rugs, that are more often associated with the Islamic world than China. In short, they learned that China was a multiethnic and multireligious society, shaped, in part, by the Silk Roads.

Professor Moore discusses the ease with which instructors and students can incorporate primary sources on the Silk Roads. The voyagers' accounts she cites are colorful and exciting and can help students to understand narrative writing as well as to assess the reliability of what on the surface seem fantastic accounts. In short, study of these texts promotes critical thinking and the development of criteria for assessing reliability. Professor Moore also provides a useful compilation of the best translations of the travelers' accounts. Professor Wendelken adds a pedagogical essay that covers an often neglected but vital feature of the Silk Roads—proper consideration of geography. Silk Roads trade and cultural interactions cannot be understood without a clear knowledge of the environments through which merchants, pilgrims, missionaries, envoys, and entertainers traveled. Descriptions of the hardships they endured and the triumphs they experienced are essential for insights about topography, climate, and economy. Professor Wendelken also offers a guide to maps, which provides the needed insights and shows how instructors can use these graphic representations to bring the Silk Roads to life.

In the final chapter, Professor Zhang gives a vivid account of Khotan, one of the most important sites on the Silk Roads, to which she and her family were sent during the Cultural Revolution in China. She shows both the idealism that influenced many Chinese during this era but also the bleakness of the Silk Roads oases. Her frightening description of getting lost in the Taklamakan desert echoes the recollections of many survivors and probably reflects the thoughts of those not fortunate enough to have found the right path to safety.

In sum, these essays provide a wide choice of approaches for introducing students to the Silk Roads. Some of the pedagogical articles describe trips and service-learning efforts that lead to active involvement in the Silk Roads region, while others provide guidance on maps, art works, and bibliographies for studying its history and culture from home. Still others emphasize content such as a consideration of the impact of the Silk Roads on Chinese history or a survey of the importance of religions or nomads in linking cultures in Eurasia. Finally, one offers a haunting, firsthand account with a marvelous sense of place of one of the major Silk Roads oases. In short, these essays offer invaluable starting points for studies of globalization, economic and political interactions among civilizations, and religious, artistic, and cultural diffusion.

Notes

1. Elling O. Eide, "On Li Po," in *Perspectives on the T'ang*, ed. Arthur Wright and Denis Twitchett (New Haven: Yale University Press, 1973), 389.

2. See Jane Gaston Mahler, *The Westerners among the Figurines of the T'ang Dynasty of China* (Roma: Instituto Italiano per il Medio ed Estremo Oriente, 1959).

3. See, for example, Liu Xinru, *Silk and Religion* (Delhi: Oxford University Press, 1996).

4. The latest work on the subject is Michael Drompp, *Tang China and the Collapse of the Uighur Empire: A Documentary History* (Leiden: Brill, 2005).

Part I

Disciplinary Approaches
to the Silk Road

Chapter 1

Weaving with Silk

Using the Silk Roads to Organize World History Surveys Before 1500

Masako N. Racel

Historians today no longer teach world history as simply a collection of regional histories, but now attempt to present history as an integrated whole that allows students to see beyond the confinement of national, regional, or even continental boundaries. I can best describe this fairly recent concept with an analogy. History is like a massive piece of cloth that spreads out to the horizons. When we look at it closely, we see that the cloth is composed of myriad individual threads that combine with each other to form an ever-tightening weave. This weave binds together the individual threads to form the tapestry of human interaction. The rich colors of various cultural, religious, and social characteristics are apparent in the fabric, but we can only observe the true pattern by stepping back and viewing the whole from a distance. The world history survey is where we are able to provide that wide perspective.

Departmental needs determine how many professors organize their courses. Most college-level survey courses are supposed to serve two major objectives. First, they provide freshman non-history students with the essentials of cultural literacy in world history. In this role, faculty must provide students with a basic understanding of history, so it is easier to cover broad topics and concepts without getting bogged down in details and minutiae. Second, such courses must also serve as introductions for those seeking to take upper division history courses, which are typically organized by regional, chorological, and/or thematic basis, such as "Medieval Europe," "China before 1600," "Mughal India," etc.; and require a much more detailed knowledge of specific regions, people, and events. This juxtaposition of needing to keep the course focused on the overreaching concepts of history, while also providing the necessary details for those wanting a deeper and more specialized understanding creates a challenge for most instructors, especially when you consider that no one is an expert on all time periods and regions. My personal approach in addressing this problem has been to combine both the regional and world history approaches by first offering a big picture, followed by regional histories, and then weaving the regional histories together using the larger concepts of a world history approach. With this in mind, the Silk Roads and other trade routes in Eurasia offer an excellent way to organize world history lessons for the period before 1500.

At Kennesaw State University, all students are required to take a one-semester world history course that covers everything from prehistory to the present. Since this is only a one-semester, three-credit course that meets twice a week for sixteen weeks, there is certainly a huge restraint on time that I can spend on each lesson. With such a short course that covers all of human existence, clear organization is the key for students to categorize and comprehend the major points of world history. To that end, I have divided the course into three units or epochs. The first two units focus on Afro-Eurasian History (commonly known as the Old World), while the third unit deals with the era of global integration whereby the so-called New World becomes a major part of world history. The first unit covers the time period from prehistory to circa 500 CE. The second unit explores the time period following the collapse of the classical civilizations (Roman Empire, Han Dynasty of China, etc.) and before the age of global integration (c. 1500). The third unit closes out the course with everything from the age of exploration (with a discussion of American civilization) to the present. I incorporate the three major eras of the Silk Roads into the first two units of the course.

Silk Roads: Three Eras

Even though we commonly use the singular form "the Silk Road," the term generally refers to the collection of Eurasian roads and trade routes that connected the Mediterranean Basin in the west to China in the east. Some would apply the term *Silk Roads*, to refer not only to the overland route that traveled through the oasis cities of Eurasia, but also the northern steppe routes and various sea lanes. The original travelers along the Silk Road did not know it by that name; German explorer Baron Ferdinand von Richthofen coined the term much later in the nineteenth century. Although silk was probably among the most important commodities, and perhaps the only product that actually traveled the entire length of the roads, other goods, such as spices, glassware, medicinal plants, and musical instruments were also traded via the Silk Roads.[1]

It is hard to identify exactly when the Silk Roads came into existence, but it is relatively easy to identify high points in their history. The first major era for the history of the Silk Roads was during the period in which the Roman Empire to the west and the Han empire to the east both flourished. These two empires did not connect directly, but a series of overlapping trade circuits ultimately linked the two empires together indirectly. The second great age came about with the emergence of the Umayyad and Abbasid Caliphates on one hand, and the reunification of China under the Sui and Tang dynasties on the other end of Eurasia. The third great age began with the creation of the Mongol empire that encompassed much of the Eurasian landmass during the thirteenth and fourteenth centuries. For the first time, the land routes of Eurasia were controlled by a single government, providing a mechanism to facilitate trade and travel across all of Eurasia.[2] With the spread of the plague in the fourteenth century, the decline of the Mongol empire, and the opening of new ocean trade routes in the 1500s, the importance of the Silk Roads generally declined.

First Great Era of the Silk Road Trade

The first unit establishes the foundation of world history by covering the time period from prehistory to circa 500 CE, the epoch often referred to as the ancient and classical periods. A few of the major issues I address in this unit are the Neolithic Revolution and the emergence and development of complex societies in Afro-Eurasia. After covering several specific regional societies (Nile River Valley, Mesopotamia, South Asia, East Asia and the Mediterranean Basin), I add one lesson entitled "Cross-Cultural Encounters and the Spread of Ideas and Technologies" in order to pull together the different regions of Afro-Eurasia, and to better incorporate the importance of the Silk Roads during the classical era.

This lesson introduces some of the essential concepts of world history, such as the importance of cross-cultural encounters as agents of change, while providing the context in which such encounters and exchanges may take place. I explain the general pattern of change, where new ideas and/or technology may be first *adopted*, and then *adapted* to fit the needs and tastes of a certain locality. As a part of process of adaptation, I also introduce the term "syncretism," in which new "foreign" ideas are combined with old indigenous ideas, resulting in new blended ideas and concepts. I also discuss the tendency for large, stable empires to create conditions favorable to trade here, leading to the eventual development of the Silk Roads that connected the Han empire in the east to the Roman Empire in the west.

This era corresponds well with the traditional Chinese accounts of the opening of the Silk Roads when Emperor Han Wudi sent Zhang Qian (Chang-ch'ien) to the "western territory" in 139 BCE, in order to make an alliance with a nomadic people from Central Asia that the Chinese referred to as the Yuezhi (Yueh-chih). At the same time, the demand for silk garments was very high among Roman elites. Greeks and Romans had known of silk since at least the fourth century BCE, and following the Battle of Carrhae in 53 BCE when the Parthians startled the Roman soldiers with their silk banners, silk grew in popularity. Despite various attempts to limit its use to the aristocracy there was a healthy demand for trade that allowed the Silk Roads to flourish while these two great empires served as anchor points on opposing ends.[3] With the decline and eventual collapses of both the Han and Roman empires into smaller and less stable regionally based kingdoms, the Silk Roads' importance faded as trade slowed to only a trickle.[4]

HIST 1110: World History

UNIT 1: Prehistory and Afro-Eurasian World to. c.500CE

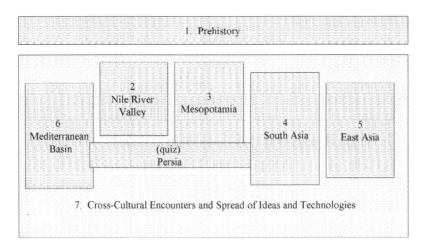

Figure 1.1. A geographic representation of Unit I showing both regional and cross-cultural lectures.

I introduce general patterns of long distance trade; with nomadic peoples, such as the Xiongnu and the Sogdians, playing the critical role as middlemen. These middlemen never traveled all the way from China to the Eastern Mediterranean and vice versa, but instead only traveled particular sections of the Silk Roads that they were familiar with, trading with similar people, ultimately connecting one end of Eurasia to another. I mention the popularity of the silk among Roman elites, but also include other goods that traveled the Silk Roads. The importance of domesticated animals, such as camels, donkeys, and horses for trades, as well as the dangers travelers faced from banditry, dehydration, and sandstorms can also be included in this section.

Centering the discussion on the Silk Roads offers many opportunities to introduce important world history concepts that a regional history approach would otherwise overlook.[5] The Silk Roads were not only important for the exchange of goods; they also served as a conduit for the transmission of ideas. Buddhism flourished along the Silk Roads, as the famous Dunhuang caves and statues of the colossal Buddhas of Bamiyan attest. The case study of the spread of Nestorian Christianity along the Silk Roads, in particular, serves as an excellent way to show how a heterodox sect could survive official condemnation by spreading

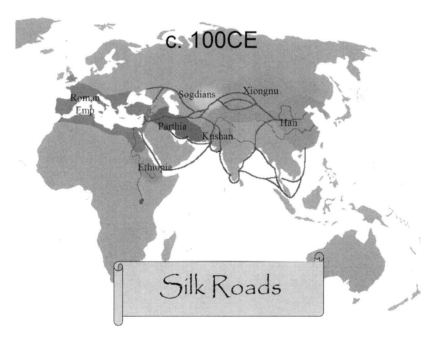

Figure 1.2. Trade routes in the Classical Period.

into areas where religious authorities were unable to impose restrictions. The case of Manichaeism, which emerged in third-century CE Mesopotamia, then part of Persian empire, offers a great example of syncretism in which elements from Zoroastrianism, Christianity, and Buddhism all merged together to form a new religion.[6] Not all transmissions along the Silk Roads were beneficial: travelers also transmitted diseases. We can link the outbreak of plagues in both the Roman Empire and the Han empires during the second and third centuries to the Silk Roads.[7] The disintegration of the Han and Roman empires, due in part to epidemic disease, resulted in a general decline of the Silk Road trade which did not fully revive until the seventh and eighth centuries CE.

The Second Era: The Societies along Three Trade Routes

My second unit covers the period between c.500 and c.1500 CE, which I divide roughly into the time period before and after the emergence of the Mongol empire. For coverage of pre-Mongolian Afro-Eurasia, I still use a regional and thematic history approach for lessons on East Asia, Western and Eastern Europe, and the Islamic world (I group the last three together as "Western Eurasia and North Africa" and focus on the transition from a Mediterranean-based society that splits into Western and Eastern Christendom, and Dar-al-Islam). I integrate regional and thematic histories with a lecture on the three trade routes of Afro-Eurasia, including the Silk Roads (overland), the Indian Ocean trade network and the trans-Saharan trade network. By organizing the lesson along these trade routes, I can easily incorporate areas that a regional history approach might neglect, such as Southeast Asia. Furthermore, this approach allows me to address important world history issues, such as the existence of "world" economic systems in premodern eras.

   I intentionally insert this lesson after covering Imperial China (the Sui, Tang, and Song dynasties) and the Umayyad and Abbasid Caliphates since these two areas became the new anchor points of the Silk Roads on both ends of Eurasia, much like the Han and Roman empires during the earlier era. A purely regional approach tends to overlook the fact that these two regions were thriving simultaneously and at one point were adjacent to each other. China, after approximately four hundred years of division, was reunited under the short-lived Sui Dynasty (581-618) and pivotal Tang Dynasty (618-907). The Islamic empire experienced phenomenal growth after its founding c. 622 and quickly unified a vast region stretching all the way from the Indus River valley to the Iberian Peninsula. The Battle of Talas River in 751 CE, during which the newly established Abbasid Caliphate and the Tang empire clashed over

UNIT 2: Afro-Eurasian World
c.400CE- c.1500CE

Western Eurasia and N. Africa			11 Afro-Eurasian World Along Trade Routes (Silk Roads, Indian Ocean Sea Lanes, and Trans- Saharan Routes)	8 East Asia
9 Western Christendom	(quiz) Byzantium	10 Islamic World		
Crusades				

14 Western Europe Late Middle Age Renaissance Reformation	12. Turco-Mongolian Empires	
	(quiz) Islamic Empires (Ottoman, Safavid, and Mughal)	13 East Asia

Figure 1.3. Geographic representation of Unit II lectures.

a territorial dispute, clearly demonstrates the contact between the two cultures. Not only was the Battle of Talas River important as a military confrontation, it also deserves the credit for the introduction of paper-making technology into the Islamic world, since some of the Chinese captured there were skilled paper-making artisans.

The period of the High Caliphate (c. 661–945) was a time of intercontinental contact and cooperation when the transmission of ideas and technology spread throughout the Islamic World. Historians normally attribute this astonishing spread of culture and ideas to the fact that the early Islamic empires controlled a vast territory that included the Indus River Valley, Persia, the Arabian Peninsula and North Africa, and the Iberian Peninsula. Islam's teaching about the hajj, which encouraged its followers to visit the holy city of Mecca at least once in their lifetimes, created favorable conditions for intercultural encounters and exchanges since people from the farthest regions all traveled to a central location, bringing with them different cultures and ideas.[8] Dar-al-Islam (the abode of Islam) served as a conduit for knowledge and technology. The Arabs adopted and adapted the numerical system developed in the Indus River valley, which we know as arabic numerals. At the other end of the empire, the Muslims also learned of Greek scholars and translated

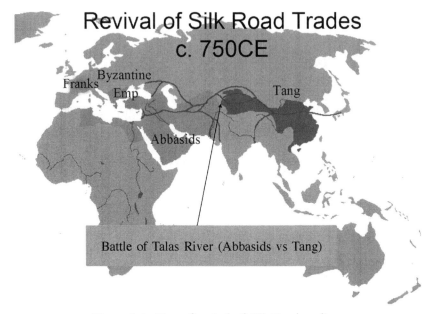

Figure 1.4. Map of revival of Silk Road trading.

ancient Greek works into Arabic. Such developments within the Islamic world eventually traveled back to Western Europe via the direct contact that resulted from the Crusades of the eleventh to thirteenth centuries. While most world history texts mention the impact of Islam on Western Europe, they often overlook the fact that much of the overland Silk Road that ran through Persia, and east to central Asia, also fell under the control of Islamic empires. As a result, nomadic pastoralists and merchants in the surrounding regions, such as the Turks and Sogdians, adopted Islam, adding to its international character. The revival of Silk Road trade thus helped the spread of Islam.

The conversion of the nomads along the Silk Roads also contributed to the cosmopolitanism of Tang China. This period is noteworthy since it is the time when famous Chinese monk Xuanzang traveled to India and bought back Buddhist scriptures, using the Silk Roads.[9] Unlike the allegedly more insular China of later periods, the Tang era was exceptionally open to foreign people and cultures. Muslims began establishing communities within China around c. 650 CE. Famous stoneware figurines from the Tang era, such as those depicting camels and Central Asians, provide clear evidence of China's connection with the Silk Roads. An Lushan, who set off a famous rebellion, was a Turkic-Sogdian general from the frontier guard. Such individuals are indicative of the multiethnic character of the Tang era that resulted from the flourishing trade along the Silk Roads.

In addition to the overland Silk Roads, the sea lanes of the Indian Ocean were prosperous at this time. Organizing a lesson along the Indian Ocean network is an excellent way to break away from the normal regional or continental models. Southeast Asia, which most textbooks tend to neglect, is easy to incorporate as a part of the Indian Ocean Trade network. Since this network included Swahili cities of East Africa, teachers can avoid a continental perspective that tends to isolate Africa from the rest of the world. Although the Indian Ocean approach can separate the coastal regions from the rest of Africa, it is possible to avoid this problem by showing the connection between the Swahili city-states and the inland economy, the most notable example of which was the rise of the Monomopata empire during the fifteenth century. Additionally, I show the interconnectedness of world trade, since the cowrie shells many African societies used for currency came from the Maldives Islands in the Indian Ocean. While I have students thinking outside of the box, I include a discussion of the Austronesian migration, which resulted in populating parts of Southeast Asia, the Pacific (including Hawaii and Easter Island) and even Madagascar, which is usually treated as part of Africa.

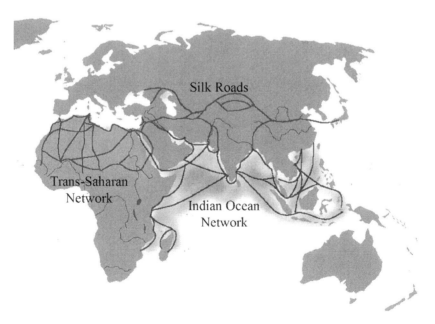

Figure 1.5. Silk Roads and trans-Saharan trade routes.

I am also able to incorporate the trans-Saharan routes into my lecture about societies existing along trade routes. I explain the rise of empires along the Sahalian belt, such as Ghana, Mali, and Songhay, in connection with the rise of the trans-Saharan trade. This is a great opportunity to break free from the myth that Africa was an isolated continent by demonstrating sub-Saharan Africa's connection to the Islamic world as well as Europe. The introduction of Islam into West Africa is another major theme for this section. Indeed, all three trade routes—the Silk Roads, the Indian Ocean trade network and the trans-Saharan trade routes—offer ways to explain the spread of Islam through trade. In my opinion, this is one of the most important factors contributing to the spread of Islam. This section offers an opportunity to debunk the myths of forced conversion to Islam that many students seem to subscribe to. It also provides an excellent opportunity to talk about the patterns of "social conversion" Jerry Bentley discusses in *Old World Encounters*, where the conversion of urban elites precedes conversion of the masses.[10]

The Third Era: The Mongols

The almost-complete unification of the Eurasian landmass under the Mongol empire marks a distinct stage in the history of the Silk Roads. Never before the emergence of the Mongol empire had a single political entity controlled the Silk Roads. The period of Pax Mongolica (Mongolian Peace), the thirteenth century, was marked by the unprecedented ease of travel across Eurasia. According to Marco Polo, there were supply stations throughout the empire that would provide lodging, horses, and other supplies for travelers:

> You must know that the city of Khanbalik is a centre from which many roads radiate to many provinces, one to each, and every road bears the name of the province to which it runs. The whole system is admirably contrived. When one of the Great Khan's messengers sets out along any of these roads, he has only to go twenty-five miles and there he finds a posting station. . . . At every post the messengers find a spacious and palatial hostelry for their lodging. . . . When the messengers are traveling through out-of-the way country, where there are no homesteads or habitations, they find that great khan had posts established even in these wilds. . . . But here stages are longer, posts are thirty-five miles apart and in some cases over forty miles . . .[11]

This system of waystations, known as *yams*, was supported by the use of a tablet, known as *paiza* or *gerege,* which authorized one to use the *yam*.[12] The new ability to travel allowed many peoples, such as merchants, missionaries, and others to go to lands where they had never dared venture before. Examples of such travelers included Marco Polo (1254–1324), a merchant from Venetia who served in the court of Khubilai Khan; Ibn Battuta (1304–c.1370), a Muslim *qadi* (judge) from Morocco who traveled all over Afro-Eurasia; and Rabban Sauma (c.1260–1313), a Nestorian Turk born in Northern China, who traveled into Europe.[13]

I use a chart from *Culture and Conquest in Mongolian Eurasia* by Thomas T. Allsen to show the degree of interculturalism within the Mongol empire.[14] Such evidence indicates an increased volume of cross-cultural interaction during the Mongol Era of the thirteenth century, even though there are some skeptics, such as Frances Wood, who argue that Marco Polo did not go to China and that the Pax Mongolica was "no more than one of those brilliant simplifications that can serve as chapter title for world history books."[15]

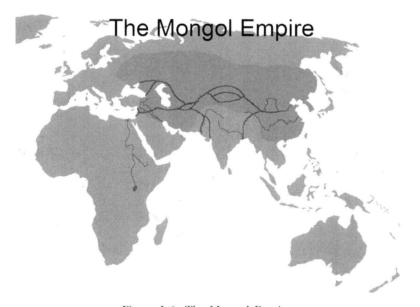

Figure 1.6. The Mongol Empire.

It is also possible to place the Mongol episode into a Western European historical context, even though the Mongols never directly controlled Western Europe. Many scholars accept that the Crusades of the eleventh, twelfth, and thirteenth centuries were key events that ended Western Europe's isolation. As a result of the Crusades, the volume of trade with cultures outside of Europe began to increase, giving the cities of Italy a geographic advantage over other areas of Western Europe. When the Mongols established their empire, a new circuit in Central Asia that would directly connect the Eastern Mediterranean and East Asia emerged, likely increasing the volume of trade with Europe.[16] The Europeans had mixed feelings about the Mongols, seeing them both as a possible invader and as a potential ally. The Crusader Kingdom of Jerusalem (1099–1291) was constantly threatened by the surrounding Muslim populations, and Christian Europeans thought the Mongols, who had conquered much of the Muslim population in the Middle East, might come to their aid. The stories of John of Plano Carpini (1180–1252) and William of Rubruck (c. 1220–1293) do a particularly good job of illustrating this point.[17] This is also a good time to discuss the transmission of key ideas and technologies in the fourteenth century, such as gunpowder and the printing press, as well as bubonic plague, demonstrating how one can teach "world history" in a manner that transcends regional boundaries.

Conclusion

By combining the normal regional history approach with some lessons on the trade routes, world history teachers can present a "connection" between various regions of the world that would otherwise be left out of the history of human communities. Many of the important topics I have covered in my discussion of these three main periods of the Silk Road would be almost impossible to present if one were to take a strictly compartmentalized and regional approach to teaching world history. The history of the Silk Roads offers a rich and invigorating new way to organize premodern Eurasian history that provides not only a connecting thread to tie all the various cultures together, but also provides opportunities for including many neglected areas we would not otherwise have the opportunity to teach.

Suggested Readings

Abu-Lughod, Janet L. *Before European Hegemony: The World System A.D. 1250–1350*. Oxford: Oxford University Press, 1989.

Allsen, Thomas T. *Culture and Conquest in Mongolian Eurasia*. Cambridge: Cambridge University Press, 2001.

Bennison, Amira K. "Muslim Universalism and Western Globalization," in *Globalization in World History*, ed. A. G. Hopkins. New York: W. W. Norton, 2002.

Bentley, Jerry. *Old World Encounters: Cross-Cultural Contacts and Exchanges in Pre-Modern Times*. New York and Oxford: Oxford University Press, 1993.

Bentley, Jerry, Herbert Ziegler, and Heather Streets. *Traditions and Encounters: A Brief Global History*, 1st ed. New York: McGraw-Hill, 2006.

Budge, E. A. Wallis, trans. *The Monks of Kublai Khan Emperor of China*. Brooklyn: AMS, 1975.

Dawson, Christopher. *Mission to Asia*. Toronto: University of Toronto Press, 1980.

Dunn, Ross E. *The Adventures of Ibn Battuta: A Muslim Traveler of the 14th Century*. Berkeley and Los Angeles: University of California Press, 2005.

Foltz, Richard C. *Religions of the Silk Road: Overland Trade and Cultural Exchange from Antiquity to the Fifteenth Century*. New York: St. Martin's Griffin, 1999.

Larner, John. *Marco Polo and the Discovery of the World*. New Haven and London: Yale University Press, 1999.

McNeill, William H. *Plagues and Peoples*. New York: Anchor Press, 1976.

Morgan, David. *The Mongols*. Cambridge, MA: Blackwell, 1986.

Polo, Marco. *The Travels*. New York: Penguin, 1958.

Wood, Frances. *Did Marco Polo Go to China?* Boulder: Westview, 1996.

————. *The Silk Road: Two Thousand Years in the Heart of Asia*. Berkeley and Los Angeles: University of California Press, 2002.

Wriggins, Sally Hovey. *The Silk Road Journey with Xuanzang*. Revised and Updated version. Boulder: Westview, 2004.

Notes

1. Frances Wood, *The Silk Road: Two Thousand Years in the Heart of Asia* (Berkeley and Los Angeles: University of California Press, 2002), is a good introductory book with many color illustrations.

2. Not all scholars see the Mongolian era as a distinct era in the Silk Road Trade. For example, Frances Wood argues that creation of the Mongol empire did not contribute to creating conditions favorable to travel and trade (*Silk Road*, 116). My argument is based on studies such as Janet L. Abu-Lughod's *Before European Hegemony: The World System A.D. 1250–1350*. (Oxford: Oxford University Press, 1989), which argues that new trade circuit that connected one end of Eurasia to another emerged as a result of creation of the Mongol empire.

3. The Silk Foundation, "History of Silk," http://www.silk-road.com/artl/silkhistory.shtml, Accessed August 16, 2007.

4. Jerry Bentley, Herbert Ziegler, and Heather Streets, *Traditions and Encounters: A Brief Global History*, 1st ed. (New York: McGraw-Hill, 2006) is the textbook I use in my class. Chapter 9, entitled "Cross-Cultural Exchanges on the Silk Roads," is a particularly useful chapter for this era.

5. Unless otherwise noted, I created all of these maps myself using Photoshop. I started with a generic world map from Wikipedia.com, and cut out North and South America so as to show only the Eastern Hemisphere. I made these maps because I was not happy with ones you can get from textbooks—they usually only show sections (such as the trans-Saharan trade route map that shows only Africa, and the Islamic world map that shows only the Mediterranean and Indus Valley). I thus consulted numerous publications to draw these maps as I wanted them. For other ideas on maps, please see Rebecca Wendelken's essay elsewhere in this volume.

6. Richard C. Foltz, *Religions of the Silk Road: Overland Trade and Cultural Exchange from Antiquity to the Fifteenth Century* (New York: St. Martin's Griffin, 1999), offers a general introduction to this subject, although I found his coverage of Buddhism to be insufficient. For example, he attempts to delve into Buddhism's interaction with other cultures and religions (such as the Gandhara synthesis and its Hellenistic influence), but he fails to explain the impact these influences had on Buddhism and instead ends up just providing a simple and uninspiring explanation of different Buddhist sects in the region (40–42, 52–54).

7. Bentley, Ziegler, and Streets' *Traditions and Encounters: A Brief Global History* takes such a position. William H. McNeill's *Plagues and Peoples* (New York: Anchor Press, 1976), also suggests that four separate disease pools developed in Middle East, India, China, and the Mediterranean basin respectively, converging together in the first century CE when trade routes that connected these four areas were firmly established (124).

8. A good discussion on this topic is in Amira K. Bennison, "Muslim Universalism and Western Globalization," in *Globalization in World History*, ed. A. G. Hopkins (New York: W. W. Norton, 2002), 73–98.

9. For basic discussion of Xuanzang's travel, consult Sally Hovey Wriggins's *The Silk Road Journey with Xuanzang*, revised and updated version (Boulder: Westview, 2004).

10. Jerry Bentley, *Old World Encounters: Cross-Cultural Contacts and Exchanges in Pre-Modern Times* (New York and Oxford: Oxford University Press, 1993), 5–20.

11. Marco Polo, *The Travels* (New York: Penguin, 1958), 150–51.

12. Some discussion of *paiza* can be found in David Morgan, *The Mongols* (Cambridge, MA: Blackwell, 1986), 103–107.

13. For more discussion on Ibn Battuta, see Ross E. Dunn, *The Adventures of Ibn Battuta: A Muslim Traveler of the 14th Century* (Berkeley and Los Angeles: University of California Press, 2005). Rabban Sauma's travel account is available as *The Monks of Kublai Khan Emperor of China*, trans. E. A. Wallis Budge (Brooklyn: AMS, 1975).

14. Thomas T. Allsen, *Culture and Conquest in Mongolian Eurasia* (Cambridge: Cambridge University Press, 2001), 8. The table indicates "personnel exchanges" within Mongol empire showing " 'Westerners' in the East" and " 'Easterners' in the West."

15. Frances Wood, *Did Marco Polo Go to China?* (Boulder: Westview, 1996), 116. John Larner's *Marco Polo and the Discovery of the World* (New Haven and London: Yale University Press, 1999) refutes Wood's theory.

16. Janet L. Abu-Lughod, *Before European Hegemony: The World System AD 1250–1350* (Oxford: Oxford University Press, 1989). Map on page 34 shows eight trade circuits.

17. Both John of Plano Carpini and William of Rubruck left detailed account of their travels, which can be found in *Mission to Asia* by Christopher Dawson (Toronto: University of Toronto Press, 1980).

Chapter 2

How to Use the Silk Roads in the European History Survey Course

Marybeth Carlson

It's not as if we need more topics to fill up a term's worth of European history. A Silk Roads unit is an obvious choice in a World History course or an Asian History survey. A historian of the Islamic world cannot make sense of Middle Eastern economies without examining the Silk Roads. But in many European history surveys, they earn a passing mention—perhaps in introducing the Crusades—or slip off the syllabus entirely.[1]

But the Silk Roads played a central role in shaping Europe's economy and in stirring medieval Europeans' curiosity about the wider world. This reality alone earns the topic a prominent place in a European survey. Moreover, an exploration of Europe's commercial ties to the rest of Eurasia provides students with a stimulating alternative to the traditional European historical narrative. Emphasizing interregional contacts brings Europe out of its own *sui generis* geographical box. Historians such as Marshall Hodgson, and more recently, William McNeill and Jerry Bentley, have argued that the histories of Eurasia and Africa can best be understood as a single unit.[2] Indeed, European history instructors often examine how Europe affected the rest of the world as a matter of course. But further study of the Silk Roads highlights how these interregional connections shaped the course of events within Europe as well. For example, examining how the Silk Roads linked Europe to the Eurasian economy for centuries contextualizes the confrontation between the Ottoman empire and European states.

Organizing a history survey around a conceptual narrative that recognizes the underlying unity of the Afro-Eurasian world in the preindustrial era allows for a more sophisticated analysis of change over time in European history. For example, David Christian suggests that the study of "trans-ecological exchanges" along the Silk Roads offers a valuable alternative to the more traditional "trans-civilizational exchanges," since it incorporates an appreciation of the role of environment and geography in human affairs.[3] Outsiders' views of European customs (and European travelers' notes on what they found remarkable in other cultures) can help students recognize not only what was distinctive about European culture historically, but also what linked Europe to the larger world before the sixteenth century. Hence, the Silk Roads is not merely yet another topic to try to stuff into a European history survey, but rather is of fundamental importance for understanding the European past.

This chapter examines how the themes of the conventional European history survey can be adapted to incorporate material from the Silk Roads. During the classical era, the Greeks and Romans built empires that brought them into contact with the Silk Roads. Products from Asia became very desirable commodities. In the Byzantine and Medieval eras, despite conflicts with the Islamic world, Italian merchants continued to carry luxuries from the Silk Roads to the West. By the time of the Renaissance, Europe's desire to emulate the splendor of the East inspired a number of technological and commercial innovations. Even during the development of nineteenth-century imperialism, excavation of the art treasures of the Silk Roads became another theater in which to act out imperial rivalries. The topics and readings suggested here can enliven discussions and enhance learning opportunities in European History courses.

Knowledge of the Silk Roads in the Classical Mediterranean

We know little about trade between the Mediterranean and Central Asia or between the Mediterranean and the Indian Ocean basin before Alexander's campaigns. It seems logical to assume that some novelties from inner Asia made their way through Persia to the Ionian city-states and onward to Greece—and vice versa. Herodotus passed along some Persian lore about a few Central Asian peoples, notably the Scythians, in Book IV of the *Histories*. But documented European interaction with the people and goods of the Silk Roads began with Alexander's conquests in Central Asia. The Hellenistic world not only facilitated the circulation of material goods, but it provided a common cultural sphere for diffusing ideas and artistic methods and motifs from South Asia to the Mediterranean and back again.[4] Seleucus I appears to have sent an ambassador, one Megathenes, to the court of the Mauryan empire on the Indian subcontinent, around the end of the second century BCE

Fragments of his account of Chandragupta's ("Sandrocottus") capital *are* available online.[5] Megathenes devotes considerable attention to the capture, care, and training of elephants, which Mauryan rulers sent as gifts to the Seleucids. The *Indika* described the caste system, "wool" that grew on trees (probably a reference to cotton), and other textiles made from tree bark. The latter is possibly a reference to silk, since for many centuries the Greeks and Romans continued to subscribe to the misconception that silk came from a kind of tree.[6]

The Romans encountered silk firsthand in 53 BCE, when Marcus Licinius Crassus, triumvir and governor of the Roman province of Syria, went to battle against the Parthians at Carrhae, near the Euphrates River. The battle was a devastating loss to the Romans, because arrows from the composite bows of the Parthians pierced the Romans' heavy armor. At the height of the battle, the Parthians unfurled banners of a material that shone like fire, presumably silk, terrifying the soldiers, who broke ranks and fled.[7]

Nevertheless, silk became a highly sought-after product in the Roman Empire, the source of fashionable gowns as well as senatorial togas that were more comfortable than the traditional wool. Due to the hostility between the Parthians and the Romans, as well as the Parthians' desire to forestall any direct contact between the Romans and the Han Chinese, most of the Romans' silk, spices, and fragrances were routed through the Kushan empire in South Asia (which had succeeded the Mauryan empire). Originally, Europeans were unaware of the details of Silk Road trade because merchants from the Arabian coastline acted as middlemen for these transactions. But after envoys from several Indian states visited the emperor Augustus, Europeans gained a better understanding of the silk routes. It was probably during the first century CE, that the *Periplus Maris Erythraei* (The Periplus of the Erythraean Sea) described the ports and markets of the Indian Ocean. (The "Erythraean Sea" was the Greeks' name for the Red Sea, but included the Indian Ocean and the Persian Gulf.) The Periplus credited the Greek ship captain Hippalus with the European discovery of the route to India and the knowledge of how to use the seasonal monsoon winds to navigate these waters.[8] Traders carried Roman coins, wines, and perfumes as well as glass, frankincense, and other goods from the eastern borders of the empire and exchanged them for indigo, ivory, spices, gems, silk thread, and silk and cotton textiles.

The demand for Silk Road luxuries was so high that it represented a constant drain on the Roman supply of silver and gold, according to Pliny the Elder, who complained about such profligacy.[9] The cost of importing such volumes of silk cannot have benefited the increasingly disordered Roman economy during the end of the empire. Desire for better access to the luxuries of the overland trade may even have contributed to the rationale behind Rome's wars with Parthia. Instructors can better help students understand the reasons for the Romans' efforts to expand into Armenia and Mesopotamia, not to mention the end of the empire itself, by drawing a connection between the Silk Roads and the Mediterranean.

Silk Roads–Inspired Changes in the European Middle Ages and Renaissance

Europe's links with the Silk Roads continued to shape its history in the medieval period. Demand for silk remained vigorous in the Byzantine empire, where the state maintained silk-weaving workshops to support its diplomatic maneuvers and supply palace and ecclesiastical needs. But the workshops had to import their silk thread via the Sassanian empire (which had replaced the Parthians). The Sassanians made sure that the secret of raw silk remained a mystery. Ultimately, it was the interchange of ideas as well as goods along the Silk Roads that broke the embargo. Christianity spread east along the Silk Roads in the form of Nestorianism, which emphasizes a separation between the human and divine essences in Jesus Christ. While the orthodox church considered Nestorian Christianity a heresy, this religious link between some Silk Roads peoples and the Mediterranean world provided a vector for the spread of sericulture skills to the West. According to the Byzantine writer Procopius, it was two Nestorian monks who broke the monopoly in the sixth century by smuggling silkworm cocoons to Constantinople during the reign of Justinian.[10]

Silk production techniques spread from Byzantium to the rest of Europe after the Fourth Crusade in 1204. Venetian textile merchants, who then assumed a privileged position in Byzantium, adapted the production techniques of the imperial state workshops to conditions in their own city. Venetian state agencies and guilds took on complementary roles in constructing a domestic silk industry, even creating a precedent-setting patent system. Craftsmen carried such silk fabrication techniques to other Renaissance city-states, where further technical innovations appeared. In Bologna, for example, artisans produced silk on a circular mill that included a hydraulic wheel, a mechanical winder, and bobbins, creating, in effect, a factory, two centuries before the Industrial Revolution. These inventions, freeing Europe's economy from its dependence on silk supplies from the Silk Road, transformed Europe's markets and production systems as they were carried beyond Italy.[11]

Silk was far from the only product from the Silk Roads to stimulate the growth of the European economy. The bazaars of Alexandria, Damascus, Aleppo, and other Asian entrepôts stimulated many of the technical and artistic innovations of Renaissance Europe. Italian merchants began to replace their galleys with the larger, single-masted cogs developed in northern Europe to hold more cargo. These ships enabled merchants to better meet the growing demand for goods from the Silk Roads. All of this international commerce required new ways of doing business—bills of exchange, double entry bookkeeping—all essential to the early development of capitalism. The Silk Roads carried Chinese inventions to Europe, including gunpowder, printing, paper, and porcelain, that all contributed to the transformation of the European economy by stimulating mining and metallurgy and the creation of the entire printing industry.[12] Europeans were even able to adapt water mills to paper manufacture in a way that enabled them to export cheaper, better quality paper back to the Islamic world.[13]

The Silk Roads also played a role in the development of the stock market—and ultimately, of stock market regulation—as a result of a speculative craze for tulips in seventeenth-century Holland. Caravans from the Tian Shan and Pamir mountain ranges first carried tulip bulbs across the steppe. Among the Persians, the flowers became a metaphor for perfection and female beauty, while in the Ottoman empire, tulips were regarded as one of the most valued blossoms in the garden. In the 1560s, some tulips wound up in a Flemish cloth merchant's kitchen garden, where a botanist friend admired and transplanted them. He passed them to fellow botanist Carolus Clusius, who founded the first botanical garden in the Dutch Republic at the University of Leiden. Clusius developed a number of new hybrids, which found their way across the Low Countries and beyond—sometimes as the result of thefts from his garden! In comparison to other European flowers of the era, tulips had intense colors as well as petals whose colors were sharply defined rather than shaded into each other. These characteristics inspired a passion for tulips in the seventeenth-century *bon ton,* which in turn created a commodity market for tulip bulbs in Holland. Speculators who had no intention of ever planting tulip bulbs in their own gardens bought the bulbs simply to sell them to another speculator for higher prices. Moreover, the very nature of this particular commodity persuaded novices to invest in tulip bulbs without any background in the trade and with relatively little capital. As a result, demand escalated—and so did prices. Thus, by 1635, as prices doubled or tripled every few days, speculators were trading promissory notes, buying shares of a single bulb and selling on margin. Participants in the craze traded the most prized varieties for land, houses, coaches, and all manner of valuable objects. The bubble

burst in early February 1637, leading Dutch magistrates to publish endless sermons on the folly of speculation. As a result, investment analysts
still invoke the financial mania for a flower from the passes of the Silk
Roads any time a stock market bubble seems imminent.[14]

The Silk Roads' impact on Europe during the Middle Ages and
Renaissance has been overlooked in traditional approaches to teaching.
But recent and ongoing research is demonstrating that Europeans'
desire for the products carried along the Silk Roads transformed their
economies. The skills they learned in the bazaars where they traded
helped set the stage for capitalism. Their consciousness of the splendor
of Asian cities aroused a curiosity about the world that would propel
them beyond their shores. Exposing students to such findings gives them
an understanding of a Europe that is more complex and culturally richer
than the standard narrative.

Europeans' Exploration of the Silk Roads during the Mongol Era

In the thirteenth century, Chinggis Khan unified the Mongol tribes of
the Eurasian steppe. A series of trade disputes with kingdoms along the
Silk Roads then set off Mongol expansion in Central Asia. Ultimately,
Chinggis and his successors constructed an empire that stretched from
Novgorod in the west to the Pacific Ocean in the east and south to the
Arabian Sea. The unification of the lands surrounding the Silk Roads
created a "Pax Mongolica" that made it possible for European envoys
and merchants to travel the entire length of the Silk Roads. It was at
this time that Europeans first came into direct contact with China and
their accounts of their travels provide us with valuable windows into the
European mindset, while creating opportunities for students to engage
in historiographical inquiry.[15]

Travelers' accounts from this period of history have been better
preserved and permit students to discover for themselves the worldviews
that Westerners brought to their experience of Asia. Jerry Bentley's excellent material on the *World History Matters* Web site furnishes students
with a list of analytical questions to pose in reading such narratives, as
well as a sample analysis, an annotated bibliography, and a list of travel
accounts available online.[16]

The earliest European authority on life in the Mongol empire
came from an embassy Pope Innocent IV dispatched to the Mongols in
1245, hoping to find an ally against the Seljuq Turks who were attack-
ing the Latin kingdoms of the Levant. The expedition's leader, John of

Plano Carpini, a Franciscan friar, was unable to accomplish the pope's instructions to convert his hosts, but did witness the proclamation of a new Great Khan. On his return, he described his adventures in an account that circulated in Europe in excerpts in Vincent of Beauvais' *Speculum Historiale*.[17]

The pope was not the only European ruler seeking help from the Mongols in dislodging the Muslims from the Mideast. Louis IX of France, leader of the Seventh and Eighth Crusades, sent William of Rubruck, a Flemish Franciscan on a mission to convert the Mongols and then secure their assistance against the Muslims. Rubruck and his party traveled all the way to Karakorum in a roundtrip journey that lasted most of three years. Believing King Louis was still on Crusade, Rubruck made for Syria when he returned. But the king had returned to France, and the Provincial of the Franciscans wanted Rubruck to teach in Acre. Instead, he wrote the king a report of his trip, known as the *Itinerarium fratris Willielmi de Rubruquis de ordine fratrum Minorum, Galli, Anno gratia 1253 ad partes Orientales*. The *Itinerarium* is an observant and detailed description of the Mongols' life. He reports on the presence of Nestorian Christians along the route and in Karakorum, suggesting they were the sources of rumors that occasionally reached Europe that the Mongols had converted to Christianity. Few copies of the *Itinerarium* circulated in Europe, so that despite its clarity and detail, it never achieved much influence.[18]

History students can also gain an understanding of the European past by examining the impressions of Rabban Sauma, a Silk Road traveler from China who journeyed to Rome, Paris, and Gascony. A Nestorian Christian monk who set off on a pilgrimage to Jerusalem, Rabban Sauma and a companion, Rabban Markos, found their way blocked by warfare. Instead, the ruler of the Persian Ilkhanate sent him on an embassy to Europe in search of allies against the Mamluks. While he obtained audiences with the kings of France and England and with Pope Nicholas IV, soon after his election in 1288, Rabban Sauma did not succeed in winning anyone's commitment for the alliance. He returned to the Ilkhanate, and his embassy faded from memory, except for a few brief references in the archives of the Vatican and of England and France. But a Syriac translation of his journals turned up in Iran in 1887 and was translated into English in the 1920s.[19]

Meanwhile, Venetian merchants were making the most of the Mongol conquest of the steppes to extend their commercial networks. Traders such as Maffeo and Niccolò Polo made their way to Venice's outposts along the Black Sea to do business. The brothers Polo, however, found themselves diverted along the route home and ended up in the Great

Khan's new capital of Khanbaliq (now Beijing) in 1266. After returning home, they made a second journey in 1271, bringing Niccolò's son, Marco, along for the adventure that Marco then described to a cellmate after his return, years later. Those recollections, known as *The Travels of Marco Polo* in English (and as *Il Milione*, the "Million Lies" by scoffing Italians) were widely circulated in Europe (in sometimes conflicting translations), even before the invention of printing presses. His travels inspired mapmakers and European sea explorers, notably Columbus, who is known to have owned a copy of the Latin edition.[20]

The Travels of Marco Polo also offers European history students an opportunity to examine how historians use a critical reading of sources to construct an understanding of the past. In this case, the class examines the debate over the authenticity of Marco Polo's work. Frances Wood, in *Did Marco Polo Go to China?*, doubts that Marco Polo actually traveled through the Mongol empire, arguing that his tale was more probably cobbled together from others, with a sizeable dose of fantasy added. She observes that no one has found a reference to the famous merchant of Venice in any of China's archives, which do mention other Westerners. There are a variety of Chinese customs that were so startlingly different from Europe's culture that one might expect Polo to have commented on them—the Chinese style of writing, chopsticks, tea drinking, or woodblock printing. But he ignores all of these in his memoir.[21] On the other hand, in *Marco Polo and the Discovery of the World*, John Larner logically points out that if the account had been plagiarized from other sources, then those sources must also have been fraudulent. If Marco Polo had been a minor Mongol official rather than the "governor" his memoirs style him as, then it is logical that the archives do not note his presence in the empire. Polo's book contains so much detailed information about the world beyond Europe that it would represent a remarkable feat of research indeed, if he actually had never gone.[22] These contrasting arguments—both written in a lucid and attractive style—offer students models of historical argument.

The disintegration of the Mongol hold over Asia made it difficult for the market centers along the Silk Roads to maintain a defense against both bandits and a lack of natural resources. Advances in shipbuilding and seafaring technologies in Europe made commerce along ocean routes safer and less expensive than by means of caravan. The mood in Venice turned gloomy after Vasco da Gama made his trip around the Cape of Good Hope to Calicut: "[A]ll the people from across the mountains who once came to Venice to buy spices with their money will now turn to Lisbon . . . because they will be able to buy at a cheaper price."[23] New discoveries and new products continued to instigate change in Europe's economy and culture, but the Silk Roads' commercial networks were no longer a key element in those changes.

Foreign Devils on the Silk Road in the Age of Imperialism

Even after seaborne empires replaced overland trade, the concept of the Silk Roads can still be a useful device in modern European history courses. An examination of the beginnings of Western exploration and excavation of the Silk Roads in the early twentieth century can stimulate students' interest in the age of imperialism. Sven Hedin, Aurel Stein, and other adventurers traveled deep into the Taklamakan and Gobi deserts to unearth the remains of once-powerful market towns and cave temples. These explorations took place within the context of the "Great Game," a struggle between the British and Russian empires for political control in Central Asia. It was the published accounts of these explorations which created the modern consciousness of the scale of the transcontinental caravan trade, long forgotten by that time. Their expeditions turned up literally tens of thousands of Buddhist art treasures and ancient scrolls in Central Asian territory only nominally under the control of China's Qing Dynasty by this time. An international race to cart off as many of the artifacts as possible to vaults in European museums ensued, since the Qing Dynasty at the time was far too feeble to have stopped them. Peter Hopkirk's *Foreign Devils on the Silk Road* is a lively, readable account of these exploits. His book questions the ethics of such cultural pilfering, but also presents the then-current defense of views about saving the material for posterity, providing a rich source of material for class discussion.[24]

At present, the European Union is debating the admission of Turkey. Arguments against Turkish membership tend to emphasize a unified European culture, and, for members of some Christian Democrat parties, a Christian identity. Will increased Turkish immigration throughout Europe, the inevitable result of its membership, challenge that identity? What does it mean to be European, after all? These debates make the study of the Silk Roads ever more relevant in a European history survey. The Silk Roads, which so often acted as a link between Europe and Asia, can provide students with a new perspective on historical relationships that play a role in contemporary issues.[25]

Including the Silk Road in the European survey will help remind us that globalization has never ignored Europe. It is not merely a twenty-first-century construct, a product of the Internet, or a side effect of the actions of multinational corporations and Hollywood. Europe's knowledge of and contacts with the rest of the world, have always shaped its history, and thus the Silk Roads should be an integral part of any European survey.

Suggested Readings

Brotton, Jerry. *The Renaissance Bazaar: From the Silk Road to Michelangelo.* Oxford: Oxford University Press, 2003.

Delanty, Gerard, ed. *Europe and Asia beyond East and West* (Routledge/ESA Studies in European Societies). New York: Routledge, 2006.

Foltz, Richard C. *Overland Trade and Cultural Exchange from Antiquity to the Fifteenth Century.* New York: St. Martin's Press, 1999.

Larner, John. *Marco Polo and the Discovery of the World.* 1999. Reprint, New Haven: Yale Nota Bene Paperback, 2001.

Lin, Xinru, and Lynda Norene Shaffer. *Connections across Eurasia: Transportation, Communications, and Cultural Exchange across the Silk Roads.* New York: McGraw-Hill, 2007.

Mola, Luca. *The Silk Industry in Renaissance Venice.* Baltimore: Johns Hopkins University Press, 2000.

Rachewiltz, Igor de. *Papal Envoys to the Great Khans.* Stanford: Stanford University Press, 1971.

Rossabi, Morris. *Voyager from Xanadu: Rabban Sauma and the First Journey from China to the West.* Tokyo and New York: Kodansha International, 1992.

Notes

1. Two outstanding resources for nonspecialists who want to use the Silk Roads in a European survey are Xinru Liu, *The Silk Road: Overland Trade and Cultural Interactions in Eurasia, Essays in Global and Comparative History* (Washington, DC: American Historical Association, 1998) and Morris Rossabi "The Silk Roads: An Educational Resource," *Education about Asia* 4 (1999): 16–20, as well as those sources referenced in the other chapters of this book.

2. Marshall G. S. Hodgson, "The Interrelations of Societies in History," in *Rethinking World History: Essays on Europe, Islam and World History* (Cambridge: Cambridge University Press, 1993), 3–28; William H. McNeill, "World History and the Rise and Fall of the West," *Journal of World History* 9 (1998): 215–36; and Jerry H. Bentley, "Hemispheric Integration, 500–1500 CE," *Journal of World History* 9 (1998): 237–54.

3. David Christian, "Silk Roads or Steppe Roads? The Silk Roads in World History," *Journal of World History* 11 (2000): 1–26. The essays in *Europe and Asia Beyond East and West (Routledge/ESA Studies in European Societies)*, ed. Gerard Delanty (New York: Routledge, 2006) offer a number of suggestions for rethinking how Europe fits into larger Eurasian historical patterns.

4. Richard C. Foltz, *Overland Trade and Cultural Exchange from Antiquity to the Fifteenth Century* (New York: St. Martin's Press, 1999).

5. Megasthenes, *Indika* (http://www.mssu.edu/projectsouthasia/history/primarydocs/Foreign_Views/GreekRoman/Megasthenes-Indika.htm, accessed July 1, 2007). This material is taken from John W. McCrindle's *Ancient India and Described by Megasthenes and Arrian* (1877; reprinted New Delhi: Munshiram Manoharlal, 2000). Also useful is Jean-François Salles, "Achaemenid and Hellenistic Trade in the Indian Ocean," in *The Indian Ocean in Antiquity*, ed. Julian Reade (London: Kegan Paul International, 1996), 251–67.

6. Liu, *Silk Road*, 4.

7. Robert Collins, "The Deadly Banners of Carrhae," (http://www.silkroad.com/artl/carrhae.shtml, accessed July 3, 2007). Collins also reports that, "[i]n 36 B.C. a Chinese force attacked and captured a Central Asian town, Li-chien, some 3,700 miles east of Rome. It had been held by another band of barbarians, the Huns, but in the town the Chinese captured 145 foreign mercenary soldiers. There were three peculiar aspects to this town. The name, Li-chien, was one of the Chinese names later applied to the Roman Empire. It was protected by wooden stockades, a Roman technique. Its soldiers employed the testudo formation of overlapping shields." The details suggest that the town's defenders may have been survivors of the 10,000 Romans captured at Carrhae.

8. The Periplus is available online as "The Voyage around the Erythraean Sea" at the Silk Road Seattle Project (http://depts.washington.edu/silkroad/texts/periplus/periplus.html, accessed June 30, 2007). The Internet Ancient History Sourcebook also has it (http://www.fordham.edu/halsall/ancient/periplus.html, accessed June 30, 2007). Both are drawn from William H. Schoff, tr. and ed., *The Periplus of the Erythraean Sea: Travel and Trade in the Indian Ocean by a Merchant of the First Century* (1912).

9. Xinru Liu and Lynda Norene Shaffer, *Connections across Eurasia: Transportation, Communications and Cultural Exchange across the Silk Roads* (New York: McGraw-Hill, 2007).

10. "Introduction of Sericulture into the Byzantine Empire" in Anna Muthesius, *Studies in Silk in Byzantium* (London: Pindar Press, 2004). For the passage from Procopius, see The Internet Medieval Sourcebook, *Procopius: The Roman Silk Industry*, http://www.fordham.edu/halsall/source/550byzsilk.html.

11. Luca Mola, *The Silk Industry in Renaissance Venice* (Baltimore: Johns Hopkins University Press, 2000); and Carlo Poni, "The Circular Silk Mill: A Factory before the Industrial Revolution in Early Modern Europe," *History of Technology* 21 (1999): 65–85. On the diffusion of silk textile manufacturing technologies, see, for example, Lien Bich Luu, "French Speaking Refugees and the Foundation of the London Silk Industry in the 16th Century," *Proceedings of the Huguenot Society of Great Britain and Ireland* 26, no. 5 (1997): 564–76 or Natalie K. Rothstein, "Canterbury and London: The Silk Industry in the Late Seventeenth Century," *Textile History* 20, no. 1 (1989): 33–47.

12. Jerry Brotton, *The Renaissance Bazaar: from the Silk Road to Michelangelo* (Oxford: Oxford University Press, 2003).

13. Jonathan M. Bloom, "Revolution by the Ream: A History of Paper," *Saudi Aramco World* 50 (May/June 1999) 28–39. Also available online at http://www.saudiaramcoworld.com/issue/199903/revolution.by.the.ream-a.history.of.paper.htm. Accessed July 1, 2007.

14. Mike Dash, *TulipoMania: The Story of the World's Most Coveted Flower and the Extraordinary Passions It Aroused* (New York: Crown Publishers, 2000) and Simon Schama, *The Embarrassment of Riches: An Interpretation of Dutch Culture in the Golden Age* (New York: Knopf, 1987).

15. The Web site, "The Mongols in World History," (http://afe.easia.columbia.edu/mongols/index.html, accessed July 9, 2007) offers students descriptions of the key figures in the establishment of the empire, analyses for their success, and an assessment of the Mongols' influence on world history, as well as an assortment of maps and images.

16. See http://chnm.gmu.edu/worldhistorysources/unpacking/travelmain.html. Another list of Silk Road travelers, along with an annotated bibliography, can be found at http://www.silk-road.com/toc/index.html.

17. I. de Rachewiltz, *Papal Envoys to the Great Khans* (Stanford: Stanford University Press, 1971). For a full version of Friar John's narrative, see "The long and wonderful voyage of Frier Iohn de Plano Carpini" (full version: http://etext.library.adelaide.edu.au/h/hakluyt/voyages/carpini/complete.html, accessed July 8, 2007) or for excerpts, see "The Journey of Friar John of Pian de Carpine to the Court of Kuyuk Khan, 1245–47" (http://depts.washington.edu/silkroad/texts/carpini.html, accessed July 8, 2007).

18. "First Europeans Traveled to Khan's Court" (http://www.silk-road.com/artl/carrub.shtml, accessed July 2, 2007). His report can be read online, "William of Rubruck's Account of the Mongols" (http://depts.washington.edu/silkroad/texts/rubruck.html, accessed July 2, 2007).

19. Morris Rossabi, *Voyager from Xanadu: Rabban Sauma and the First Journey from China to the West* (Tokyo and New York: Kodansha International, 1992). For Sauma's account, see "The History of the Life and Travels of Rabban Sawma, translated from the Syriac by Sir E. A. Wallis Budge (1928)" (http://depts.washington.edu/silkroad/texts/sauma.html, accessed July 2, 2007).

20. *The Travels of Marco Polo* (New York: Penguin Classics, 1958). A version is also available at Project Gutenberg (http://www.gutenberg.org/etext/10636 and http://www.gutenberg.org/etext/12410).

21. Frances Wood, *Did Marco Polo Go to China?* (Boulder: Westview, 1996).

22. John Larner, *Marco Polo and the Discovery of the World* (New Haven: Yale University Press, 1999; reprinted Yale Nota Bene Paperback, 2001). An earlier authority is Igor de Rachewiltz, "Marco Polo went to China," *Zentralasiatische Studien* 27 (1997): 34–92; Additions and corrections, 28 (1998), 177; Rachewiltz summarizes his arguments at http://dspace.anu.edu.au/bitstream/1885/41883/1/Marcopolo.html. See also Rossabi, "Did Marco Polo Really Go to China?" at http://afe.easia.columbia.edu/mongols/pop/polo/mp_essay.htm.

23. Brotton, *Renaissance Bazaar*, 170.

24. Peter Hopkirk, *Foreign Devils on the Silk Road: The Search for the Lost Treasures of Central Asia* (Oxford: Oxford University Press, 1980).

25. Ulrich Beck and Gerard Delanty, "Europe from a Cosmopolitan Perspective," in *Europe and Asia Beyond East and West*, 15.

.

Chapter 3

The Silk Road and Chinese Identity, Past and Present

Robert W. Foster

Courses in Chinese history often emphasize China's relative isolation and stress the internal developments of the civilization. However, when we bring the Silk Road into Chinese history, we bring China out of its "splendid isolation" and make it both a contributor to and recipient of Eurasian culture. Placing Chinese history in this broader context helps us avoid projecting the vision of a modern nation-state with stable borders and a clear identity back into the past. Rather than thinking solely about the internal developments leading to contemporary "China," we look at East Asia as part of Eurasia and see how the tides of peoples, ideas, and technology shaped the cultures of the continent.[1] Furthermore, underscoring the historical importance of Central Asia in the Chinese worldview makes the nineteenth-century confrontation with the West more understandable. We see that the Chinese were not ignoring a Western threat, but were dealing with Westerners within their traditional worldview, placing greatest emphasis on the nations close by. China's West was not Europe, but the Silk Road of Central Asia, which profoundly shaped Chinese culture and continues to shape Chinese identity and policy today.

The traditional Chinese account of the Silk Road's origins is that Han Dynasty Emperor Wudi (r. 141–87 BCE) sent his general, Zhang Qian, to campaign against the nomadic Xiongnu people to the north of Han and so "opened the Silk Road." This created a paradigm with China serving as the creator of the Silk Road to achieve Wudi's desire to have access to the "heavenly horses" of Central Asia. Wudi wanted these horses either for his cavalry or for himself, since they were grand animals, faster than Chinese mounts, that "sweated blood" when they ran. Though colorful, this account overlooks the long-standing flow of technology and ideas through Eurasia from well before the Han dynasty.

This China-centered view developed out of the vision in the Chinese sources themselves. There was a tradition of viewing the world divided between China, the "Central Kingdom," and surrounding non-Chinese, who had either fallen under the sway of Chinese culture (referred to as "cooked barbarians") or had not ("raw barbarians"). In the twentieth century, many historians argued for the relative isolation of Chinese civilization and its development independent of other civilizations. In part, this was a reaction to initial Western studies of China that suggested the literate Chinese could only have developed from the ancient civilizations of the Middle East.

Redressing this view of an isolated China (or Europe, for that matter), while not falling into the trap of suggesting all civilization has its roots in the Middle East, is well under way. The development of the chariot, bronzes, and writing in China illustrates the varying degrees of influence the rest of Eurasia had upon China's history. Archaeology has been particularly important in this regard. It seems clear now that one of the key technologies of the Bronze Age, the chariot, was a Middle Eastern, or Central Asian, invention that spread along the steppe to China. Archeologists have discovered fully formed chariots buried in elite tombs from the twelfth century BCE, but no prior evidence to suggest that it was an indigenous invention. Thus, the chariot, which was central to the military power of the Shang dynasty (ca. 1600-ca. 1045 BCE), is most likely a foreign import. Bronze is a good example of a technology that local cultures adapted and transformed. There is little doubt that Chinese bronzes are different in form and function from Middle Eastern bronzes. But was the actual technology for making bronze independently discovered in the Mediterranean and in China? Here, too, there seems to be evidence that techniques for smelting bronze diffused across Eurasia, but were employed differently in China, an area rich in the tin and copper needed to make bronze. The early Chinese cultures used the new metal technology to shape vessels that conformed to their traditional pottery styles. However, the last of the Bronze Age discoveries in China, writing, appears to be an entirely independent invention. Unlike the chariot, archaeological evidence—pottery markings and oracle bones, in particular—demonstrates the evolution of writing within the Chinese context. The different levels of Eurasian influence that are apparent in the archaeological record force us to rethink old paradigms. To lean too far toward cultural autonomy or too far toward cultural diffusion from the Middle East does not fit the evidence we currently have.

At the same time, products from what is now China flowed both east and west. Scholars have found jades from Khotan in the Tarim Basin (modern Xinjiang province in the PRC) at Hongshan cultural sites dating to 3000 BCE in Manchuria. Chinese silk has been found at Sapalli in Bactria, dated to ca. 1900–1700 BCE. It is better for us to think of the Han dynasty's "opening" of the Silk Road not as a moment of increased international awareness among the Chinese, or a Chinese creation based upon their desire to open trade between East and Central Asia, but as an attempt by Han Wudi to control an ancient trade network for the greater profit of his empire.

As Han dynasty awareness of Central Asia grew, we see in Han sources a desire to demarcate what was distinctively "Chinese" from barbarian. The official histories of the period note how the Xiongnu were everything the Chinese were not: "they" ate uncooked meat, did not respect the elderly, and wore skins. The portrayal spoke volumes for not only what the Han historians viewed as barbarian customs to the north, but perhaps even more about what it ought to mean to be Chinese. Only recently have scholars of China dealt seriously with the Xiongnu by looking beyond the deprecatory Chinese sources and depending more upon archaeology to describe an advanced semi-nomadic society that benefited from its position as middleman between East Asia and West Asia.[2]

Perhaps one of the great ironies for those who would argue for China's cultural autonomy is the reality that for most of the region's history, a significant proportion of Chinese have been ruled by non-Chinese from the north. The other side of this relationship, though, is that these non-Chinese rulers often shifted from being "raw" to "cooked" by adopting Chinese customs, language, and political systems. After the decline of the Han dynasty in the early third century CE, much of northern China was occupied by Turkic peoples. Under their patronage, Buddhism, which had entered China along the Silk Road during the Han, flourished. Incredible Buddhist grottoes and cave complexes were developed throughout northern China at sites such as Longmen, Yungang, and most famously at Dunhuang. The caves at Dunhuang are an excellent example of the blending of peoples and cultures as expressed through devotional art. We can trace the tides of control at Dunhuang through the various families that sponsored the Buddhist art in the caves. At times Turkic people held sway, at times Chinese, and at times Tibetans. Consequently, the caves are awash with different artistic styles and doctrinal representations of varying schools of Buddhism. Other sites farther west in the Tarim basin mark the transfer of Greco-Roman artistic styles from Gandharan culture, a remnant of Alexander's Asian empire, and its fusion with Chinese techniques as the styles mixed in sites such as Dunhuang.

Beyond providing an interesting point for the introduction of artistic cross-fertilization, Buddhism is also an excellent means for examining intellectual exchange between very different cultures. The world's major religions were all transported along the Silk Road with the merchants and missionaries who carried their faiths with them. Buddhism is certainly the religion most associated with the Silk Road, though it was later supplanted by Islam in Central Asia. While scholars of China tend to focus on the Indian origins of Buddhism, we also need to recognize that Buddhism was widely accepted in central and southwest Asia prior to the rise of Islam. This fact is abundantly apparent in the Buddhist art of monastic centers in Afghanistan, such as the recently destroyed colossal Buddhas of Bamiyan. Buddhism arrived in Persia well before China. In fact, based on oasis art that shows Buddhist figures clothed as Persians, some now argue that Buddhism spread outward from northern India into southwest Asia and then along the trade routes to China. Along the way, Buddhism adapted to the cultures it encountered and vice versa. For China, the classic cases are early translations of Buddhist sutras and the transformation of Avalokitesvara.

In order to make the new religion comprehensible to the Chinese, Central Asian monks, such as Kumarajiva (344–413), attempted to "match concepts" between Buddhist doctrine and traditional Chinese ideas. The consequence was that early in its existence in China, Buddhism was closely associated with Daoism. Translators and missionaries spoke of a Buddhist Dao, or "Way," in the same sense that the Daoists and Confucians each had a Way. By using Chinese terms to relate Buddhist ideas, the translations made new concepts more accessible, but also obscured their original meaning. There were clear areas of conflict between Buddhism and Chinese culture. First and foremost was the conflict between the Buddhist call to renounce the world and join a monastic community and the Chinese belief in the continuity of the family. How could one both be a true, celibate pursuer of enlightenment and nirvana, while at the same time fulfilling one's duty to parents and ancestors? It is no surprise that the Chinese found Vimalakirti so appealing. Here was a disciple of Buddha who was both an enlightened being and an accomplished businessman and father. In China, Buddhism became worldlier with fewer distinctions between monks and lay believers.

The transformation of Avalokitesvara is also a case in point for the power of Chinese culture to shape Buddhism. In India, Avalokitesvara was a male figure, the bodhisattva of compassion. As his story moved into China, the early conceptual match seems to have been the Queen Mother of the West. Avalokitesvara, known in Chinese as Guanyin (Kan-non in Japanese) became more and more feminized the farther east and the later in history he/she went. While Buddhism undoubtedly brought new ideas into Chinese culture, China also shaped the Buddhist traditions that were to prevail in East Asia. This has led modern scholars to debate whether Buddhism conquered China, or China conquered Buddhism.

The tension between original doctrine and cultural adaptation of religion is not simply one modern commentators note. A number of Chinese Buddhists were also concerned that their translations were tainted by native ideas, or that the transmission of Buddhist ideas was incomplete, leading to confusion among the Chinese. Spurred by the desire for clarity, Chinese monks embarked upon pilgrimages to the home of Buddhism. Most famous of these traveling monks were Faxian (fl. 399–414) and Xuanzang (ca. 596–664). Both men left records of their journeys that are valuable accounts of the history of the Silk Road. In them we read of the dangers of travel, the mixture of cultures, and the intermingling of religions in the period before Islam's rapid rise and spread through Southwest and Central Asia.

Xuanzang, concerned that Chinese Buddhism had strayed from the original teachings, undertook his journey at the height of the Tang dynasty's influence in Central Asia. However, the emperor had banned international travel, so Xuanzang had to sneak out of the empire in his pursuit of knowledge. Over nearly twenty years Xuanzang traveled through Central Asia and India. In India, he found to his shock that Buddhism had, in fact, greatly declined in popularity, while many of its ideas were incorporated into Hindu practices out of which Buddhism originated. At the same time, Indian Buddhists were impressed by the Chinese pilgrim and asked him to stay and teach at the Buddhist university in Nalanda. One interesting point about Xuanzang's time in India is that he brought with him sutras that were popular in China, believed to be original teachings of Buddha, but of which there were no Indian versions. Most likely these texts were created in China as part of the adaptation of Buddhist doctrine to Chinese society, but Xuanzang brought them "back" to India. When Xuanzang returned to Tang China, he was welcomed by the emperor, who supported the construction of the Big Goose Pagoda in Chang'an (modern Xi'an) to serve as the repository for the numerous texts Xuanzang brought back. Yet his return perhaps also underscored how different Chinese Buddhism had become from Indian Buddhism, since, despite imperial support, his "Consciousness Only" school of Buddhism never supplanted other, more Sinified, schools such as Tiantai and Pure Land.

Xuanzang's Tang dynasty marks a high point in Silk Road exchange. The imperial family, the Li, was made up of part-Turkic northerners strongly influenced by Central Asian traditions. The more effete culture of southern China that stressed scholarship and artistry for elite men and demure submissiveness for elite women is not evident in the tomb murals of the imperial family. Court life mixed artistry and activity. The murals depict orchestras with musicians playing instruments of Central Asian origins, such as the lute and *yang-qin* (literally the "barbarian zither"), and courtly gentlemen and ladies engaged in mounted hunting expeditions or polo matches.

The Tang capital of Chang'an was a huge cosmopolitan city laid out on an orderly grid. The Western Market near the city walls was a lively area inhabited by those engaged in Silk Road trade. A number of residents there were merchants from Central Asia (Uyghurs, Sogdians, and Persians among others) who were allowed to establish places of worship for native religions. We have evidence that Manichaeism, Zoroastrianism, and Nestorian Christianity were practiced in the city. A number of leading figures in Tang seem to have been Central Asian immigrants to Asia's wealthiest city. One of China's most beloved poets, Li Po, was born in what is now northern Afghanistan. In the mid-eighth century, two of the leading generals in the Tang armies were foreign: An Lushan, a Central Asian Sogdian, and General Gao, a Korean. This was also the time when Japanese rulers sent emissaries to the Tang court, some of whom stayed in the capital to serve the dynasty or to study before returning home. This is, perhaps, the origin of some of the Central and Western Asian objects that made their way into the Shoso-in storehouse in Nara, Japan, when it was founded in 756. Goods from Persia, India, and the Eastern Mediterranean were dedicated to Todai-ji Buddhist temple for the spiritual benefit of the recently deceased Emperor Shomu. Therefore, we should not think of Chang'an as the eastern terminus for the Silk Road, but rather the major East Asian entrepôt.

Tang's grand cosmopolitanism came to an end when An Lushan rebelled in 755. The rebellion demonstrates again how deeply enmeshed with its neighbors Tang China was. The rebellion, led by a Sogdian ex-general cum usurper, forced the Li family to call upon non-Chinese allies such as the Uyghurs to contain the rebellion. However, the center was destabilized and Tang control of the Silk Road west of Chang'an was lost to the Tibetans, who competed with various Turkic peoples for the route's control. If we once again focus upon the oasis at Dunhuang, there is a wealth of material, both in terms of texts and religious art, that demonstrates the shifting suzerainty of the area. The story of the northwestern oases during the eighth century is an excellent case study of a power vacuum forming after the collapse of a great power. Examining the interplay of the Uyghurs, the Tibetans, the Turks, and the Kirghiz is also important for understanding some of the current political controversies surrounding the relations of these peoples who still form significant minorities in the present People's Republic of China.

Similar to the period following the collapse of the Han dynasty, the fall of Tang ushered in a time when non-Chinese controlled the northern reaches of the former empire. We can use the subsequent Song dynasty as an example of a state forced to develop internally due to the dearth of foreign trade. In 1004, the Treaty of Shanyuan underscored the relative weakness of the Song state in the face of its northern neighbors, the Liao dynasty of the Khitan people. The treaty referred to the Song emperor as the "younger brother" of the "elder brother" Khitan emperor and subsequently, the Song had to pay a large tribute in silk and gold to keep peace along its northern borders. Yet the closure of the borders also spurred tremendous internal development. If the Tang marked a high point in Chinese expansion into Central Asia, and its capital was symbolic of its polyglot culture, the Song marked a peak in technological development and its capital became the center of a resurgent nativist Confucianism. Developments in agriculture led to increased production, which spurred more highly developed trade networks to move goods through the smaller empire. Song scholars became less concerned with understanding non-native cultures and focused on reexamining their own literary and philosophical traditions as a means of defining the empire's culture and developing its institutional framework. Modern scholars once believed that Buddhism went into decline in the Song after its Tang dynasty heyday. Recent work, however, argues that Buddhism remained a strong intellectual and social force, but that more people were attracted to the Chan tradition, which was less concerned with scriptures than direct experience. While not rejecting the utility of sutras for teaching, Chan Buddhists did not see the need to go beyond China in search of new texts.

As Chinese in the Song turned to native traditions, the Japanese sent fewer and fewer embassies to China. Aside from occasional religious exchanges, Japanese elites did not return to the mainland to study the latest artistic styles, political models, or philosophical texts. It is really from the ninth century on that the Japanese, while still admiring the culture of the fallen Tang, began forging their culture exclusive of trends on the continent.

While the Tang reached farthest into Central Asia, the Song were cut off from those influences by the pastoral-nomadic empires to the north and west. This relative isolation (it was not, of course, complete) became even more severe when another northern neighbor, the Jurchen Jin dynasty, invaded Song territory in 1125, and the Song lost the northern half of their empire. The Jurchens also took their capital at

Kaifeng, capturing the emperor and heir-apparent along with numerous members of the imperial family and bureaucracy. A prince of the royal family eventually reestablished a "temporary capital" in the south: Xingzai, Marco Polo's Kinsai and present-day Hangzhou. The court's stated, yet unrealized, goal was always to regain the north. Some have argued that from this point onward, the Southern Song "turned inward." Politics became more autocratic, philosophy more self-directed, and the scale of painting more diminutive. Southern Song is an interesting case study of an empire under duress. While politics and philosophy (in terms of neo-Confucianism) became more centralized and codified, the economy continued to flourish, though bound to a smaller region. This continued production fed a highly developed military on land and water. It would be a mistake to hold to the traditional view that the Song was militarily weak and so lost the north. Instead, we should remark how much better organized and more powerful the states to the north had become. In contrast to Tang suzerainty over the eastern Silk Road, the Song had to engage in multistate relations, at times trying to play one northern state against another in hopes of surviving.

This policy of "using barbarians to defeat barbarians" meant the Song watched in anticipation as the Jurchen were themselves invaded by a newly organized nomadic group in the thirteenth century. Chinggis (Genghis) Khan had gradually built a coalition of tribes through conquest and alliance and formed the Mongol nation. The Mongol empire is rightly famous for its explosive military expansion from relative obscurity. In less than fifty years, the Mongols ruled Eurasia between Korea and Hungary. That the Song was one of the last places to fall to the Mongols, in 1279, speaks to both their own military skills and technology and to the Mongol cavalry's initial inability to attack walled cities in a landscape dominated by hills and flooded rice fields.

The Mongol conquests reopened the overland flow of goods to and from China. The "Pax Mongolica" led to increased contacts, with Europe in particular. But it came at a high cost. The darker side of the conquest for Central Asia was the destruction of many major cities that had resisted Mongol rule. One theory for the decline of the overland Silk Road after the Mongol period is that the Mongols so devastated the infrastructure of Central Asian states (such as the underground irrigation systems) that post-Mongol rulers were never able to revive their economic power.

The Mongol Yuan dynasty (1279–1368) brought new Silk Road influences to China. Not fully trusting the Chinese to work within their government, the Yuan created an ethnic hierarchy with Mongol allies at the top, Central Asians next, then Northern Chinese, and Southern

Chinese—who had resisted longest—at the bottom. Since there were only a few million Mongols in total, they had to rely upon the help of others to rule the hundreds of millions of people throughout Eurasia. Consequently, a number of Yuan officials, particularly those in high office, were not Chinese. More subtle and salutary influences also worked their way along the trade routes in this period. For example, Chinese landscape painting influenced Persian artists' portrayal of clouds and mountains, while Persian use of cobalt blue glaze for porcelains made its way to China.

The Mongol empire broke up through a combination of internecine warfare and internal rebellion of subject peoples. In China, the Mongols were never vanquished, but flowed back to the steppe from the capital city they had created at Dadu, present-day Beijing. Consequently, the Mongols presented a constant threat on the northern border. During the subsequent Chinese Ming dynasty (1368–1644), the Mongols even captured a Ming emperor who was campaigning against them. Perhaps to get around the Mongols, the Ming dynasty explored the maritime trade routes and sponsored a series of expeditions between 1404 and 1433. The exact rationale for the voyages of Admiral Zheng He remains unclear. Scholars have alternately suggested their goal was to look for a deposed Ming emperor who fled from his usurping brother, to scout Mongol movements and alliances in their remaining empire, to demonstrate the power of the new regime in China, or to explore links on the "maritime Silk Road" of the Indian Ocean and South China Sea. Zheng He's fleets comprised more than two hundred vessels of various sizes and purpose: massive flagships; supply ships with food, water, and livestock; faster scouting ships; and heavier military vessels. These voyages have recently come under a great deal of scrutiny, due to a theory that the fleets, which predated the European "voyages of discovery" by several decades, actually circumnavigated the globe in the 1420s. Though many contend that this thesis is based more on speculation rather than fact, it is true that the Chinese fleets established trade routes and diplomatic links from China to the east coast of Africa. Aside from establishing outposts in the Malacca Straits, the fleet brought ambassadors to the Ming court, and even engaged in a war with a king in Ceylon when he attacked the fleet, taking him to China in chains.

Despite the success of these voyages, they were terminated under pressure from the imperial bureaucracy, which saw little purpose in far-flung voyages that did not benefit the people of the Ming empire, drained resources from the imperial treasury, and distracted attention from the Mongol threat from Central Asia. Certainly this bears witness that the pattern of Chinese foreign relations centered on the Silk Road was deeply ingrained and difficult to change. It is an interesting historical question, as yet unanswered, how influential the voyages of Zheng He were on the European voyages of discovery. While it is unlikely that we can draw direct links, it is possible that there is an indirect connection between the activity of the fleets and the European expansion into maritime Asia. Perhaps the withdrawal of the treasure fleets created a power vacuum in the Indian Ocean during the fifteenth century, which allowed for the relatively easy entry of the European powers, such as Portugal. Be that as it may, the Ming pulled the fleets back home, destroyed the records, and later pursued an antimaritime policy. This antimaritime stance raises another counterfactual for the historian to ponder: did the centuries-old fixation of the Chinese with Central Asia blind them to the economic possibilities of opening trade with other groups plying the South China Sea? By choosing not to develop a maritime presence, even though Zheng He had successfully employed the technology, the Chinese drew others, who were attracted by China's wealth, to their coast.

The Ming dynasty collapsed due to internal rebellions, but we can directly link these rebellions to the Ming economy's dependence upon silver, particularly from the New World mines of the Spanish. The government collected taxes in silver, which was easily accessible along the coast due to the maritime trade, but not in the interior, which lacked silver mines or access to New World silver. Consequently, as the price of silver rose in the interior, it became too expensive for farmers who could not pay their taxes, and many rebelled. The final rebellion of Li Zicheng in the 1640s culminated not only in the overthrow of the Ming royal family, but also the full-scale invasion by the Manchus from northeast Asia. Ostensibly, the Manchus came in to help put down Li's rebellion, but they continued their push until all of China was under their control, leading to the creation of China's last dynasty, the Qing (1644–1911).

The borders of today's China were established as the Qing came into direct contact with expansionist Russia and Great Britain. The Qing's main concern was still Central Asia and the ancient Silk Road oases. In the sixteenth and seventeenth centuries, Europeans had established a presence along the southern coast of China, but the Chinese saw them mainly as an oddity. True, there was a Jesuit presence at the royal court. Many Jesuits had risen in the bureaucracy on the basis of their scientific expertise, particularly those with astronomical knowledge. But Europeans were still rare in China, and, after controversies within the Catholic Church in the eighteenth century, Jesuits eventually ceased playing a major role.

It is important to remember that the Qing was not static. It too was a growing empire during the age of European expansion. Even though more Europeans were making their way to East Asia, Qing foreign policy was firmly fixed on Central Asia as the realm of greatest concern. In the eighteenth and early nineteenth centuries, Qing forces fought a number of campaigns pushing their control farther into the northwest and incorporating Xinjiang, or the "New Territory," into the empire. The region was mostly populated by Turkic groups, particularly the Uyghurs, who had converted to Islam. Throughout the remainder of the Qing dynasty, Xinjiang became a restive place as local Turkic leaders or Muslim imams tried to reestablish local autonomy. These, and other, internal rebellions occupied the attention of the Qing court, which is one reason why they paid little heed to Lord Macartney's mission to open trade and diplomatic relations with China in 1793. From the Qing outlook, Britain was far away, had a small population, had little of value to trade with China, and was certainly not as pressing a concern as campaigning in Xinjiang, establishing suzerainty over Tibet, and suppressing internal rebellions. It is not overstating the point to say that the centuries of Silk Road trade and conflict were so deeply impressed on the consciousness of the Chinese and their Manchu rulers that they remained the chief international concern in the face of European expansion.

As the eighteenth century progressed, Britain tightened its grip on India, the Russians expanded into Central Asia and Siberia, and the Qing was brought into the "Great Game" of empire building, boundary drawing, and espionage by these competing powers. The current political problems dealing with the status of Tibet stem directly from the interaction of the three empires that came to surround it in the late nineteenth century. The Tibetans had rebuffed British attempts to map Tibet and to set up diplomatic relations (even invading the area to press their case), while the Russians and British wanted to delineate boundaries in Central Asia to avoid war between the two powers. Due to the Qing military presence in Tibet—initially requested by one of the Dalai Lamas during battles with his rivals—the British and Russians determined that Tibet fell within the borders of the Qing empire. That border remains to this day.

When the Qing collapsed in 1911, Sun Yatsen's Nationalist Party came to power and created a national flag that represented the five major ethnic groups of the new Republic of China: Han Chinese, Tibetans, Hui (Muslims), Manchus, and Mongols. This flag remained in use until 1929, underscoring the idea that "Chinese" national identity was not based upon Han Chinese ethnic identity. This is not to say that the minority groups in the west (Tibetan, Hui, and Mongol) accepted their status as part of the new Republic. Indeed, they all attempted to establish independent governments as the Republic fell into the chaos of China's warlord period. Muslims in Xinjiang founded the Republic of East Turkestan, Tibetans claimed their independence, and Mongolia became the second nation, after the Soviet Union, to be founded on the back of a communist revolution. Only the latter, due to Soviet support, was successful in maintaining independence from China. East Turkestan and Tibet had no such influential backing to press their claims internationally. Eventually, both were reincorporated through subterfuge, diplomacy, and war, in the years following the founding of the People's Republic of China in 1949. It has been a cornerstone of the Communist Party's internal and foreign policies to maintain the borders of the Qing empire, with the exception of Mongolia. Hence, the CCP sees separatist movements in Xinjiang and Tibet as "internal" affairs for the Chinese to deal with, rather than issues involving international diplomacy. Chinese national identity is still very much linked to concerns with Central Asia and the "Western Regions" that Han Wudi wanted to conquer more than two thousand years ago.

In China today, this region and the Silk Road are again significant. China's economy needs natural resources to continue its massive growth. The "Uyghur Autonomous Region of Xinjiang" provides a great deal of oil for China, though not enough. Consequently, the ancient Silk Road is becoming the modern Oil Road as China contracts deals with Central Asian republics for their oil to be piped into China via Xinjiang. The importance of this conduit colors the interpretation of the region's past and makes the PRC's government even more wary of the East Turkestan separatist movement. Given that the region's native population is predominantly Muslim, the PRC has been able to use the United States' current concern about terrorist organizations to paint the separatists as sponsored by Islamic radicals (though there seems to be little, if any evidence of this), thus diminishing American support.

Chinese goods, even silks, are once again in demand in Central Asia as the republics there are no longer supplied by the Soviet economy. Chinese merchants are marketing their goods to fill the gap left by the collapse of Soviet consumer production and the poor supply from western Russia to Siberia. This was abundantly clear immediately after the fall of the Soviet Union. The Trans-Siberian railway became a modern caravan as people from all walks of life would buy goods, particularly clothing, in Beijing, then sell them from their train compartments to people waiting at Siberian stations. Some people made their livelihood this way, others simply engaged in the trade as a means of supplementing income while on business or vacation trips.

When considering the role of the Silk Road in Chinese history, we must recognize that we cannot project the current "Chinese" nation back into the past. Chinese interchange with other parts of Eurasia over the millennia has led to the ebb and flow of peoples, technology, and ideas in all directions. The case of the "Mummies of Xinjiang" is illustrative of this point. The recent discovery and identification of a number of Bronze Age mummies (perhaps related to those who introduced the chariot to the region in Shang times) as more Caucasoid than Mongoloid has led to heated debate that has, at times, aroused nationalist passions. Yet when one considers the tides of conquest and control over the region and the trade routes, it seems unlikely that these mummies are direct progenitors of current natives in Xinjiang, or represent a challenge to Chinese claims over the area. Instead, we should view them as another sign of how ancient the movement of goods and cultures across Eurasia really is. For historians of China, it is important to recognize that we can too easily fixate upon notions of China's cultural seclusion, when for much of its history China was intimately linked to, if not directly ruled by, other peoples of the Silk Road. Similarly, an appreciation of the profound influence of the Silk Road on the development of Chinese culture gives us greater insight into the current status of China, both in terms of its relations with other nations and its position in the revival of Eurasian trade in the twenty-first century.

Suggested Readings

Di Cosmo, Nicola. *Ancient China and Its Enemies: The Rise of Nomadic Power in East Asian History.* New York: Cambridge University Press, 2004.

Hopkirk, Peter. *Foreign Devils on the Silk Road: The Search for the Lost Cities and Treasures of Chinese Central Asia.* New York: Oxford University Press, 2001.

———. *The Great Game: The Struggle for Empire in Central Asia.* Tokyo and New York: Kodansha International, 1994.

Inoue, Yasushi. *Tun-Huang: A Novel.* Tokyo and New York: Kodansha International, 1978.

Morgan, David. *The Mongols.* Edited by James Campbell and Barry Cunliffe, The Peoples of Europe. Oxford: Oxford University Press, 1987.

Ning, Qiang. *Art, Religion, and Politics in Medieval China: The Dunhuang Cave of the Zhai Family.* Honolulu: University of Hawaii Press, 2004.

Puett, Michael. "China in Early Eurasian History: A Brief Review of Recent Scholarship on the Issue." In *The Bronze Age and Early Iron Age Peoples of Eastern Central Asia,* ed. Victor H. Mair, 699–715. Washington, DC: The Institute for the Study of Man, 1998.

Rossabi, Morris. *Voyager from Xanadu: Rabban Sauma and the First Journey from China to the West.* Tokyo and New York; Kodansha International, 1992.

Schafer, Edward H. *The Golden Peaches of Samarkand; a Study of T'ang Exotics.* Berkeley: University of California Press, 1963.

Whitfield, Susan. *Life Along the Silk Road.* Berkeley: University of California Press, 1999.

———, and Ursula Sims-Williams. *The Silk Road: Trade, Travel, War, and Faith.* Chicago: Serindia Publications, 2004.

Wood, Frances. *The Silk Road: Two Thousand Years in the Heart of Asia.* Berkeley: University of California Press, 2002.

Useful Web Sites

Silk Road Seattle: http://depts.washington.edu/uwch/silkroad/
International Dunhuang Project: http://idp.bl.uk/
The Silkroad Foundation: http://www.silk-road.com/toc/index.html
The Digital Silkroad: http://dsr.nii.ac.jp/

Notes

1. Despite calling into question the use of "China" for the premodern civilization, it is still easiest to use "Chinese" to refer to products of the area now within the borders of the modern nation-state.

2. In particular see Nicola Di Cosmo, *Ancient China and Its Enemies: The Rise of Nomadic Power in East Asian History* (New York: Cambridge University Press, 2004).

Chapter 4

Silk Road Studies in the Political Science Classroom

Rick Parrish

Although we may think of the Silk Road as an ancient phenomenon, it is alive and well even today. During the past few years, I have discovered that this 3,500-year-old pan-Eurasian web of social, economic, and political interaction is a rich source of inspiration for infusing exotic but relevant new material into all my political science courses. From freshman-level Introduction to Political Science to senior seminars, nearly every course I teach has benefited from the incorporation of Silk Road material into its syllabus. I have found that strategically integrating Silk Road Studies into these courses enhances students' understanding not only of Eurasian politics, but also of globalization, identity politics, international political economy, political theory, and other major themes in political science. In this chapter I intend to elaborate on these and other themes that Silk Road Studies can bring to political science classes, with the intention of inspiring other political scientists to find their own ways of incorporating this fascinating field into their own courses.

Although Silk Road Studies may seem rather distant from political science, the fundamental, unambiguously political lesson of the field is that globalization is an ancient phenomenon. It is common in international relations and international political economy to compare today's globalized world with the European colonial networks and capital flows of the late nineteenth century, but we can easily expand this insightful pedagogical technique beyond its Eurocentric framework to embrace the centuries-old globalization of the Silk Road. At even the most cursory of glances, the breadth and depth of interaction along these ancient Eurasian trade routes yields a slower, but no less intense web of interaction than today's global community.

Advanced forms of international political and economic activity
are an almost primeval aspect of Eurasian life. A brief elaboration of
the relations between China and Rome may serve as a case in point.
Although both primary textual sources and physical evidence hint at
direct commercial exchanges as early as the first century BCE, there
was no confirmed direct official contact between them. Even so, robust
indirect exchange between these two poles of Eurasia occurred for many
years before, with goods passing through Parthian, Kushan, and Xiongnu
hands before reaching their final destination. The first large quantities
of silk came to Rome through Parthian merchants in the first century
BCE, and grew so popular that the Roman Senate became concerned
about the quantity of gold flowing out of the country.

China and Rome nearly made direct diplomatic contact at the
end of the first century CE, when Gan Ying, the first Chinese envoy
to Rome, journeyed as far west as Parthian Mesopotamia. The Parthian
government, worried that direct Sino-Roman relations would hurt their
own position as intermediaries, misinformed Gan Ying, telling him that
Rome lay another two year's journey away. Gan Ying returned home
without reaching Rome itself, but provided a secondhand account of
Rome's government and economy, as well as its peoples and customs. In
166, a group of Romans claiming official status made their way to China,
but they were likely only merchants from the Roman Near East.

Inspired by both Roman and Chinese sources, some researchers
are investigating the possibility that during this period Roman soldiers
fought against the Chinese on at least one occasion. One Chinese
account of their battle against the Xiongnu in Ferghana reports soldiers
using classic Roman military tactics. When the Parthians defeated the
Romans at the Battle of Carrhae in 53 BCE, they captured several
thousand soldiers whom, some scholars suggest, the Parthians may have
relocated to their eastern border in Central Asia. The Xiongnu may
have then captured the Romans from the Parthians or employed them
as mercenaries in their fight against the Chinese. Some researchers have
suggested that these displaced Romans established the town of Liqian,
in contemporary China's Gansu province. These contacts demonstrate
that even two thousand years ago, political, military, and economic ties
bound together Asian states in an ancient international system.

The close economic ties between the Mongolian Golden Horde,
which ruled much of northern Central Asia during the thirteenth and
fourteenth centuries, and the Italian city-state of Genoa, provide another
demonstrative example of historical globalization in Eurasia. Soon after
conquering the Black Sea region, the Golden Horde gave the Genoese exclusive rights to trade in their newly won ports. Several cities in

Crimea, including the major trading centers of Kaffa and Sarai, became in effect Genoese colonies within Mongol territory. Through these and other collaborative cities a wealth of goods and knowledge flowed both east and west across the Golden Horde.

The close ties between the two governments also served strategic political purposes. By allying with Genoa, the Golden Horde was able to maintain links through the Mediterranean with the Mamluks of Egypt, their allies against the Ilkhan empire of present-day Iran and Iraq. Genoa, in addition to its near-exclusive European access to Silk Road trade, also gained a powerful military ally. The depth of integration between Genoa and the Golden Horde is perhaps best demonstrated by the international coinage they developed during the late thirteenth century. Facilitating trade between these two states and providing a material token of their cooperation, these coins included the Khan's inscription on one side and the seal of the Genoese Bank of St. George on the other. The coins were stamped in Kaffa, Genoa's largest trading city within the Golden Horde's territory, and have been found throughout the region.

Grasping the historic globalization of the Silk Road will help students develop a more rigorous understanding of contemporary Central Asian politics. The United States' recent (and belated) involvement in Central Asia, focused mostly around its open wars and other less visible antiterrorist activities there, has engendered increased coverage of that region in political science courses. Yet just as Central Asia experts have criticized the U.S. government for its insensitivity to the political history of this region, so have many political science professors ignored the understanding and predictive capacity their students can gain from knowledge of Asia's three-thousand-year-old international system.

One issue of major contemporary relevance is the trade of nuclear materials, knowledge, and equipment across Central Asia. Although rightfully concerned at the threat this trade represents, both our governments and our educators seem surprised by its success in the face of the region's complex tangle of languages, border crossings, currencies, and physical dangers. Yet nuclear material is simply a modern commodity in an ancient web of exchange. That small bands of furtive, poorly provisioned traders can overcome these obstacles would come as no surprise to those who understand that such trade is the antique quintessence of Central Asian life.

Many travelers far less formidable than gangs of armed nuclear weapons smugglers have made successful journeys through Central Asia. Among the most unlikely was Faxian, a fifth-century Chinese Buddhist who, at the age of sixty-five, walked from central China across the Taklamakan desert, over the Pamirs, and throughout India. During his three-year journey he passed through more than twenty countries, avoided several battles, and learned to navigate the vast Taklamakan by the mounds of dried animal bones left by previous travelers. Xuanzang, a young, inexperienced seventh-century Chinese Buddhist, defied an imperial order banning foreign travel by walking to Tashkent, Samarkand, and Kashmir in search of religious texts. For much of his journey, he hid during the day and traveled at night to avoid government officials who were trying to stop him.

On foot, horseback, or camel, large trading caravans have also routinely braved the hazards of Central Asia since at least the first century BCE. Regularly overcoming the difficulties of deserts, mountain passes, crime, government regulations, language barriers, and monetary exchange, these merchants traveled along many of the same routes in use today, to conduct business in many of the same centers of both legal and illicit Central Asian trade. Oasis cities such as Kashgar, Bukhara, Samarkand, and Damascus would be as familiar to Sassanian or Tangut entrepreneurs as they are to the region's contemporary merchants.

Of course, business did not always go smoothly. Extant letters from fourth century Sogdian traders refer to the difficulties of conducting business in China, wracked by famine, civil war, peasant uprisings, and invasions. Other documents throughout history refer to the loss of personnel and products due to weather disasters, robbery by bands of criminals, extortion by local officials, taxes and fines, and even wild animals. Whether during the chaos of the twelfth century or the Pax Mongolica of the thirteenth, the Soviet domination of the late twentieth century or the weak states of the early twenty-first, enterprising merchants have continued to trade products of all sorts along Central Asia's Silk Roads.

Nuclear material is more valuable today than silk was years ago, so it should come as no surprise that traders continue to brave the region's dangers to traffic in one of its native commodities. Kazakhstan alone possesses about one-fourth of the world's uranium ore, and both Kazakhstan and Uzbekistan are among the world's most prolific producers of yellow cake, a form of slightly enriched uranium. Kyrgyzstan has plans to restart its own dormant uranium mining operations, and Pakistan intends to expand its own mining to three new sites. In recent years the former Soviet republics of Central Asia have transferred their Soviet-era nuclear arsenals back to Russia, but an array of Soviet nuclear facilities remain.

This wealth of nuclear material has proven an irresistible temptation for black market traders throughout Central Asia, and a series of high profile smuggling cases have highlighted the increasing sophistication of the illicit nuclear trade across the ancient Silk Road. In one recent case, several ounces of weapons-grade uranium changed hands multiple times as they made their way from Siberia, across Russia and Georgia, and into small village close to where the borders of Georgia, Azerbaijan, and Armenia meet. Trade of all sorts flourishes there, despite official government animosities.

Illegal drug smuggling represents a far greater portion of today's Silk Road economy. Afghanistan is the world's largest producer of opium, with most of it following the ancient trade routes across Central Asia to Europe. The drug trade accounts for major portions of the gross domestic products of Afghanistan, Pakistan, Tajikistan, Kyrgyzstan, and Turkmenistan. In fact, there is evidence that drug money in large part financed the Kyrgyz revolution of 2005. The drug trade also engenders widespread political corruption, further undermining the internal stability of several other weak Central Asian states.

The multinational smuggling syndicates that control much of the black market Silk Road trade in nuclear materials, drugs, slaves, and other illicit commodities often control large swaths of countryside, crossing borders at will and acting with impunity against the region's weak states. These non-state actors have been a far greater source of violence than the Central Asian states themselves. By one widely accepted count, since 1989 there have been 107 civil wars in Central Asia, each involving at least one non-state actor, but there have been only seven interstate wars. Multinational corporations also often overshadow the states that host them. In the strategically important Ferghana valley, divided among Uzbekistan, Tajikistan, and Kyrgyzstan, and rife with religious extremist groups, one of the strongest military units is the security staff at the Daewoo Textile factory. Countries come and go, but the Silk Road remains, and today's Central Asian states are in many ways eclipsed by the political economy that they inherited from time immemorial.

Intergovernmental organizations such as the Shanghai Cooperation Organization, major players in contemporary Central Asian politics, are another aspect of contemporary Asian politics that we can better understand through Silk Road Studies. The Chinese government's formal interest in Central Asia extends back more than two thousand years, when it began cultivating a system of diplomatic and military influence with the states on its vulnerable western and northern borders. China set up its first Central Asian protectorates during the first century CE, sending armies to garrison important trading centers and protect caravan routes as far west as the Pamir Mountains. The Protectorate of the Western Regions, the government office responsible for administering these territories, continued under various names until the fourth century.

Today's Karakoram and Pamir Highways, the two highest paved roads in the world, follow ancient trade routes through this region.

Chinese power receded after the Han, but its interest in controlling the important Silk Road trade routes through Central Asia remained. Early in the Tang Dynasty (618–907), China extended its control as far west as Samarkand and Kabul, and as far north as Lake Balkash, in modern Kazakhstan. Although parts of modern Xinjiang province were under Chinese control during the Han, China's claim to control over the bulk of Xinjiang descends from this later era. With these vast areas of direct control augmented by satellite states in Iran and Afghanistan, China dominated Central Asia until the mid-eighth century, when a rebellion under An Lushan, a Tang general of Sogdian ethnicity, brought Chinese expansion to a halt.

This trend of Chinese expansion and contraction has continued to the present day. Recovering from losses to nineteenth-century colonialism, China has expanded its direct control over Central Asia, including Xinjiang and Tibet, to one of the greatest extents in its history. Having learned from long experience, China understands that both its safety and its economic prosperity depend in large part upon strong relationships with Central Asian states—relationships in which it has long considered itself *primus inter pares*. Today, China and Russia (which also has a historic interest in Central Asia) use the Shanghai Cooperation Organization to maintain their traditional influence over the comparatively weak Central Asian states. The SCO itself is a new organization, but its mission statement could apply just as easily during the Tang Dynasty as it does today. Using the ancient techniques of direct control and diplomatic pressure, China continues to pursue its interests in Central Asia.

The next political theme into which we can productively incorporate Silk Road Studies is identity politics. Centuries of intensive interactions among Central Asia's porous patchwork of ethnicities have yielded fascinating case studies for both research and teaching. Perhaps the broadest of these cases is the meaning of "Chinese," which remains a highly contested concept with contemporary relevance. Throughout "Chinese history" (itself an extremely political, retroactive category), Chinese identity has been shaped by interaction with cultural and political Others from throughout the Silk Road region, such as various nomadic groups like the Xiongnu and Mongols, more sedentary societies like the Persians and Sogdians, and of course Europeans who arrived by either land or sea. Between the Liao (Khitan), Jin (Jurchen), Yuan (Mongol), and Qing (Manchu) Dynasties, China has spent most of the last thousand years ruled by "non-Chinese" peoples. Even so, mainstream Chinese ethnic identity maintains a robust distinction from other national groups both within and outside of the current borders of China itself.

One aspect of the continued salience of Chinese identity politics is evident in the treatment of ethnic minorities, such as the Hui and Uyghur, in China's westernmost provinces. Since the 1999 announcement of its Great Western Development Program, the Chinese government has focused on mainstreaming and sinicizing these groups through economic development and state building programs. Seen through the lens of Silk Road Studies, the GWDP is only the latest manifestation of a tradition that began with the Han Dynasty's Protectorate of the Western Regions, a tradition aimed at controlling, absorbing, or eliminating the ethnic groups of this region, which, as we have seen, has only been an intermittent part of the Chinese state.

The ethnic groups of contemporary China's Central Asian provinces, such as the Hui and Uyghur, are themselves interesting case studies in identity politics. These Turkic Muslim groups inhabit the poor, mountainous Xinjiang Province, far from mainstream Chinese society in the east. Culturally, historically, and politically, they have more in common with the Tajiks and Uzbeks than they do with the "Chinese." There is little connection between today's Uyghurs and the powerful Uyghur Kaganate of 745–840 CE, which ruled much of Central Asia, including the Ferghana valley, Mongolia, and northern Xinjiang. Even so, the existence of this empire (and two brief periods of independence during the mid-twentieth century) is among contemporary Uyghurs' arguments for independence from China and the restoration of their independent homeland.

Interestingly, a similar disjunction currently exists in Mongolia, where the government, as well as some nationalists, has begun invoking the twelfth and thirteenth centuries' Mongolian empires in order to press political, economic, and social goals. But as with the Uyghurs, there is little connection between the imperial Mongols of eight hundred years ago and those of today. In both cases, these fictions are essential to the construction of their contemporary national identities and the pursuit of national initiatives.

Perhaps even more significant for Central Asian identity politics is the issue of Tibet. Contrasting Tibetan nationalist and Chinese accounts of Tibetan identity represent a fascinating duel for the hearts and minds of that region's people, with ongoing political implications for both sides. Tibet's relations with China have been turbulent since its unification in the seventh century, when the two vied for control over much of Central Asia. Following victories by an alliance of Tibetan and Uyghur forces, Tibet even briefly occupied the Chinese capital. Tibet's Central Asian empire continued into the ninth century, when it finally dissipated under continued outside pressure. As countries of the Silk Road, Tibet and China continued their close trading relations until the Yuan Dynasty under Khubilai Khan conquered Tibet in the thirteenth century.

After the collapse of the Yuan in 1368, the Tibetans overthrew the Mongol-supported regime and three successive native dynasties ruled the country. Although Tibet was independent until the Qing Dynasty invaded in 1717, it maintained a tributary relationship with China. By the mid-nineteenth century, Britain had expanded its area of influence northward from India, and held considerable sway over Tibet, then officially part of the Chinese Manchu empire. Tibet became practically independent again after the 1911 Chinese revolution, although both China and Britain made claims to it. Colonial politics between Britain and China gave rise to a dispute over the southern border of Tibet, which precipitated the Sino-Indian War of 1962 and the unresolved disagreement over the border.

After the Chinese civil war, the Communist government began reimposing control over those regions that had declared their independence. This included Tibet, which the Chinese military entered in 1950. Under Chinese pressure, the following year the Tibetan leadership officially affirmed China's sovereignty over Tibet. In 1959, the Chinese suppressed a revolt against their rule, and since then there have been no organized, large-scale military uprisings against Chinese control.

Yet many Tibetans struggle to maintain a distinctive identity in the face of projects designed to permanently integrate Tibet and its people into the Chinese state. The opening of the Qinghai-Tibet Railway in 2006, which runs from Beijing to Llasa, is only the latest in a series of such high-profile projects. For decades, the Chinese government has encouraged (or forced) members of China's Han ethnic majority to relocate to Tibet for the purposes of diluting the region's ethnic distinctiveness and forging closer political, economic, and cultural ties with the rest of China. China has also constructed more than twenty thousand miles of roads, hydroelectric power plants, and schools. These schools are a good example of the ambivalent status of such projects. Although Chinese-built schools have raised Tibetan literacy from 2 to 95 percent, they also teach government-approved curricula that instill mainstream Chinese culture in Tibet's youth. Recently, China announced a 40 percent increase in infrastructure spending in Tibet, including the construction of the world's highest airport. Tibetan nationalists may welcome the economic advantages of a new airport, but they are concerned that easier tourism and business travel from more mainstream parts of China will further dilute Tibet's distinctive identity.

Less palpable, but equally important, is the continuing debate between Iranian and Persian identities, both within the state of Iran and among that country's expatriate groups abroad. In the United States, for instance, it is common for individuals who emigrated from Iran to identify themselves as Persian, so as to distance themselves from recent political and social developments there and foreground their rich cultural past. Since at least 550 BCE, the Persian state has been a federation of multiple ethnicities, dominated by a Persian ethnic majority. The term *Iran* derives from Aryan, a broader ethnic group to which most citizens of modern Iran belong. Changing the country's name from Persia to Iran in 1935 was in part an attempt to deemphasize Persian ethnic identity and create a larger Iranian civic identity. This Iranian identity has been a source of stability in multiethnic Iran, but many émigrés from Iran shun it. Some of Persian ethnicity have never accepted the Iranian civic identity, while others seek to disassociate themselves from Iranian politics. Still others perceive that their daily lives in the United States will be easier if they identify themselves as Persian, rather than as Iranian, which may cause backlash by some Americans who feel negatively toward Iran. As these examples illustrate, we can better understand issues in contemporary identity politics by supplementing mainstream political science with the deep historical perspective of Silk Road Studies.

Silk Road Studies can also provide valuable insights into post-9/11 security politics. Again, the Uyghurs in China's Xinjiang province and across the border in Afghanistan are of primary significance. Before 9/11, the Chinese government agreed that there was no terrorist activity among Uyghur separatists. After 9/11, however, China successfully linked Uyghur separatism to the global war on terrorism. Although official Chinese records indicate that until recently there had been no significant political violence in Xinjiang since the late 1990s, it continues to raise the specter of Uyghur terrorism, executing an average of nearly two Uyghurs per week for various political offenses.

The Uyghurs are also relevant to the U.S. campaigns in Central Asia. Soon after 9/11, the United States added the East Turkestan Islamic Movement (ETIM), a militant Uyghur separatist group, to its list of terrorist organizations. According to the United States, ETIM soldiers fought alongside the Taliban in Afghanistan, and in 2002 two ETIM members were accused of planning to attack the U.S. embassy in Kyrgyzstan. Twenty-two Uyghurs were detained by the United States at its detention facility in Guantanamo Bay, Cuba. In 2006, five of these men were released and resettled in Albania, the only country that would take them. In 2009, ten more were released to Bermuda and Palau. The Uyghurs refused to return to China, for fear of political persecution.

International political economy, both historical and contemporary, is another theme by which Silk Road Studies can intersect political science. Just one major example is TRACECA, the Transport Corridor Europe-Caucasus-Asia, informally known as the "New Silk Road." This project, one of the largest international building ventures in the world, is the product of cooperation among several Eurasian states. Begun in 1993, this network of roads, railways, pipelines, and fiber optic cables is intended to link major economic centers across Eurasia both to each other, as well as to the economically disadvantaged areas in between. One of these roads, Asian Highway One, will span the three thousand miles between Istanbul and Urumqi, in China's Xinjiang Province. Once complete, TRACECA's 87,000 miles of infrastructure will update many ancient trade routes in order to further facilitate the movement of people and goods across Eurasia, leading to deeper economic relations among the states it traverses. TRACECA consciously promotes this perception of these new infrastructure projects as part of an ancient Silk Road tradition. The organization's Web site stresses this theme, even referring to TRACECA as the "renaissance" of the Silk Road. Journalists and researchers, whose reports on TRACECA often refer to it as an "update," "revitalization," or "modernization" of the Silk Road have also embraced this narrative. Even official government statements incorporate this theme, with ministers from Azerbaijan, Georgia, Russia, and the United Nations explicitly referring to TRACECA as the "New Silk Road."

Silk Road Studies may even be useful in political theory courses. Tangible commodities such as tools and textiles were not the only products that diffused throughout Eurasia. The Silk Road also involved the intellectual exchange of ideas, including political theories. Alexander the Great's possible patronage of Aristotle, which may have included gifts of documents and artifacts from his travels throughout Asia, is only the most obvious of these. Whether or not Alexander supplied Aristotle with foreign goods, Aristotle expressed knowledge of India and other regions of Asia. Despite what the Achaeans themselves liked to believe, Greece did not stand alone. It was an intimate part of the Silk Road, and its intellectuals were influenced by it. There is even evidence that the Trojan War, so iconic to the ancient Greeks, was actually about controlling trade routes to the Black Sea.

Of course, Aristotle was not the only great intellectual to absorb ideas from the Silk Road. For instance, there is evidence that Anaximander (c.610–c.546 BCE), a pre-Socratic philosopher and native of Miletus, may have been influenced by Persian ideas. The port city of Miletus, located on the coast of Asia Minor in present-day Turkey, had close ties with both Persia and Greece. As a major eastern Mediterranean harbor, Miletus even had regular contact with Babylon and Egypt, and both goods and ideas from all corners of the Silk Road passed through it. The first evidence of Persian influence on Anaximander is his cosmological notion that the universe was created out of a formless, boundless, inexhaustibility. This idea that all determinable objects arise from limitless possibility was a common Persian religious notion that Miletans would have known well. Anaximander also believed that the stars were the closest celestial bodies to Earth, followed by the planets, with the sun farthest away. Although this theory may seem counterintuitive, it was a concept known to Persian astronomers. Anaximander was also reputed to be the first person to draw a map of the world. On this map, of which we have only descriptions, the Earth is round, with its landmass surrounded by ocean. The Mediterranean Sea is in the middle, dividing Europe and Asia. The areas of Asia Minor, Greece, Italy, and Spain are on one side, while northern Africa, Persia, and Assyria are on the other, perhaps implying equality between the two sides. Although debates continue about the extent of Persian influence on Anaximander, it seems clear that life in a Silk Road city had at least some effect on the philosophy, astronomy, and philosophy of this important pre-Socratic thinker.

Political theorists who venture outside European thought in their courses can benefit from Silk Road Studies by exploring the spread of Confucianism and the sinicization that often accompanied it to places like Korea and Japan. Also fascinating is the interaction between Confucianism and Buddhism, which yielded the various Neo-Confucianisms that themselves spread along the trade routes, influencing Korea, Japan, and Southeast Asia. One such interaction shaped the ideas of Ogyu Sorai (1666–1728), a member of Japan's samurai class during the Tokugawa period. Rejecting the study of later Confucian writings, Sorai returned to the ancient Confucian classics for guidance. Applying Confucian teachings to political and social issues, he was a proponent of the samurai as rulers and civil servants.

We can also consider Al Farabi, perhaps the single greatest political theorist of the Muslim world, as a product of the Silk Road. He was born in either Afghanistan or Persia in the ninth century, was schooled in Bukhara and Baghdad, two of the most cosmopolitan Silk Road cities, and traveled extensively. Influenced by Plato, Aristotle, and philosophers from as far afield as India, he wrote widely on political topics and remains one of the most influential political theorists of all time.

Silk Road Studies are not only useful for expounding on specific political theorists. They can also yield intriguing investigations of political concepts, such as nomadic versus sedentary notions of ownership, boundaries, and governance. Shifting focus from the well-known sedentary civilizations like Greece, China, and Persia, to relatively obscure nomadic peoples such as the Xiongnu and Sogdians, we might even entice students to reconsider concepts such as power and distinctions like center versus periphery. After all, these nomadic cultures provided the connective tissue that linked the great intellectual centers of the past, making possible the ancient urban golden ages by providing them with foreign products and ideas.

One of the most interesting examples is the Mongols, who conquered the sedentary cultures of Asia with their superior cavalry tactics, developed over generations of nomadism. Their empires, extending from Eastern Europe to the Pacific, engendered the intermixing of people and ideas on unprecedented levels. The first Europeans to reach China did so during this period, and subsequent travelers, such as William of Rubruck and the Polos, brought back tales and technology that challenged thirteenth-century Eurocentrism. These encounters incited the development of new ideas in Europe, helping give rise to the Renaissance. By the eighteenth century, China had become a fixture in political theory, with philosophers from Leibniz to Rousseau using China as a foil against which to measure Europe—John Stuart Mill was even director of the British East India Company. It is no accident that the Renaissance began after the infusion of new ideas into Europe. In *The Republic*, Plato himself noted that a real conversation about justice could not take place in conservative Athens. It had to occur in Piraeus, the nearby cosmopolitan harbor city, site of international festivals and host to foreign traders and their stimulating ideas from around the world.

Finally, the term *Silk Road* may itself serve political science as a new metaphor, replacing the tired and wooly "Clash of Civilizations" as the catchphrase of the increasingly global twenty-first century. As a metaphor, the Silk Road comprehends a much greater variety of international interaction, a global community of peoples complete with cooperation and conflict, opportunity and peril. The speed of the world's connectivity has certainly increased, and just as a banking crisis in Southeast Asia can affect the North American economy, so can an anonymous Iraqi blogger become an American celebrity. Yet the globalization these examples represent is nothing new. It was just as real in the fourth century, when the Chinese invention of block printing caused a revolution that spread throughout Asia, and just as important in the twelfth century, when the death of the Great Khan in Mongolia saved Europe and Egypt from certain conquest beneath the hooves of Mongol armies. There have always been clashes of civilizations, but these are simply one aspect of the ancient, contemporary, and future global Silk Road.

Suggested Readings

Atabaki, Touraj, and Sanjyot Mehendale, eds. *Central Asia and the Caucasus: Transnationalism and Diaspora.* London: Routledge, 2005.

Chang, Chun-shu. *The Rise of the Chinese Empire: Nation, State, and Imperialism in Early China*. Ann Arbor: University of Michigan Press, 2007.

Kaiser, Markus. *Eurasia in the Making: Revival of the Silk Road*. Bielefeld: Transcript Verlag, 2007.

Olcott, Martha. *Central Asia's Second Chance*. Washington, DC: Carnegie Endowment for International Peace, 2005.

Shambaugh, David, ed. *Power Shift: China and Asia's New Dynamics*. Berkeley: University of California Press, 2006.

Shankman, Steven, and Stephen W. Durrant, eds. *Early China/Ancient Greece: Thinking Through Comparisons*. Albany: State University of New York Press, 2002.

Starrs, Roy, ed. *Nations Under Siege: Globalization and Nationalism in Asia*. New York: Palgrave Macmillan, 2002.

Thakur, Ramesh, and Edward Newman, eds. *Broadening Asia's Security Discourse and Agenda: Political, Social, and Environmental Perspectives*. Tokyo: United Nations University Press, 2004.

Chapter 5

Teaching the Silk Road in Comparative Politics

Gang Guo

Even for those who are interested in international affairs, on the surface the Silk Road would seem to be among the most irrelevant subject matters to comparative politics that one can think of. To begin with, it is so ancient that by the time most of today's nation-states came into existence the Silk Road had already faded away into history and become of interest only to archaeologists. Why should we even mention the Silk Road alongside those great wars, revolutions, and reforms that have fundamentally shaped the political landscape of the major countries? Besides, what can we possibly compare the Silk Road with? How could the Silk Road have anything to do with politics, institutions, interests, policies, or really be even remotely related to the important political issues that concern people in today's world?

If we think long and hard enough there are actually answers to the above questions.[1] However, that is not the point that I am trying to make in this chapter. In my opinion, the key purpose of incorporating the Silk Road into comparative politics courses is to use the Road as a metaphor to elucidate the complexity of understanding domestic politics around the globe. The Silk Road itself is certainly a fascinating historical topic, yet more importantly for the teaching of comparative politics it challenges students' long-ingrained paradigms of thinking about politics and political development. The very core of the teaching and learning experience in college involves constantly challenging and sometimes reformulating paradigms, and encouraging independent, mature, and sophisticated thinkers.

In this chapter I shall discuss in turn the two greatest contributions that the incorporation of the Silk Road into undergraduate courses

73

in comparative politics can make, and illustrate them with examples of my past blunders in teaching. First, the Silk Road as a metaphor should constantly remind us of the need to teach and to learn across and beyond boundaries. Our minds have been thoroughly programmed by our education and experience to frame immediately any domestic political issue within boundaries. Physical, geographic boundaries, social, cultural, political boundaries, and boundaries between nation-states, between academic disciplines, or between teaching and learning are all so meticulously engrained into our habits of thinking that most of the time we are not even aware of their impact. Most of us are either unwilling or unable to go beyond or across boundaries, physical or artificial, for fear of losing the security or comfort of the territory most familiar to us. However, such an approach to teaching and learning can be rather misleading to our students. We are preparing them for careers in an increasingly complex, dynamic, and globally interdependent world, and compartmentalized thinking is the last thing that they need to get ready for this new environment.

Second, the Silk Road as a metaphor also exposes the oversimplification of the path to domestic political development that students of comparative politics often succumb to. Physically the Silk Road was not one single road like the historic Route 66. To borrow a modern term in computer science, the Silk Road (or Roads) is rather like a mesh network of nodes and paths. The Silk Road was not even a road, as the routes ancient caravans took between oases or trading posts were constantly shifting. On one level, that can be a good metaphor for comparative political development. On a higher level, we can also think of the Silk Road as symbolizing an ongoing process of culture arising interculturally for millennia. Through this process, diverse peoples on the Afro-Eurasian landmass have all contributed to the maturing and enrichment of the human society as a whole in their respective unique ways. Early global exchanges of goods, services, people, science, technologies, religions, and ideologies resulted in remarkable progress in the premodern world. Everybody was directly or indirectly affected by and often benefited from that process. There was no such thing as a superior development model that all civilizations had to follow sooner or later, and it did not make much sense to array societies along a developmental continuum with some country posited as the world's historical end.

The comparative description, examination, and analysis of different political systems are intellectual traditions that we can trace back at least to the era of Aristotle in ancient Greece. Comparative politics is an important subfield of political science that regularly attracts a large following of scholars and students alike. In the American Political Science

Association, comparative politics is by far the largest organized section, with 1,631 members as of August 2006. In contrast, none of the other sections has more than a thousand members. Unlike American politics or international relations, the phrase *comparative politics* directly conveys a certain method of study, namely, comparison. The field encompasses diverse approaches such as large or small N-analysis and single case studies; and varied subject matter such as political institutions, cultures, interests, policies, and so on. Nation-states in the world, big or small, rich or poor, democratic or authoritarian, are all of interest to the comparative politics community.

Teaching comparative politics is especially challenging. Many students choose to major in political science with a view to a future career in law. A small minority plan to pursue employment opportunities in the federal government or to work toward an advanced degree. Understandably, it often comes as a shock to many undergraduate students when they realize that comparative politics is a required course for all political science majors. Besides the introductory course to the field, there are a wide variety of upper-level undergraduate and graduate courses in comparative politics for students to choose from. However, the motivation for a lot of students to take those courses is purely practical, namely that they need at least a C grade in the course in order for it to fulfill the requirements for graduation with a bachelor's degree in political science. "Why do I have to know anything about the politics of this or that particular country?" is one of the common reactions to the comparative politics courses that they have to take. Thus, convincing them of the need to study the Silk Road seems a daunting task, but one that provides great rewards.

I developed most of the ideas for this chapter during the time when I attended the National Endowment for the Humanities 2006 Summer Institute entitled "The Silk Road: Early Globalization and Chinese Cultural Identity" at the East West Center in Honolulu, Hawaii. I almost literally jumped at the opportunity to participate in the program. The institute constantly challenged my paradigms about comparative politics, world history, and undergraduate teaching, which prompted me to rethink the design of my courses. Having trained as a political scientist in the positive theory tradition, I got used to building game theoretic models and analyzing large-N statistical data sets, to the extent that my name is actually listed on the Mathematics Genealogy Project. Throughout all my courses, I try to instill the teachings of a basic quantitative understanding. I often ask my students to describe, interpret, or analyze data presented in various forms. However, I have realized quantitative skills are just one set, albeit an essential one, in the students' academic tool box. They deserve to, and must, acquire many more skills and much more knowledge to remain competitive after they graduate from college.

Teaching and Learning across and beyond Boundaries

Speaking from my own experiences I now firmly believe in the concept of "teaching across boundaries," with boundaries meaning not only national geographic boundaries but also disciplinary boundaries between social sciences and the humanities, as well as the boundary between research and teaching. Like millions of other people, I received my formal school education in two countries that are half a globe apart. I have had a personal passion for historical and geographic studies ever since high school but have never received any formal training in either subject since I graduated from college. My favorite course in college was an elective, The History of China's Foreign Cultural Exchange, taught by Professor Zhang Zhi. To a twenty-one-year-old college student who had hardly ever seen any foreigner, let alone other kinds of foreign experience, it was quite a mind-boggling experience to learn that so much of what I had taken for granted as being uniquely "Chinese" actually came from India, Mongolia, Japan, and elsewhere. Likewise, so much of what I had thought were distinctively Japanese, Vietnamese, and Korean also came from other cultures in ancient times. It turns out that the Silk Road played an essential role in forming what has become known today as "Chinese," "Japanese," "Korean," and so on. I was thoroughly fascinated by the fact that one can hardly finish a sentence in modern Chinese without using a word, such as *world*, *society*, or *economy*, that had been borrowed from Sanskrit, Japanese, or some other language, often through communications made possible by the Silk Road. I started to have some doubt about the utility of my former conceptual framework or mentality of "us versus them" in understanding contemporary political issues.

After completing an undergraduate degree in Beijing in international relations I went to the University of Rochester in upstate New York to pursue graduate study in political science, concentrating on comparative politics and international relations. The rigorous training at Rochester prepared me well for the scientific study of politics, yet since I started teaching at the University of Mississippi in 2002 I have continually felt the need to hone my teaching skills, especially in the study of history and culture. The first course I taught was POL 324: Politics of China, an advanced-level undergraduate course in the comparative politics subfield. In preparing the course materials, I realized that I could not simply teach the politics of China without devoting a substantial portion of the course to the long history of China. A course in American politics can start with the U.S. Constitution, introducing the three branches of government, followed by other political institutions such as parties, elections, interest groups, etc. and specific policy issues. In contrast, we cannot understand Chinese politics today by just reading the 1982 constitution of the P.R.C. The United States has had one constitution for more than two centuries, while China has seen nearly one in every decade since the end of World War II. More importantly, the fundamental features of the Chinese political system today have resulted from diverse traditions and legacies, some dating back to Confucian philosophy, some to the Qin dynasty (221–207 BCE), some to the former Soviet Union, and probably most to the Maoist era. Without being explicitly so, the course on Chinese politics had to become an interdisciplinary course that blended elements of both social sciences and the humanities.

The necessity of teaching and learning across and beyond boundaries became even more clear and urgent to me after I was first asked to teach courses at the Croft Institute for International Studies four years ago. My current position is a joint appointment between the Department of Political Science and the Institute. While the former tends to emphasize research the latter is devoted to undergraduate teaching. My teaching activities at the Croft Institute include being instructor of both the required core course and some elective courses in international studies as well as being a mentor of senior theses on various topics related to East Asia. Enrollment at the Croft Institute has grown now to well over a hundred students since its first full year of operation eight years ago. In addition to one of three regional foci, namely East Asia, Europe, and Latin America, Croft students select a thematic concentration. Over time the thematic concentration of social and cultural identity (SCI) has become the most popular, encompassing almost 30 percent of Croft graduates so far, but few courses in that concentration concern East Asia.

My teaching responsibilities have constantly necessitated endeavors beyond the confines of my disciplinary background. For instance, when I first taught INST 203: East Asian Studies, which we require of all Croft students, I covered a sketch of Chinese political history from Confucius to present. But it would have been ideal to discuss the mutual cultural nourishment between China and its ancient neighbors in that course, thus exposing the myth of a monolithic and static Chinese culture. In my political science courses I sometimes tried to bring historical and comparative perspectives into the discussion of current political issues yet often found myself lacking a solid and systematic pedagogical knowledge of ancient Chinese culture. My courses POL 337: Asia in World Affairs and POL 387: Political Economy of East Asia predominantly covered events and issues after the cold war, which left many important historical questions unanswered for the students.

Before I attended the Summer Institute on the Silk Road I did not feel confident enough to venture beyond the established curriculum. I have since realized that I can substantively strengthen both of my political science courses with a series of lectures on the Silk Road as a case study of early Asian globalization. I also help my students in POL 324: Politics of China by examining the big picture of the Chinese cultural context before branching out to the various contemporary political institutions and processes. The addition of some elements of the humanities into the social science curriculum and the broader dialogue between the hitherto quite separate general fields can be beneficial to the humanities as well. The peculiar emphasis of social sciences on the specification of variables and causal linkages and the interpretation of current events can all usefully supplement the approaches of the humanities. An interdisciplinary undergraduate course on globalization and cultural identity can better meet the substantial and growing needs of students on this campus, especially at the Croft Institute. My study of the Silk Road therefore, will provide me with a precious opportunity to fill in a curricular gap and make a considerable contribution to my home institution.

The implications of the Silk Road are apparently far more than just the grasp of the long-underutilized factual information about the historic Road. Most often scholars use words such as *isolation, exclusion,* and so on in reference to Oriental civilizations, but those words probably describe more a state of mind than the actual physical condition. Such artificial boundaries surrounding these civilizations in Asia have always given outsiders an impression of exoticism, mystery, and implied desirability. They also have given insiders feelings of security, comfort, and even pride. Therefore, the myths and illusions of isolation and exclusion of the various Asian civilizations were maintained and even carefully guarded by both outsiders and insiders. Historically, even the Chinese themselves were often unaware of the extent of communications and exchanges between China and the rest of the world. Long before Zhang Qian opened the Silk Road in the second century BCE, bamboo and cloth from Sichuan had already made their way to Central Asia through India, and Zhang Qian found out about it only after he saw them in Central Asian markets and then reported to the emperor.

Similarly, many long-established boundaries are artificial but have been so deeply engrained into our paradigms of thinking that we simply take those boundaries for granted and conveniently use them as points of departure in our intellectual endeavors. For example, the sovereign nation-state is one of the most important concepts in political science and has become the standard theoretical and empirical foundation for political science research. However, most of the nation-states in the world today have been constructed only in the most recent decades. That period of time would seem like a wink compared with the history of human civilizations. It was the Europeans who drew most of the boundaries between contemporary nation-states at one point or another. Therefore, the concept of exclusive sovereignty rights strictly within those artificial but sacrosanct political boundaries would sound quite foreign to many of the traditional societies that European colonialists conquered or divided.

Obviously, comparative politics as a field is inherently cross-border, yet the teaching of undergraduate courses in comparative politics has often become some sort of "island hopping": conducting a well-rounded survey of the political system of one country and then starting all over again for another country. The advantage of such a teaching method is obvious. It is easy, convenient, and flexible. Instructors who divide their courses in comparative politics into separate country-modules can quickly adapt them to various configurations of each class or semester. Students are immersed in detailed information about a political system as well as the wider socioeconomic context in which politics operates. Therefore, they may be able to absorb more specific knowledge about a particular country. For example, for convenience sake I turned my Introduction to East Asian Studies into essentially two separate introductions to China and Japan. Like many other teachers I started the course with an introduction to the geographic background of China, emphasizing the "isolation" of China from the rest of the world as well as the Yellow River basin as the "cradle" of the Chinese people. Now I realize that both assumptions are problematic or at least incomplete. On one hand, the discoveries of the oldest human remains in the southwest of China clearly demonstrate that the infant Chinese civilization may have had multiple "cradles." On the other hand, the relative isolation of China has to be balanced by the numerous historical and archeological pieces of evidence of the Chinese contacts with the rest of the world from the earliest times. After all, human beings are among the most mobile species on earth, and human ancestors managed to spread from East Africa to all inhabitable corners of the world, from the Arctic tundra to the South Pacific islands. Deserts, mountains, rivers, straits, or even vast oceans, all examples often cited to prove China's exclusion from the outside world, never stopped the early *Homo sapiens* many thousands of years ago. Why should those physical boundaries "isolate" any civilization at a much later age?

Before I knew it I had team-taught the required course three times. Unfortunately, that means that before I became enlightened at the NEH institute I had already misled well over a hundred students about East Asia! My other courses on Asian or world politics were also country-by-country surveys of political development and institutions, which now seem to me grossly inadequate and misleading for the students. By taking a simple geographical approach, we are consciously or unconsciously projecting the contemporary concepts of nation-state to every historical period, even though we can probably best think of historical China, Japan, or for that matter any other country, as a continuous and unending process.

An alternative method of teaching comparative politics is to organize the course by thematic topics, such as parliamentary versus presidential systems, federal versus unitary systems, political parties and electoral rules, interest articulation and aggregation, and so on. When discussing each topic, I bring in specific political systems as examples to illustrate how the thematic subject operates in practice. This approach, however, also has its own pros and cons. By putting a special emphasis on the themes, concepts, and theories in comparative politics, the students can gain conceptual clarity up front and integrate their knowledge of political phenomena. The thematic approach also makes it possible to cover more countries during the course of a semester. On the other hand, the drawbacks of this approach are obvious. Without the incorporation of intensive investigation of a few countries, students may have difficulty referring to a set of cases that show the application of the concepts to actual political systems in the world today. Besides, teaching comparative politics by themes often gives students insufficient exposure to the unique social and cultural contexts in which each political system operates. For instance, if I bring in China as simply a specific case of a Communist Party state established in a developing country, students would miss a large part of the picture in Chinese politics today, especially at the grassroots level.

After teaching several courses in comparative politics, I have found that it is probably better to strike a balance between these two methods of teaching. What seems to work the best is to formulate the course contents into a crisscross pattern so that throughout the semester the instructor and the students constantly fill in the remaining empty cells in the cross-tabulation of knowledge nodes. This intertwined method of teaching that attempts to combine the best of both worlds still leaves something to be desired. Specifically, it still conforms to the traditional compartmentalized thinking and thus does not pay enough attention to the interconnectedness between the political systems or between the thematic topics. I now have both ambitious and realistic plans for the teaching of all my existing courses in comparative politics. The students in those courses will benefit from the addition of a module on the interconnected nature of political development that can help them better understand the progress of various societies and how they have shaped each other through external relations. I will also incorporate the early cross-cultural developments in Asia that have a profound impact on the socioeconomic landscape of the region today into our required INST 203: East Asian Studies course.

Finally, the boundary between teaching and research also seems further blurred to me after systematically studying the Silk Road. Besides nicely fitting my teaching needs, I have gained deep insights and a well-rounded understanding of Chinese culture and Asian history, which have also readily informed my current research in contemporary Chinese politics. Many of the issues related to the Silk Road, such as the reactions to globalization, the intricate interplay of socioeconomic factors and politics, and the cultural context of political decision making, have clear contemporary counterparts.

Rethinking the Political Development Path

Besides promoting the study of comparative politics across and beyond various artificial boundaries, the metaphor of the Silk Road can bring other fresh perspectives into the teaching and learning of comparative politics. By incorporating the Silk Road into courses on comparative politics, we not only actively challenge the compartmentalized thinking that takes boundaries for granted but also bring into question some of the fundamental assumptions in understanding political development and democratization. To use the metaphor of the Silk Road again, the Road was not just a bridge that went across and beyond boundaries. It was also an organic catalyst that contributed to the continuous maturing and enrichment of the human experience, society, and culture as a whole. Peoples along the historical Silk Road exchanged commodities, technologies, knowledge, religions, and ideas, which contributed to their social, economic, cultural, and political progresses in various ways. All these different civilizations along the Silk Road can thus probably be more appropriately thought of as distinctive participants in the global exchange, interaction, and progress. However, the existing conceptual frameworks in the study of political and economic transitions often assume that we can easily array societies along a developmental continuum with the same ideal historical end for everyone.

Generations of scholars have described and attempted to design the ideal political system, and governments and international organizations have focused their time and effort on helping underdeveloped countries to achieve this ideal universal pattern of government. For decades after the founding of the modern discipline of comparative politics, mainstream scholars in this inchoate field took much of their inspiration from the Prussian state as the model of good governance and proper public administration. The brutal realities of World War I apparently shattered that ideal model. Since World War II, the United States has become the new model for the world, the historical end of mankind, and the "shining city upon a hill." Some people believe that in time they can fulfill this mission of social and political engineering around the globe, by force if necessary.

This vision of the world has probably brought about tremendous progress to human society. However, it may not be the best conceptual framework to describe and to understand political and social development in much of the non-Western world. The historical role the Silk Road has played illustrates what Tang Junyi called "the inseparability of the one and the many, of uniqueness and multivalence, of continuity and multiplicity, of integrity and integration." Rather than "one nation under God, indivisible," we can at best describe the historical entities connected by the Silk Road as "multiple nations under various men, gods, Buddha, etc." We often apply inappropriate conceptual framework to the understanding of other societies without realizing that there may not be one single easy answer to every question. The traditional Chinese worldview of "tianxia" (under heaven) gave Western Christians some reason to celebrate that they had found the counterpart of God, yet the Chinese idea of "heaven" is fundamentally different from the Western idea of God. Likewise, in teaching Chinese political history I used to tell my students that Confucianism was the dominant political ideology in China for more than two millennia. If I had told them a far more complicated story they would probably have been unable to remember anything about traditional Chinese political ideology, but the dominance of Confucianism is still a misleading concept. We should not only introduce the various schools of political thought in Chinese history besides Confucianism but also convey to the students a sense of the interconnectedness and mutual influence among the different ideologies. We should also emphasize the often stark contrast between the ideal and the reality in Chinese political history.

On a broader scale, we need to be aware of the near-tyranny of the ideology of democracy in studying political development in the non-Western world. Most scholars and politicians assume that every country will inevitably follow the modernization route of the West, that is, establishing free-market capitalism and liberal democracy. The question of free market and democratization is not whether they will happen, but how and when. They cite the triumph of free-market capitalism and liberal democracy around the world as proof that we can conveniently ignore all the differences between societies in following this one single model of development. However, a closer examination of the political economic systems among these countries turns up a wide variety of ways in which capitalism or democracy operates.

Historically, the Silk Road provides multiple examples of the complexity of social progress that belie the universal and linear development path. More than two thousand years ago, Buddhism traveled along the Silk Road into China during the Han dynasty, yet by the Tang dynasty Chinese Buddhism had already evolved almost beyond recognition. Dissatisfaction with that reality prompted Xuanzang (602–664) to go on a quest for the "authentic" Buddhism in its place of origin in India. However, later Chinese Buddhists paid scant attention to the Buddhist works brought back by Xuanzang. In a sense, by then China had become an independent source of Buddhist ideas and no longer relied on the Indian model for inspiration. In other words, only several hundred years after the initial introduction of Buddhism, China became one of the participants in the generation, exchange, interaction, and progress of global Buddhism.

Likewise, different civilizations along the historical Silk Road contributed in their unique ways to the advancement of technology. The ancient peoples on the Central Asian steppes were experts on chariot and cavalry warfare, which in time spread to other civilizations, altering the outcome of many historical battles. The ancient Chinese left their mark in history by contributing many of the technologies that were central to the literary experience that they valued, such as paper making and printing. In this sense, ancient civilizations along the historical Silk Road were all participants in global technological progress. No one had the perfect answer to every problem, and each people, no matter how far advanced they were, could still benefit from the exchanges with others and improve themselves in the process.

It is our responsibility to challenge our students to rethink the political development path in a comparative politics course. As the historical experiences of the civilizations connected by the Silk Road illustrate, there may not be one single perfect path of development, and no one nation may hold the one absolute truth or superior model for progress. Each society can contribute to the perfection of political economic systems in its unique way, and the world community can thus move continually forward. The traditional intellectual mission of designing and engineering the ideal political system may be losing its appeal. The normative and judgmental elements of comparative politics have proven to be less helpful than many had believed. A more productive way of political inquiry may be to try first to study in detail and to understand how the different existing political systems operate and why they work in their respective unique ways. Then we shall have a firmer basis for understanding what changes may be both desirable and feasible.

Suggested Readings

Blyth, Mark. "Great Punctuations: Prediction, Randomness, and the Evolution of Comparative Political Science," *American Political Science Review* 100, no. 4 (November 2006): 493–98.

China Institute in America. *From Silk to Oil: Cross-Cultural Connections Along the Silk Road, A Curriculum Guide for Educators*. 2005. <http://www.chinainstitute.org/educators/silkguide.html>.

Christian, David. "Silk Roads or Steppe Roads? The Silk Roads in World History," *Journal of World History* 11, no.1, (Spring 2000): 1–26.

Richards, David L., and Neil J. Mitchell. "A Makeover for the Introductory Comparative Politics Course: Revising the College Board's Advanced Placement Program (AP) Course in Comparative Government and Politics," *PS: Political Science & Politics* 39, no. 2 (April 2006): 357–62.

Rossabi, Morris, ed. *Governing China's Multiethnic Frontiers*. Seattle: University of Washington Press, 2005.

Note

1. Rick Parrish offers a number of excellent suggestions elsewhere in this volume.

Chapter 6

Art and the Silk Road

Joan O'Mara

Although trained as an Asian art historian, I did not become interested in the Silk Road until my encounter with Yo-Yo Ma's Silk Road Project a number of years ago and since then, that interest has grown. I visited sites along the Silk Road in China in 2004 and studied it further at the NEH Summer Institute in 2006, revisiting the Mogao caves in 2008. After teaching a course on the arts of the Silk Road twice, once as an upper-level seminar and then as a freshmen-only seminar, I have decided that, in one form or another, it deserves a regular place in my teaching schedule. Why is the Silk Road so important? The response of one freshman on an end-of-term course evaluation sums up the reason for my decision quite succinctly: "I had no idea." Any course that focuses on the Silk Road, or at least introduces it into the discussion, offers a view of the past that is more globalized—and thus more appropriate for the beginning of the twenty-first century—than the worldview with which most of us were raised. Such a globalized perspective is no less important for art history than it would be for any other academic discipline, as we try to encourage students to look at the past in a way that recognizes contributions beyond those of the Western tradition.[1]

A second question that we might ask is: Why should we regard art as important to the study of the Silk Road, which may seem to have more to do with economic development, or with the transmission of religion, than it does with the history of art? One of the things that students hear in all of my classes is that art history, far from being a frivolous add-on to their educations, can be vital to their understanding of any of the humanities and also relevant to what they are learning in the social sciences. The arts—especially when we understand them to include the results of archaeological excavation—provide a visual gateway to understanding a civilization. Nowhere is this more true than in a consideration of the Silk Road, for its arts and archaeology are keys to understanding both the continuities and the changes that have occurred over the millennia of its existence.

Art and, especially, archaeology along the Silk Road have revealed much about its oases and city centers, about the people who lived there and traversed its various routes, and about the kinds of trade goods they handled. Excavations dating back a century or more have rediscovered long-abandoned towns such as Loulan, which flourished during the Han Dynasty but declined and failed in the third or fourth century, due to the intermittent supply of water in the lake of Lop Nor in the Taklamakan Desert. In 1906, the site was excavated by the Hungarian-born British archaeologist and explorer Aurel Stein (1862–1943).[2] There, Stein found perishable objects dating from about the time of the site's abandonment, preserved because of the aridity of the region that had been the city's downfall.[3] His finds included a bale of yellow silk, along with wooden measuring instruments used to standardize the size of such bales; many documents on paper illustrating trade and contact with other foreign cultures; and wooden architectural fragments utilizing Ionic and Corinthian capitals, sure signs of an exchange taking place between Asia and the Mediterranean world of that period.

Two more archaeological sites that have yielded evidence of international exchanges are the ruins of the once-great cities of Gaochang (Khocho) and Jiaohe (Yarkhoto), not far from the present oasis town of Turfan. Gaochang was founded in the first century BCE, and came under Chinese control during the Han Dynasty; Jiaohe, closer to Turfan and raised from the surrounding terrain on an impressive, arrowhead-shaped plateau, was a capital of the Jushi people before the Chinese assumed control, also during the Han dynasty. Both were major, cosmopolitan centers during the Tang dynasty, with evidences for all of the major population groups and religious beliefs traversing the Silk Road at the time, and both were destroyed in wars of the thirteenth century.

In addition to the excavations at ruined cities such as Loulan, Gaochang, and Jiaohe, excavations at burial sites along the Silk Road have unearthed finds that provide scholars with much information about the lives of those buried there, and about Chinese burial practices in general. Buddhists, of course, practiced cremation, but burials that predate the advent of Buddhism, and non-Buddhist tombs after its introduction, have yielded remarkable troves that tell us much about details of life at the time. Clay architectural models and other objects found in Han tombs, for example, provide evidence for architectural practice during the Han, and allow students to see the connections between Chinese domestic architecture—houses and hunting towers (or watch towers)—and the image halls and pagodas that later evolved for Buddhist temple architecture in China, Korea, and Japan. Such models can also provide information about daily life for peasants in the Han. Models of pigpens, with sows sometimes suckling their young, and occasionally adjacent to one- or two-seat privies, are particularly interesting in this regard.

Archaeology at later Han tombsites has brought to light evidence for the success of efforts to secure what was, from China's point of view, its most keenly sought-after object of trade. Numerous tomb figures depict the "heavenly horses" that were first acquired from Ferghana (Ch.: Dayuan), a region now divided between Uzbekistan and Kyrgyzstan. The most remarkable of these tomb figures are the iconic bronze *Horse Flying on the Back of a Swallow* and the high-stepping retinue that follows him, from the tomb of a Han general that was excavated at Wuwei in the Gansu corridor in 1969.[4] The characteristic energy of the horses of Han is easily detected in many other examples, as well (Fig. 6.1). Described as "fire-breathing," "blood-sweating," and "able to travel 1,000 *li* without tiring," these newly introduced horses transformed the Chinese cavalry, which had previously gone into battle with much stockier ponies serving as mounts and pulling chariots.

Figure 6.1. Celestial horse, bronze with traces of polychrome; Han dynasty; Minneapolis Institute of Arts, Gift of Ruth and Bruce Dayton.

Other tombs from the Han and succeeding periods, especially the Tang dynasty, have yielded a variety of substitution burial objects of animals and figures which demonstrate the cosmopolitan nature of life in this period. Figures of Sogdian riders on camels (Fig. 6.2) with their triangular peaked caps and obvious Caucasoid features—large noses, heavy facial hair, and bulging eyes—stand out as clearly foreign from a Chinese point of view. Accompanying them are similar substitution burial figurines of those who served the Chinese as grooms tending horses, or as musicians and entertainers, including dancers known for their performance of the "Sogdian swirl." The latter performers were much in demand at the Chinese courts.

A particularly significant excavation site, the Astana cemetery located near Turfan, reflects the importance of this region during the Tang dynasty when Gaochang and Jiaohe were flourishing. This Tang cemetery, consisting of more than four hundred tombs that have yielded over ten thousand objects, was excavated by Japanese explorer Kozui Otani in 1902 and 1910, by Aurel Stein in 1914, and by the Chinese from 1959 onward. The aridity of the air, as at Loulan, has preserved mummified bodies and many usually perishable materials, including

Figure 6.2. Sogdian on a Camel, clay with traces of polychrome; Tang dynasty; Minneapolis Institute of Arts, The John R. Van Derlip Trust Fund.

wooden tomb figures dressed in cloth and paper, artificial flowers made of silk, and textiles with patterns and motifs that bear resemblance to textile patterns brought across the Silk Road from Persia.[5]

Raw commodities used in the production of works of art also made their way to and from China via overland routes and, later, via maritime routes from the New World. The story of the smuggling of silkworm eggs out of China in the headdress of a Chinese princess being married to a second-century king of Khotan, is a well-known one that is depicted in a painting from Dandan-Uiliq, a site near the Khotan oasis that flourished from the fourth to the eighth century.[6] Whether the story is historically accurate or not, knowledge of the silk-making process, once a closely held secret in China, did in fact reach Khotan around the second century CE, and silk production subsequently became a mainstay of the Khotanese economy.

Silver was a commodity in much shorter supply in China than gold or the metals used in the production of bronzes. The Chinese therefore valued it more highly than gold, a reversal of the traditional Western preference for gold over silver. Thus, the proliferation of silver objects among the decorative arts of the Tang Dynasty may be seen as a reflection of the prosperity of that period, brought about in part by foreign trade.

The "lion and grape" mirror, typically silver, or silvered bronze, with one polished, reflective surface and a back decorated with lions circling the mirror among clusters of grapes and their vines, used both a new material and new motifs, for Chinese mirrors had heretofore traditionally been made of bronze, sometimes inlaid with gold, and neither the lion nor the grape was native to China. We may think of the lion now as an exclusively African animal, but the Asiatic subspecies of the lion used to live all over southwest Asia, and it appears as early as the ninth century BCE in Assyrian reliefs from Nineveh.[7] After the introduction of the grape, also from the Near East, vineyards were planted at oasis sites such as Turfan, where grapes are still an important agricultural product today.

Another commodity that reached China from the West over the Silk Road was cobalt. The Chinese used cobalt from Persia in the production of cobalt oxide, used for the painted blue underglaze motifs of the "blue and white" wares of the Ming and Qing dynasties. The cobalt decoration of earlier wares of the Yuan dynasty had often had a grainy quality; the result of using locally supplied Chinese cobalt that was inferior to Persian supplies. The Chinese clearly preferred Persian cobalt, which yielded the clear blue color found in the underglaze decoration of later porcelain wares. As China acquired cobalt from Persia, so too, the

Chinese and the Persians exchanged ceramics, and the blue and white wares that were traded back and forth across Silk Road land routes reciprocally influenced each others' shapes and design motifs, as well.

Studying the art of the Silk Road not only demonstrates the interconnectedness of cultures but it can also enhance our understanding of how ideas spread and evolve. We can see art functioning in the service of religion, as we consider the evolution of the Buddha image and its spread from India in the Kushan Dynasty (50–320 CE) and later, across the trade routes to Central Asia and China. We can also see evidence for early contacts between Asian and Western cultures as we consider the manner in which that image of the Buddha was presented to worshipers.

Some of the earliest Buddha images come from Gandharan India. Located in present-day Pakistan and Afghanistan, the Gandhara region in the second and third century CE was under the control of Kushan India. It was there that the Kushan rulers, who had come out of Central Asia when they first invaded India, sought the relative coolness of the region for their summer capital. By that time the Romans, following in the footsteps of Alexander and his Asian empire, had established a colonial presence in the provinces of western Asia. Those who traded with them, and those who had worked for them there, carrying out sculptural commissions, also produced work for Kushan patrons in Gandhara who admired many aspects of Roman culture. Thus, some of the earliest images of the Buddha (Fig. 6.3) show him wearing a full-length, toga-like garment that the Buddha would never have worn during his earthly existence, both because of the heat of the Indian subcontinent and because a toga was only intended for Roman citizens—something that the historical Buddha assuredly was not.[8] That originally Roman garment, worn by the Buddha, made its way across the Silk Road along with Buddhism, as the religion spread from India through Central Asia and then to China, Korea, and Japan.

Numerous cave sites along the Silk Road document the spread of Mahayana Buddhism between the third and the ninth centuries. The sites are generally in the vicinity of various oases, as travelers and later pilgrims made the overland journey through barren, water-parched, and robber-infested wildernesses. Those who governed such oases provided patronage for Buddhist sites there. Added to their dedications were commissions by returning pilgrims, thankful for a safe journey.

One of the best known of these devotional patronage sites is at Bamiyan, in present-day Afghanistan. There, situated among smaller devotional caves, stood two colossal, toga-clad figures of the Buddha, one 120 feet tall, the other 175 feet, that had looked out on the valley

Figure 6.3. Standing Buddha, gray schist; Kushan dynasty; The Avery Brundage Collection, B60S593. © Asian Art Museum of San Francisco. Used by permission.

for more than a millennium and a half, until the Taliban destroyed them in March 2001, for anti-iconic reasons. The smaller of the two sculptures had probably been carved during the fourth century, and the larger one may be a bit later, dating from the late fourth to early fifth century. They reflected a provincial version of the Gandharan style, crudely cut from the rock and then coated with mud, followed by stucco to model the details of drapery folds. At one time, they may have been gilded. It had been a long time since those Buddhas had watched pilgrims come and go, on their way to and from the Holy Land of Buddhism, but Buddhists throughout the world, as well as the art community, widely regarded their destruction as an unconscionable act.[9]

Another important Buddhist patronage site along the southern route of the Silk Road through Central Asia was the fortified town of Miran. As at Loulan, remains at Miran show influences coming from the West. In 1906, Aurel Stein discovered there, in the third-century ruins of a square building that had housed a stupa, wall paintings of garland-bearing figures reminiscent of garland-bearing *putti* from Roman sarcophagi, another point of comparison with the arts of the late Roman world.[10]

Other sites along the route that skirts the northern edge of the Taklamakan Desert reveal international influences on Buddhism and Buddhist art. The site at Kyzyl is especially important. In caves there that date from the fourth to the seventh centuries, there is a remarkable amalgam of painting styles, ranging from figural types in the Indian fashion where shading suggests three-dimensional volume, to more purely linear Chinese styles where striping replaces the subtler shading of Indian practice.[11] It is interesting to note the degree to which the Chinese reliance on the brushed line of calligraphy and painting transformed the appearance of this relatively new subject matter.

The Caves of the Thousand Buddhas at Bezeklik, outside Turfan, consist of more than eighty caves, forty of which contained paintings. The caves are not in the best state of preservation today. Some paintings were carried off to museums in Berlin at the beginning of the twentieth century. Many of these were destroyed in the course of bombing raids during World War II. A number of the images still *in situ* have been defaced—literally de-faced, with jagged gashes across the facial features, thus rendering the images ineffective as icons. There is one interesting, undamaged portion of a painting of the Parinirvana (a scene depicting the death of the historical Buddha) that was painted in the ninth century, at a time when the Uyghurs were in control of the region. The Parinirvana scene shows musicians of various nationalities among the mourners, reflecting the ethnic mix present in and around Turfan at that time.[12]

The most important of all of the Buddhist cave sites along the Silk Road is that of the Mogao caves, also called the Caves of the Thousand Buddhas (Fig. 6.4), located a short distance across the desert from the important oasis town of Dunhuang. Dunhuang was first established in 111 BCE as a Han command post, and was the point of departure, and return for all of the trade routes across Central Asia. In the centuries succeeding the Han, Dunhuang was governed by a series of non-Han rulers who, having embraced Buddhism, commissioned caves at Mogao, until the return of Chinese governance under the Sui.

At a site marked by more than seven hundred caves, almost five hundred numbered caves are filled with painted and sculptural examples of Buddhist art, beginning in the fourth century and continuing into the Yuan dynasty. The caves were cut into a cliffside of gravel conglomerate not particularly suitable for carving. As a result, the sculptural groupings

Figure 6.4. Mogao Caves at Dunhuang, General view. Photo by Joan O'Mara, 2008.

at the Mogao Caves, unlike rock-cut sculptural groupings at contemporary sites such as Yungang or Longmen, were modeled on wooden and straw armatures, and covered with clay that was then painted, and sometimes partially gilded.

Significantly, Dunhuang was under the control of the Tibetans during the latter part of the Tang dynasty, and thus the provincial site escaped the effects of the ninth-century promulgations of the Tang against foreign religions that resulted in the widespread destruction of the metropolitan Buddhist temples, and their painting and sculpture. As a result, the Mogao Caves at Dunhuang preserve examples from almost the entire history of Buddhist patronage, although earlier examples do not have the same sense of sophistication that the art of the metropolitan temples would have provided.

Beginning in the fourth century during the Six Dynasties period, the earliest commissioned caves at Dunhuang were decorated in a fairly provincial manner, with thick outlines for the contours of painted figures. As at Kyzyl, such striping was the Sinicization of an Indian painting technique, and it did more to flatten and patternize the figures than it did to suggest three-dimensionality. Patronage was by the Tuoba Wei and other non-Han Chinese groups active in northern China during this period, and subject matter often focused on the historical Buddha Sakyamuni, or on Maitreya, the Buddha of the Future whose coming was expected to follow the life of Sakyamuni by one thousand years and was thus anticipated and expected during the Six Dynasties period.

After four centuries of disunity, the Sui dynasty (581–618) brought a reunification of China and a burst of patronage to the cave site. Trade revived, travel became safer, and was a practice much encouraged by one of the Sui emperors. A disproportionately large number of caves date from this brief, thirty-seven-year time period. Commissions of the succeeding Tang dynasty often focused on a new devotion to Amitabha, and the pursuit of the goal of rebirth in his "Pure Land," the Western Paradise, or in paradises associated with other Buddhas. Gone was the provincial character of the caves of the Six Dynasties period. The sculpture and painting of the later, Tang caves rank with the most important examples of Tang Buddhist art, as the *bodhisattva* that is now in the Sackler Museum at Harvard (Fig. 6.5) makes clear. That sculpture was

Figure 6.5. Kneeling Attendant Bodhisattva (sculpture removed from Cave 328, Mogao Caves, Dunhuang, Gansu province), molded clay stucco over wooden armature, gesso-covered surface with polychromy and gilding; late 7th c., Tang dynasty; Harvard Art Museum, Arthur M. Sackler Museum, First Fogg Expedition to China (1923–24), 1924.70; photo credit: Imaging Department © President and Fellows of Harvard College.

removed from an altar grouping by an American, Langdon Warner, who came as part of a 1924–25 Harvard expedition. Although he claimed that he was rescuing it from possible damage by White Russians fleeing the Bolshevik Revolution in Russia, the complete altar grouping was presumably no less at risk at the time, and tour guides at the caves still make a point of noting the place originally occupied by the sculpture before Warner took it.

There was also a trove of many thousands of Buddhist scroll paintings, sutras, and other calligraphic texts, that had been sealed—for protection from impending invasion by Islamic forces at the beginning of the eleventh century, according to one theory; on the arrival of a new version of Buddhist scriptures, according to another theory—in a so-called library cave, a small sub-cave (Cave 17) located on one side of Cave 16. The library cave was opened in 1907 by Aurel Stein, who carried off more than twenty thousand of its scrolls, justifying his actions on the grounds that they were suffering deterioration from having been stored on the ground, and from having been packed so tightly into such a small space. Stein was followed closely by French Sinologist Paul Pelliot (1878–1945), whose ability to read Chinese enabled him to pick and choose many more of the scrolls that he considered to be of the greatest interest, from what Stein had left behind,. Others followed, including Aurel Stein again, returning for more scrolls in 1913. When Chinese authorities finally closed the library cave and cleared it, the choicest examples had been long gone, much to the dismay of the present Chinese stewards of the site.[13]

Buddhism was not the only religion to spread its beliefs and practices along the Silk Road. Christianity, too, took to the Silk Road some centuries later, brought there by traders who were practitioners of Nestorianism. Nestorianism, or Syriac Christianity, as it is also called, was a form of Christianity deemed heretical at the Council of Ephesus in 431 CE, but which was still widely practiced in Persia. Its practitioners established Nestorian communities in trading posts across the Silk Road, and eventually in the Tang capital of Chang'an (Xi'an). There, it established itself as a syncretistic manifestation of Christianity in China. At the top of the so-called Nestorian Stele, a stone dedicatory monument preserved in Xi'an, a lotus gives rise to a cross, flanked by what appears to be the Daoist "fungus of immortality," and below that design, an inscription in Chinese and Syriac tells of the establishment of Nestorianism in China, and of the founding of a monastery in the seventh century.[14]

What remains of this monastery, called Daqin Si, is a recently discovered pagoda, oriented east-west in the manner of a Christian church rather than north-south in the Buddhist fashion, that was established on the grounds of a Daoist monastery outside of Chang'an (Xi'an).[15] Nestorianism flourished for a time, and may have been influential in the establishment and spread of Pure Land Buddhism, because the Chinese seem to have regarded it as a variant form of Buddhism—and why not? From a Chinese point of view, Nestorian Christianity, like Buddhism, had been brought from the West. Both focused on the moral teachings of a great spiritual leader. Nestorians also believed in a rebirth in heaven for the faithful believer, and that would have seemed quite compatible with evolving Pure Land hopes for rebirth in Amitabha's Western Paradise. Since such a hope seems far removed from the original teachings of the historical Buddha, it could even be argued that the prominence of the idea in Buddhism of the Tang dynasty could be connected to a Chinese misunderstanding of Nestorian Christianity, as a variant form of Buddhism.

Nestorian texts are among those discovered in the "library cave" at Dunhuang. Remains of a Tang dynasty Nestorian worship space were also discovered in the abandoned city of Gaochang, which was excavated in 1904–05. Fragments of a wall painting from that building depict a Nestorian priest carrying out what may have been a Palm Sunday observance.[16] So, it would appear that Nestorianism was a flourishing religion in China during the Tang dynasty. At the close of that dynasty, however, it died out, felled like much of Buddhism by the ninth-century decree outlawing foreign religions.

Along with Buddhism and Nestorian Christianity, there are also traces of Judaism, Manichaeism, Zoroastrianism, and, finally, Islam along the Silk Road. Scholars have found Manichaean illustrated texts, for example, in Gaochang.[17] Islam still flourishes among the Uyghur minority in Xinjiang Province in northwest China, and the architecture of Chinese mosques reflects both Islamic and native Chinese architectural styles. An early mosque in Chang'an, for example, resembles the layout and appearance of a Chinese Buddhist temple, but other mosques in Xinjiang Province bear a closer resemblance to more traditional Islamic examples. It should be no surprise to find evidences of all of these religions, as their adherents traveled, traded, and worshipped as they crossed Asia.

Even in Western art history classes, or in European civilization courses, knowledge of the Silk Road can enhance students' understanding of the period they are studying and the materials that they are seeing. Art historians often interpret Dutch still life paintings in terms of moral allegory, with tulips and other flowers in a vase, along with the insects that will destroy their beauty, standing as moralizing examples of *vanitas* that point to the inadvisability of putting too much stock in the transient pleasures of this world. So too, the partially consumed food in Dutch "breakfast pieces" conveys a similar message. But the items on these tables and in other Dutch still life paintings also deliver another meaning. In the seventeenth century, the Dutch were important traders on the high seas, importing many Silk Roads products. Works of art were themselves objects of trade. This was especially true of ceramics; and such items, along with the maps on the walls in other paintings, can point to the importance of maritime trade with the Indies, China, and Japan, as a source of Holland's material prosperity. An awareness of the ups and downs of the tulip trade, facilitated by the Silk Road, should also inform any understanding of the Dutch floral still lifes of that period that include tulips.[18]

The Dutch were by no means the first to trade with China to acquire its porcelain. The greatest impact of the Chinese export of ceramics, however, came from the rise of the later, maritime Silk Road, when the Portuguese, followed by the Dutch and then the English, Americans, and other Western powers engaged in maritime trade, established footholds in Chinese port cities. Anyone teaching the later history of China, the history of Western colonialism, or early economic history, can benefit from a study of Chinese ceramic exports to the West. During the Baroque era and continuing through the nineteenth century, Europeans, and then Americans, placed a high value on the porcelain being exported from China along maritime trade routes.

Prior to the introduction of porcelain, Europeans had eaten their meals on pewter services, crude wooden trenchers, and common earthenware, but they quickly became accustomed to the practice of eating from porcelain dinner services. They regarded this new ceramic medium as quite a wonder: thin-walled but durable, and elegantly decorated. Eventually, they learned how to produce it themselves. The duplication of the formula for true, "hard-paste" porcelain is credited to Johan Friedrich Bottger in 1707, and production in Europe officially began in a factory at Meissen, near Dresden, in 1710. Even then, the popularity of export wares from China continued, and European ceramicists adapted Chinese motifs for their own porcelain wares, producing a body of material that is sometimes referred to as "chinoiserie."

By the late Ming dynasty, the Portuguese had established themselves at Macao, not far from the city of Guangzhou, at the mouth of the Pearl River. There, they functioned as middlemen: their so-called Black Ship came annually from Goa, on the coast of India, and the Spice Islands, bringing pepper and other spices to China, where they were traded for silk and porcelain in Macao. During the Qing dynasty, Portugal continued to wield power and influence in Macao, but without its former primacy in the maritime Silk Road trade. The main distribution point for Chinese export porcelain from the inland kiln site of Jingdezhen was the nearby port city of Guangzhou (better known in the Western world as Canton). The *cohongs* (trading houses) of that city are depicted on the outside of a punch bowl, with flags identifying the various countries, including the United States, which had established footholds there by the eighteenth and nineteenth centuries (Fig. 6.6).

One of the most popular types of export ware was the armorial dinner service, a good example of which is the family armorial service (Fig. 6.7) commissioned by Eldred Lancelot Lee of Shropshire, England. Lee and his family were involved in English trade with Asia through the East India Company, and such involvement accounts for the scenes of the port cities of London and Guangzhou that alternate on the rim around the Lee family coat of arms.[19]

The export porcelain was packed in tea to cushion it, and the tea trade came to assume an increasingly larger role in maritime shipping, especially for the British.[20] Tea drinking fueled a major reform in the drinking habits of Europeans. Scholars have theorized that the drinking of tea and coffee—another import—had unanticipated consequences for public health in Europe. Boiling the water to produce those beverages cut down on the incidence of water-borne diseases, and the caffeine in tea, as well as the availability of safer water, provided an alternative to

Figure 6.6. Porcelain punchbowl with the Hongs of Guangzhou; made in China 1790–1802, Qing dynasty; Gift of Mr. and Mrs. Gerry Lenfest, Washington and Lee University, Lexington, VA.

Figure 6.7. Porcelain charger with Coat of Arms of Lee of Coton; 1700–1750, Qing dynasty; Reeves Center Acquisition Fund, Washington and Lee University, Lexington, VA.

alcohol consumption. These changes contributed in part to a population explosion in Europe, which in turn helped to fuel the Industrial Revolution there.[21] In return for porcelain and tea, what the Chinese wanted, and got, was ginseng and silver bullion, much of it from the New World. What they did not want, but nevertheless got from the British, who were ever concerned about the balance of trade, was opium.

The arts have intersected in numerous ways with the history of trade, religions, and exploration and conquest along the Silk Road. We cannot easily divorce our understanding of the Silk Road from a consideration of the arts and archaeology that reveal so much about the lives of those carrying on the trade, and the products that trade generated. Further, the arts found along the Silk Road are expressions of religious ideas that moved across its expanses, and are essential to understanding their history and practice. Finally, art objects themselves were important trade commodities, purchased and carried across the Silk Road, especially the maritime routes that brought porcelain to the West in the Ming and Qing dynasties. Beyond the specifics of archaeological sites, patronage of

Buddhist caves, or the Western craving for porcelain, however, it is clear that we have, for some time, lived in a globalized world, and no one is well served by learning the history of art, trade, religion, or any other discipline with blinders on, focusing only on the Western traditions of Europe and the United States. The study of the arts of the Silk Road is one way to broaden what we teach our students.

Suggested Readings

The Art Institute of Chicago. *The Silk Road and Beyond: Travel, Trade, and Transformation*. Museum Studies 33, 1. Chicago: Art Institute of Chicago, 2007.

Fraser, Sarah E. *Performing the Visual: The Practice of Buddhist Wall Painting in China and Central Asia, 618–960*. Stanford: Stanford University Press, 2004.

Gies, Jacques, Laure Feugere, and Andre Coutin. *Painted Buddhas of Xinjiang: Hidden Treasures from the Silk Road*. Chicago: Art Media Resources, 2002.

Juliano, Annette L., and Judith A. Lerner. *Monks and Merchants: Silk Road Treasures from Northwest China*. New York: Harry N. Abrams with The Asia Society, 2001.

Levenson, Jay A., ed. *Encompassing the Globe: Portugal and the World in the 16th and 17th Centuries*. Washington, DC: Smithsonian Institution, 2007.

So, Jenny F., and Emma C. Bunker. *Traders and Raiders on China's Northern Frontier*. Washington, DC: Smithsonian Institution, 1995.

Tucker, Jonathan. *The Silk Road, Art and History*. Chicago: Art Media Resources, 2003.

Whitfield, Roderick, and Anne Farrer. *Caves of the Thousand Buddhas: Chinese Art from the Silk Route*. New York: George Braziller, 1990.

Whitfield, Susan. *Aurel Stein on the Silk Road*. Chicago: Serindia Publications, 2004.

Notes

1. The newest edition of one of the most canonical art history survey texts, originally by H. W. Janson and titled simply *History of Art* (1962), illustrates that the effort is having at least modest success. The text is now co-authored by Penelope Davies et al. and retitled. It still does not go beyond the Western tradition, except for one chapter on the arts of Islam, but at least it no longer reflects an underlying supposition that if you are talking about art history, it must be the art of the West that is your subject. Penelope J. E. Davies et al., *Janson's History of Art: The Western Tradition*, 7th ed. (Upper Saddle River, NJ: Pearson/Prentice-Hall, 2007). A more recent basic text by Marilyn Stokstad

includes chapters on the arts of Asian, African, and New World civilizations; nearly a quarter of its total length is devoted to the exploration of non-Western traditions. Marilyn Stokstad, *Art History*, 3rd ed. (Upper Saddle River, NJ: Pearson/Prentice-Hall, 2008). The benefits of just such a globalized view of the world can also be seen in a recent exhibition on the art and commerce of Portugal and markets on three continents, including Asian ports along the later, maritime Silk Road that are relevant for this volume. See Jay A. Levenson, ed., *Encompassing the Globe: Portugal and the World in the 16th and 17th Centuries* (Washington, DC: Smithsonian Institution, 2007).

2. It may be useful to point out here that excavations at Silk Road sites in the late nineteenth and early twentieth centuries were not led or supervised by the Chinese, or others native to the sites. Any Chinese involved in such excavations were employed primarily for their knowledge of local conditions, their abilities to serve as interpreters and communicate with the locals, their actual physical labor in carrying out the excavations, and in the removal of artifacts. They could not make decisions about the disposition of artifacts. Stein and other mostly European explorers and archaeologists carried out their excavations in Asia as a tangential activity to The Great Game. Stein used a position in colonial India as a jumping-off place, serving there for thirteen years before making his first foray into Central Asia. He carried out his explorations of Silk Road sites on eight separate expeditions between 1900 and 1939, exploring its length from the Mediterranean to the cave site at Dunhuang, before his death in Kabul, Afghanistan, in 1943. Those explorations are chronicled in Susan Whitfield, *Aurel Stein on the Silk Road* (Chicago: Serindia Publications, 2004).

3. The findings at Loulan do not quite measure up to the spectacular finds at the waterlogged Han site at Mawangdui, which is beyond the geographical purview of this examination of the Silk Road, but has also yielded otherwise perishable artifacts that were preserved because of the circumstances of the burial site. What is most important, evidently, is the maintenance of a consistent environment in the tomb. It is the repeated process of wetting, drying out, then rewetting and drying again, that causes the deterioration of perishable materials.

4. Reproduced repeatedly, including Fig. 13 in Jonathan Tucker, *The Silk Road, Art and History* (Chicago: Art Media Resources, 2003), 29.

5. See, for example, Figs. 172–179 in Tucker, *The Silk Road*, 142–45.

6. The painted wood panel depicting the story of the "Silk Princess" was removed from Dandan-Uiliq by Aurel Stein, and is now in the collection of the British Museum. See Fig. 228 in Tucker, *The Silk Road*, 181.

7. For a detail of the relief *Assurnasirpal II Killing Lions*, see Stokstad, *Art History*, 40.

8. Neither was the historical Jesus a Roman citizen, yet early images of Christ also depict him wearing a toga-like robe, and for some of the same reasons.

9. The site was important for trade and worship until 1221, when the troops of Chinggis Khan came through the region. Enraged over the death

of a favorite grandson in the fighting there, Chinggis laid waste to the entire valley, killing all those who lived there and destroying all of its habitations. Images of the colossal Buddhas in August 2000, and of one of the explosions that demolished them in March 2001, may be seen in Figs. 69-73 in Tucker, *The Silk Road*, 59–62.

10. These paintings are actually associated with a name, Tita, which may have been a form of Titus, a name commonly used throughout the Roman Near East. See Figs. 219, 221, in Tucker, *The Silk Road*, 173–74.

11. In India, painters sought to render flat, two-dimensional images in as sculptural a fashion as possible, by using shading to suggest volume, rather than to suggest light coming from a directed source. For the variety of styles found at Kyzyl, see Figs. 193–199, in Tucker, *The Silk Road*, 154–57.

12. See Fig. 189 in Tucker, *The Silk Road*, 150.

13. The vast quantity of material that was removed to museums in the West means that much of it has not, even now, been thoroughly studied. There is also speculation that some of the scrolls now in the West may have been forged. Stein discovered one such forger who had been at work since 1899 in the Khotan region. More than one hundred of the painted banners and silk fragments carried off by Stein are reproduced and discussed in Roderick Whitfield and Anne Farrer, *Caves of the Thousand Buddhas: Chinese Art from the Silk Route* (New York: George Braziller, 1990).

14. A rubbing of the stele is reproduced in Fig. 104, Tucker, *The Silk Road*, 90.

15. Documented in an article by Leslie Camhi, "Ruins of an Old Christian Church on Lao-Tzu's Turf," *New York Times* February 24, 2002: AR 45.

16. Reproduced Figs. 181–182 in Tucker, *The Silk Road*, 146.

17. Reproduced front and back in Fig. 180 in Tucker, *The Silk Road*, 145.

18. An example by Adriaen van der Spelt (1632–1673) and Frans van Mieris (1633–1681) is reproduced in The Art Institute of Chicago, *The Silk Road and Beyond: Travel, Trade, and Transformation*, Museum Studies 33, 1 (Chicago: Art Institute of Chicago, 2007), 64. See Marybeth Carlson's essay elsewhere in this volume for further discussion of the tulip boom.

19. A later American descendant in that family was Confederate General Robert E. Lee, and that circumstance helps to account for the presence in the Washington and Lee University collection of a number of pieces of the Lee family armorial service.

20. The tea trade also affected those on this side of the Atlantic. Bringing a more globalized view of that trade to any tried and true discussion of the Boston Tea Party in a U.S. history class would be a service to those students.

21. Discussed by William H. McNeill in "The Historical Significance of the Way of Tea," ch. 10 in *Tea in Japan: Essays on the History of Chanoyu*, ed. Paul Varley and Kumakura Isao (Honolulu: University of Hawai'i Press, 1989).

Part II

Thematic Approaches to the Silk Road

.

Chapter 7

Incorporating Nomads into the Curriculum, One Steppe at a Time

Ronald K. Frank

In the traditional history survey, students get a narrative centered on geographically defined civilizations which tells a story of expansion, great achievements, and at times spectacular collapses. Invariably, the focus is on sedentary cultures: often on "hydraulic civilizations" that emerged in river valleys and developed into powerful overland empires with densely populated urban centers. In this standard narrative, the bulk of the Eurasian landmass comes into focus only once, when early in the thirteenth century, seemingly out of nowhere, the Mongols exploded onto the scene. Courses in world, Near Eastern, Medieval Western, Russian, or Chinese history all cover the relatively short-lived Mongol empire. Indeed, ask any premodern history class at the beginning of the semester about individual rulers students expect to hear about and more often than not the answer will be Chinggis Khan.[1]

Yet the Mongols only figure prominently in our interpretation of world history due to their easily quantifiable impact on sedentary civilizations. The Mongol sack of Kiev in 1240 is important to us because it marked the final disintegration of the Kievan Rus', likewise, the fall of Baghdad in 1252 meant a cataclysmic (though by no means final) collapse of Islamic civilization, and the final defeat of the Song dynasty in the Battle of Yamen in 1279 was a major fissure in the history of traditional China. The almost equally large and arguably more sophisticated nomadic empire of the Turks (552–744), on the other hand, did not conquer any sedentary civilizations. Perhaps for that very reason it hardly ever appears in the history books outside of specialized scholarly works.

In a historical narrative with a strong bias in favor of sedentary cultures, the Mongol phenomenon remains inexplicable. If we accept the view that great achievements in political and military organization require sophisticated exploitation of an agricultural base, there is no room for the emergence of a nomadic great power. In this context, the Mongols, like other successful so-called barbarians before and after them, remain first and foremost an alien and destructive force, something of an aberration to the regular historical development, and we hasten to point out that the course of world history soon returned to normal.

Discussing nomadic empires in their own right allows us to ana-lyze the Mongol phenomenon in a more appropriate geographical and historical context than that of its sedentary victims, and in the process reevaluate the standard narrative. Few of us have the luxury of being able to devote entire courses to the history of Central Eurasia. Nev-ertheless, no course attempting to deal with the Silk Road or any of the civilizations of the Eurasian landmass can entirely ignore the steppe frontier that all of them shared. The object of this chapter is to provide some suggestions about how to include such subject matter into existing courses, in particular in Chinese or East Asian history and Russian or Eastern European history, as these topics lend themselves all too easily to an isolationist approach.

Geography, Ecology, Linguistics, and the Frontier

The first major problem one encounters when introducing subject matter beyond the pale of established sedentary civilizations is to negotiate a bewildering variety of place names that might refer to different things at different times and that, for the most part, we cannot find on any modern map. Even the terms Central and Inner Asia compete with one another.[2] But a brief discussion of the geography of the region is essential to an understanding of nomadic peoples. The climate and ter-rain of the steppes make it difficult to grow crops but also provide few physical barriers to spatial mobility.[3] Thus, ecological conditions favor a steppe economy that is largely based on nomadic pastoralism: mobile stock raising following a circuit of seasonal pastures. Steppe dwellers have to move with their livestock once a pasture is exhausted, normally returning after the vegetation cover has regenerated. This precludes the establishment of fixed dwellings, the typical dwelling being instead a dome-shaped tent made from felt on a skeleton of wooden trellises, commonly referred to as a "yurt." The pastoral economy is extensive and thus characterized by extremely low population density.

With such a small population and a seasonal migration pattern, there is little incentive to generate social or political organization beyond a kinship or tribal level. In short, the world of the steppe nomad is in every respect the exact opposite of that of the sedentary agriculturalists who live in fixed dwellings in densely populated areas administered by a more or less sophisticated bureaucratic apparatus.[4] Not surprisingly, the interaction between these two diametrically opposed worlds has often been a series of fundamental cultural misunderstandings. For example, Chinese sources describe the people of the north as moving about like birds and beasts, and the Mongols could see very little use in peasants tilling the soil. A nomad's wealth is measured in livestock rather than land. Pastures are useful only as long as there is grass, and pastureland normally belongs to tribes or kinship groups. Animals, however, are the property of individuals. The infamous proposition to kill off the remaining peasants of northern China after the Mongol conquest in order to convert their fields into pasture thus made perfect economic sense from a nomad's point of view.

Linguistics provides another lens through which to approach nomadic societies. There are strong linguistic ties between sedentary and nomadic societies. The words *khan* and *horde* (in Russian, *orda*) both originate in Turkic terms. The title *qaghan* not only eventually became *khân* in Mongolian, but was known and used in the West (as *caganus*) since the time of the Avars (sixth century). In 839 the Carolingian Annals recorded a visit from Byzantium of emissaries of a "*caganus rhos*."[5] Evidently, the early Scandinavian rulers of Rus' had reasons to adopt steppe terminology as well.

But sedentary cultures also made linguistic contributions to nomadic ones. There is no direct evidence of a writing system among steppe pastoralists before the eighth century CE. All of the extant scripts of steppe peoples were adopted from their sedentary neighbors. The runic Turkic script was derived from a cursive form of Aramaic, while the horizontally written Sogdian and Uyghur also appear to have Semitic roots. The traditional Mongol script, written vertically from right to left is a modification of the Uyghur writing system, but with the page turned ninety degrees. The Manchu script is a further modification of the same system, written vertically from left to right. Most of these scripts were singularly unsuited to provide an adequate phonetic rendition of the Altaic languages they were used for. In the thirteenth century, the Tibetan monk 'Phags-pa created an alternative script for Mongolian based on the Indian-inspired Tibetan script. 'Phags-pa became the official script of the Mongol Yuan dynasty in China (1279–1368). The only examples of character scripts based on Chinese are those of the Khitan Liao dynasty

(947–1125), the Jurchen Jin dynasty (1115–1234), and the Tangut state of Xi Xia (990–1227), all of whom had steppe nomadic origins. Many inscriptions from the Manchu Qing dynasty (1644–1911) provide the same text in Chinese, Mongolian, Manchu, and Tibetan, at times with a 'Phags-pa heading for the Mongolian text. Using such illustrations in class can significantly enhance the appreciation of cultural, ethnic, and linguistic diversity in seemingly homogenous civilizations.[6]

Despite frequent interaction, nomads are largely peripheral to sedentary civilizations, occupying frontier or border areas. The frontier has only marginal economic significance that cannot justify the expenditure of fully incorporating it into the political structure. But at the same time, it offers considerable opportunity for those brave enough to settle there. Frontiersmen are often socially or economically marginalized people who might want to keep their distance to the center, yet on occasion the government might use them to project the power of the state farther outward. Typically, frontiersmen are farmers as well as pastoralists and warriors; thus, they combine aspects of sedentary and nomadic lifestyles. Strategically, a frontier serves as a buffer zone between the sedentary center and the hostile steppe, home of the nomadic "barbarian." Because of its cultural, ethnic, and often religious diversity, a frontier area might emerge as a fertile ground for the exchange and amalgamation of commodities, technologies, and competing value systems.

The history of large Eurasian overland empires, such as Russia and China, provides a good illustration of the significance of frontiers and the complexity of frontier policy. Russia's rapid expansion across the Eurasian landmass in the sixteenth to eighteenth centuries was at least partially the result of a redefinition of the political center. The original core area of Rus' in the upper Dniepr Basin considered everything "beyond the rapids" (*zaporozhie* in Russian) as peripheral and potentially hostile "open field" (*pol'e*). With the shift of the political center to Moscow in response to close interaction with the Golden Horde, the former center became itself more closely associated with a frontier, as the term *Ukraina* (roughly, "on the periphery") implies. Meanwhile, Cossacks, quintessential frontiersmen of mixed ancestry, provided much of the manpower for further Russian expansion eastward while resisting (at times violently) attempts to incorporate them into the Russian state.[7] Essentially the short-term outcome was a grotesquely enlarged frontier zone that could only very gradually be incorporated into the Russian state once the technology and necessary resources became available.

Chinese frontier policy, on the other hand, was characterized by periods of active expansion in the west and containment measures in the north. Through a series of maps showing the geographical expansion of China over successive dynasties, students can easily discern what area constitutes the agricultural core ("China proper"). Only the most powerful dynasties could lay effective claim to the western frontier area, the "panhandle" extending through the Gansu corridor into Central Asia. Both the Han (202 BCE–220 CE) and the Tang (618–907) maintained garrisons along the Silk Road, the most important artery of economic and cultural exchange in premodern Eurasia. The Song (970–1279) and Ming (1368–1644) abandoned this claim, but the Manchu Qing dynasty incorporated the area for good after the destruction of the Zunghar empire, the last significant nomadic power, in 1757. Characteristically, the Chinese named the area Xinjiang, "New Frontier," but made efforts to administer it as a regular province of the empire.

It is interesting to note that no such expansion took place into Mongolia before the Manchus came onto the scene in the seventeenth century. However, the Great Wall functioned more as a defense installation in a relatively narrow, and hence often penetrated, frontier zone, than a physical expression of a linear border. By the eighteenth century, China had effectively incorporated its former frontier zones in the north and west, established imperial borderlands in Mongolia and Tibet, and begun to negotiate a linear border with Russia.

Barbarians at the Gate: Interactions between the Nomadic and Sedentary Worlds

While the word *barbarian* is of Greek origin, the concept of barbarian is present across most sedentary cultures. The fact that steppe pastoralists often appear in this category is another reason we have not taken nomads seriously. A barbarian, in Greek terms, was essentially any non-Greek speaking person. Later, Roman and Byzantine chroniclers applied the word to anyone beyond the reach of human civilization, whether they were Turks from the steppes, Slavs from the woodlands, or Scandinavian in origin. Russian sources use the word as early as the eleventh century, mostly in reference to their nomadic Turkic neighbors to the southwest. Barbarians are thus not necessarily only steppe dwellers, though nomads did appear especially alien.

The Greeks ascribed to their neighbors on the Pontic Steppes a penchant for excessive cruelty. Herodotus reported that barbarians (in this case the Scythians) took blood oaths, shaved their foreheads, sacrificed horses, and made drinking cups of the skulls of their vanquished enemies. This latter image became a staple in the Western depiction of barbarians for centuries, as well as in other sedentary cultures. Byzantine sources relate that such a fate befell Emperor Nicephorus I in 811 at the hands of the Bulgars, a Turkic people originating on the Volga steppes. Han dynasty (202 BCE–220 CE) sources mention the same custom among the Xiongnu, their major menace across the Great Wall. A correlation between nomadic lifestyle and excessive cruelty thus loomed large in the minds of all sedentary observers of the steppes.

Whether the blanket term *barbarian* represents a suitable equivalent to the many different words used in Ancient China to describe northern neighbors has been the subject of some controversy. Chinese texts from the Eastern Zhou dynasty (771–256 BCE) mention four different categories of people as living outside of the civilizational reach of the core area, namely *Man*, *Yi*, *Rong*, and *Di*. It is unclear whether these designations were ethnonyms; the important characteristic of these people was that they lived in a succession of peripheral zones designated by their relative remoteness from the royal domain (Zhou). All had customs that differ from those of the Chinese, but the *Man* and *Yi* lived closer and could be allies, while the *Rong* and *Di* inhabited uncultivated marshes and were hostile to the center. Clearly all of them were "barbarian" in the sense of not sharing core cultural values and likely language, but rendering all these different categories with a single English equivalent is problematic.[8]

In the middle of the fifth century BCE a new type of hostile outsider appeared in the Chinese sources, the *Hu*. They were pastoralists and mounted archers, stereotypical nomads in other words. The name *Hu* might have originated as an ethnic designation for a specific group, but it soon came to mean simply "nomad." It might thus be a reasonably close match for the Greek "barbarian." Neither term implies ethnic homogeneity among the people to whom it is applied; it simply marks them as "beyond the pale." The appearance of the *Hu* may be the starting point for a discussion of arguably the most important defining feature of the steppe barbarians: their skill in mounted archery. Their amazing ability to shoot arrows with reasonable accuracy from the back of a galloping horse, often directly over the horse's tail (the famous "Parthian shot") was what impressed contemporary observers in the East and West the most.

Archeological evidence from the steppes indicates that people had domesticated horses there as early as the fourth millennium BCE. Wheeled chariots appeared on the steppes by 2000 BCE and were present in sedentary civilizations before the end of the second millennium. Yet the infamous nomadic horse riders from the steppes did not appear until as late as 800 BCE. The rather large chronological gap between initial domestication of horses and their widespread use for riding points toward a gradual development from original sedentary animal husbandry on the steppes to later full-fledged nomadic pastoralism.[9] Steppe dwellers were thus not always (and perhaps never exclusively) nomadic, rather, the nomadic pastoralist component of their society increased over time as they became more adept horse riders able to stray farther away from their homestead. By the time of their first appearance around 800 BCE, the nomadic horsemen had also become adept in the use of iron technology for weapons manufacture. Horse-riding steppe barbarians thus exploited a twofold technological advantage. Moreover, as nomadic societies gradually abandoned agriculture on the steppes, placing greater reliance on animal husbandry, a larger proportion of the male population could participate in war. This change alleviated the tremendous numerical disadvantage nomads faced when engaging a sedentary enemy.

The most formidable weapon of the nomad was the compound, or composite, bow. Made out of a combination of wood, sinew, and horn in a re-curved shape with the tips bent forward, it could shoot arrows faster and further than a wooden long bow. Such bows could deliver arrows accurately and in quick succession at about sixty yards. Shooting upward at a forty-five-degree angle could increase the range. This tactic was useful for massive attacks where accuracy did not matter.[10] There is no shortage of Western, Arabic, or Chinese accounts of nomadic battle tactics. Herodotus's description of the Scythians in Book IV of his *History*, Ibn Fadlan's account of his travels across the steppe to the Rus', and Sima Qian's treatment of the Xiongnu all offer a wide variety of information on the subject and are readily available in translation for use in class.[11]

There are a number of problems with discussing ethnic and cultural connections and identities in the context of steppe nomadic societies. First, it is very tempting to assume that the existence of similar customs among different nomadic groups implies some sort of an ethnic connection. However, unrelated ethnic groups might have borrowed specific customs because of prestige associated with them, or because they had a certain utility. A good example would be the Japanese samurai, who shaved their foreheads because it made their helmets fit more securely, not because they were distant descendants of the Scythians! Second, we cannot necessarily rely on the ethnonyms sedentary societies used in their accounts about "barbarians," because the chroniclers themselves had often no idea about the ethnic backgrounds of their barbarian subjects. Terms such as *Scythian* in the West or *Xiongnu* in China became labels for all nomads, rather than ethnic distinctions. It is important to remember that until the appearance of writing on the steppes in the eighth century, all accounts of nomadic life were the product of their sedentary neighbors. Pre-Turkic nomads did not leave us any written records in their own language. Consequently, we have little more than circumstantial evidence about their ethnic background.

Nowhere is that clearer than in the case of the Xiongnu. In the context of Chinese history the Xiongnu are the archetypical steppe barbarians. All the textual evidence we have about these particular "barbarians" comes from one source: Sima Qian's *Historical Records* (*Shiji*). The historian devoted a whole chapter to the rise of the Xiongnu, their manners and customs, and their relationship with the Han empire. According to his account, the Xiongnu were known since antiquity, but made their first direct contact with the Chinese around 230 BCE, shortly before the unification of China. After reporting that the First Emperor conducted a series of campaigns against the Hu barbarians of the North, Sima Qian then turns to the rise of Modun (Maodun), the leader of the Xiongnu. The story of how this ambitious young prince trained a detachment of warriors is a must-read for any class on Chinese history. After killing anyone who failed to obey his commands first to shoot his favorite horse, and then his favorite wife, he gave the order to shoot his own father, the tribal chieftain. At that point, none of his men refused. With this blatant disregard for the rules of filial piety, truly barbarian by Confucian standards, Modun became ruler (*shanyu*) of the Xiongnu in 209 BCE.[12]

When reading Sima Qian, students should be aware of the fact that all names and titles of the Xiongnu we can find in the *Shiji* are, of course, Chinese. To what extent these Chinese names represent a faithful attempt to transcribe or transliterate the actual names remains the object of much speculation. Linguists continue to read a lot into these names and use the result to construct often fanciful theories about the ethnic origins of the Xiongnu. Thus various researchers have found "proof" for the Xiongnu being of Proto-Mongolian, Proto-Turkic, or even Indo-European stock.[13] A related issue of special significance to a world history course is the question of the relationship between the Xiongnu and the Huns. While it is beyond doubt that the words *Xiongnu* and *Hun* are related, it is less clear whether this is a case of true ethnic connection or just an instance of "borrowing" a prestigious ethnonym.

With the appearance of the Xiongnu on the Chinese political horizon, relations with the northern frontier underwent a profound change. The defeat of Chinese forces under the direct command of Emperor Han Gaozu in 199 BCE led to the establishment of a new barbarian policy that was destined to become the blueprint for all future relations between China and the steppes. The so-called *he-qin* ("pacification") policy linked the Han empire and the Xiongnu in a tributary relationship.

By providing goods to the Xiongnu, China in effect bought assurances against future Xiongnu raids. Such a policy also made costly military expeditions unnecessary. An important question that lies at the heart of this relationship is how the supposedly fully nomadic Xiongnu were able to build and maintain a lasting state-like structure. Pastoral nomads, conventional wisdom has it, lack the resources and the productivity to maintain and support a numerically large elite, which is necessary for a state to function. Yet the Xiongnu and other pastoral nomads after them had virtual empires, and what is more, they managed to build these empires at times when they were facing a strong and united China that should have been capable of holding them in check.

Recent scholarship has provided interesting plausible explanations of this problem. Nicola Di Cosmo proposes that the Xiongnu state emerged as the result of a combination of external and internal factors. The campaigns of the First Emperor brought on a crisis that led to increased militarization and the emergence of Modun as a supra-tribal leader. The relative military weakness of the early Han dynasty gave the Xiongnu the chance to impose a tributary relationship upon China that alleviated their economic crisis and provided the means to maintain a lasting political structure on the steppe.[14] Di Cosmo's theory is based on a careful analysis of available data and previous scholarship on the subject. However, it is specifically tied to the Xiongnu situation and does not attempt to offer a paradigm applicable to later interaction between China and the steppes.

Thomas Barfield has proposed the theory that barbarian states developed in response to the opportunity for raiding and especially extortion that a unified China presented. A tribal leader could assert control over other tribes and form a tribal confederation by utilizing resources that sedentary neighbors provided. The Xiongnu obtained these resources initially by raiding China and later as tribute in the framework of the pacification (*he-qin*) policy. The Xiongnu chieftain (*shanyu*) maintained his position by acting as the sole intermediary between the Han court and the steppe tribes, thus effectively monopolizing the flow of goods from China. In essence, then, it was China that provided the necessary resources to build and maintain a state structure among nomadic pastoralists. As long as China remained united and centralized under the Han dynasty, the tribal confederacy on the steppes continued to exist. When the Han dynasty disintegrated, the flow of goods onto the steppes stopped, and the Xiongnu state fell apart. According to Barfield, this model works to explain not just the Xiongnu state, but all successive pastoral nomadic empires of Eurasia. In short, successful dynasties in China rose and fell together with strong and unified barbarian states in the north.[15]

This theory has the advantage of providing a pattern that instructors can easily utilize when teaching the history of Chinese frontier relations. However, it rests on several assumptions about steppe nomadic society that appear to be questionable. According to this theory, steppe dwellers are fully nomadic and economically self-sufficient. They conduct raids primarily to obtain luxury products that they themselves cannot produce. Thus, they do not raid out of economic necessity, and raids are just a tool in a predatory foreign policy, aimed at establishing a tributary relationship with China. However, the available data suggest that while some subsistence agriculture was present in all pastoral societies on the steppes, most nomadic raids had not only the object of capturing luxury goods, but grain and livestock as well. Most researchers agree that nomadic pastoralists raided each other and their sedentary neighbors primarily out of economic necessity, to alleviate chronic or acute food shortages.

A useful element in Barfield's theory is his distinction of two different types of "barbarians" on China's northern frontier, which he calls "predator" and "scavenger" barbarians. According to this typology, nomadic pastoralists from the Mongolian steppes usually pursued a predatory foreign policy toward China, alternating raids and negotiations in order to maximize their bargaining position with the Chinese states. The Chinese essentially financed barbarian empires on the steppes. The Xiongnu, Turks, Uyghurs, Mongols, Oirats, and Zunghars belong to this category. Their lack of agriculture is what set them apart from the inhabitants of Manchuria, where tribes practiced agriculture alongside animal husbandry. Barfield posits that these other "barbarians" from Manchuria were able to conquer and administer parts of northern China, by in essence, scavenging on the remnants of both the Chinese and the nomadic empires after the collapse of both. In periods of Chinese disunity, the north of the country was ruled by barbarian "conquest" dynasties (e.g., the Tuoba Wei kingdom, the Khitan Liao dynasty, and other "scavengers") that had the expertise to rule a sedentary population of agriculturalists. In contrast to these conquerors from Manchuria, nomadic pastoralists from the Mongolian steppes conducted raids, but as a rule had no interest in conquest. This pattern provides a very intriguing alternative to the "dynastic cycle" model in that it incorporates China into a wider geographical and historical context.

The most feared barbarians of late antiquity in the West, the Huns, appeared suddenly on Pontic Steppes in the mid-fourth century CE. Whether they were the same people as the Xiongnu, distant relatives, or completely unrelated, their role in the history of the West is comparable to that of the Xiongnu in China. The Huns were the first major pastoral nomadic group that represented a threat to the sedentary civilization of the West. Roman accounts that depict them as a fearsome, alien, and incomprehensible force are numerous and widely available in print.[16] Interestingly enough, the common name for the Huns in writings of the time was Scythians, though Marcellinus in book 31 of his *Res Gestae* does refer to them as Huns. Reading his account about Hunnish customs alongside Sima Qian's description of the Xiongnu makes for an interesting comparative exercise in a world history course. Unlike the Xiongnu in China five centuries before, however, the Huns faced a Roman Empire in steep decline. Having established a home base on the Pannonian Steppe they soon found themselves embroiled in civil wars involving Roman factions and assorted Germanic "barbarians" who had already established a foothold in parts of the Roman Empire. By 454, the Hun empire disintegrated as a result of revolts by Germanic subject populations.

At the same time, a comparable situation existed on the other end of the steppes. After the fall of the Han dynasty, the Xiongnu confederation disintegrated. From the beginning of the fourth century northern China was ruled by a succession of conquest dynasties originating in Manchuria and known as the Xianbei. These tribes were at least partially nomadic and presumably speakers of a Turkic language. Perhaps the most significant of these states was the Northern Wei (386–534). The founders of this state belonged to a nomadic tribe known from Chinese sources as Tuoba, most likely a corruption of the Turkic *Tabgach* ("origin"). In Barfield's theory, they belong to the category of scavenger barbarians who were capable of conquering and administering sedentary civilizations. Though they were themselves barbarians in the eyes of the Han Chinese, the Northern Wei dynasty had its own barbarian problem in the north.

Very shortly after the establishment of the Northern Wei dynasty in northern China the nomadic pastoral tribes inhabiting the Mongolian steppes united into a confederation known from Chinese sources as "Rouran" or "Ruan-ruan." Although relatively obscure, this confederation deserves mention in class for a variety of reasons. First, they appear to be the earliest consistent users of the title *qaghan*, which appears in Chinese sources as "kehan." Second, they are the immediate predecessors of the Turks on the steppes. Lastly, they may possibly be related to the Avars who played an important role in the history of early medieval Europe.

The rapid disintegration of the Rouran confederacy in the mid-sixth century sent shockwaves all across the Eurasian steppes. In 552, a subject people of the Rouran known in Chinese sources as Tu-jue overthrew the last Rouran qaghan in a violent revolt. The Tu-jue were none other than the Turks who shortly formed the largest overland empire in Eurasia before the Mongols. The Rouran virtually disappeared from the record after the wholesale slaughter of their aristocracy by the Turks in 555. This event is a particularly noteworthy case study in the succession of one group of steppe nomads by another. As a rule, remnants of the previously dominant group or tribe were incorporated into the new confederation. Presenting the history of the steppes as a sequence of ethnonyms alone (as in Xiongnu—Xianbei—Rouran—Turks) is misleading insofar as it implies complete physical replacement or destruction of one group by the next.

The rise of the Turks on the Mongolian steppes in the mid-fifth century was a typical example of a subject population overthrowing the dominant tribe in a confederation. The Rouran had referred to the Turks as "blacksmiths," and iron technology indeed became the hallmark of the Turkic empire. Thus, the Turks had a reputation for a highly valued and strategically important technology. They swiftly subjugated tribes from Manchuria to the Black Sea, soon controlling the entire length of the Silk Road. In fact, much of their interaction with their important sedentary neighbors China, Sassanid Persia, and Byzantium came from their desire to establish a Silk trade monopoly in Eurasia.

News of the ascendance of the Turks reached the West in 557 when a people calling themselves Avars appeared on the Eastern frontier of the Byzantine empire. These Avars claimed that they were refugees from the Turks and asked for protection and fertile lands to settle on. Emperor Justinian reportedly granted their request and the Avars became a major power in Eastern Europe for the next 250 years. As a result, the Byzantine empire became heavily involved in steppe politics.[17] The timing of their appearance in Byzantium has led many scholars to believe that the Avars are in fact the very same Rouran, though even some contemporary Byzantine observers disputed such claims. Though they were initially allies of Byzantium against the Bulgars, yet another group of Turkic-speaking steppe nomads originally from the Pontic steppes, the Avars soon turned against Constantinople. Thus, they became the natural allies of Sassanid Persia in the context of the Byzantine-Sassanid rivalry, while their enemies the Turks in turn became allies of Byzantium.

In the long run, both Avars and Bulgars relied increasingly on agriculture, and consequently adopted a sedentary lifestyle. The Avars occupied Pannonia, and were finally defeated by Charlemagne in 796. The Bulgars eventually became acculturated to their Slavic subject population whose language and customs they adopted in the ninth century. The spell of the menace from the steppes appeared to be finally broken with the decisive defeat of the last steppe raiders, the Magyars, in 955 in the Battle of Lechfeld. The historical legacy of this second wave of steppe nomads was the establishment of Hungary as the only non-Slavic state in Eastern Europe and the revolution in mounted warfare brought on by the stirrup, first introduced by the Avars.

The Turkish empire split into two parts of roughly equal size upon the death of the founder of the empire Bumin (or Tumen) in 553. The eastern half under the rule of Bumin's son Mukhan (d. 572) contained the old home of the Turks in the Altay region and remained the preeminent part of the empire. Bumin's brother Istemi (d. 576) expanded the western half all the way to the borders of Byzantium. Thus, in terms of size, or at least extension from east to west, the Turkish empire can claim parity with the Mongol empire six hundred years later. Like its Mongolian counterpart, the Turkish empire also became embroiled soon in internecine wars. It is in this context that the steppe nomadic characteristics of the political structure of the empire become apparent. In the eastern half, where traditional lateral succession pattern prevailed, a large number of pretenders to the position of *qaghan* tried to establish themselves as charismatic leaders of a devoted fighting force. The best way for a nomadic chieftain to do so was to conduct successful raids into neighboring sedentary areas in order to gain resources. The result was a series of large-scale raids into China in the early 580s. When the Sui dynasty managed to reunify China in 589, it incorporated the Eastern Turks into a tributary relationship. In fact, the Sui court employed Turkish forces in the conquest of the Khitans, a Tungusic-speaking people from Manchuria, early in the seventh century. The refusal of the Turks to furnish troops for later campaigns ultimately contributed to the fall of the Sui dynasty in 618 and its replacement by the Tang (618–907).

A good way to illustrate the strong influence of the Turks on China is to focus on the personality of Li Shimin (599–649). As Emperor Tang Taizong (r. 626–649) he was arguably the greatest ruler of the Tang dynasty, supposedly exhibiting all the characteristics of a true "Son of Heaven." Yet he came to power after personally murdering his brothers and their sons and unceremoniously forcing his father, Emperor Tang Gaozu (r. 618–626) to abdicate. He led his forces into battle and was known as an excellent horseman and archer. His battle tactics displayed a profound knowledge of steppe warfare. Reportedly he even challenged the Turkish *qaghan* to a duel when the latter arrived with a raiding party near Chang'an, the Tang capital. Shortly after ascending the throne in 626 he succeeded in personally negotiating a peace deal with the Turks. Three years later, the Tang court staged a massive intervention in a civil war that had broken out in the Turkish empire. This was by far the most successful military expedition China had ever undertaken on the steppes. The *qaghan* became a Chinese prisoner and the Turks remained under Chinese control until 682. Tang Taizong oversaw the settlement of the Turks in the Ordos region, handpicked a new aristocracy to head the different tribes, and thus incorporated the Turks into the Tang administrative structure. Turkish horsemen fighting for the Tang achieved most of the dynasty's territorial gains in Central Asia.

Tang Taizong thus achieved what no Chinese ruler before or after could claim: he neutralized the barbarian threat from the north. The main reason for his success was that he exhibited all the behavior that nomads would expect from a charismatic warrior chieftain—prowess in battle, swagger and fearlessness in the face of the enemy, and the willingness to do away with any contenders for power. He was perhaps the one Chinese emperor who truly understood the barbarians, and they in turn recognized him as "Heavenly *Qaghan*." That the allegiance of the Turks was personal rather than institutional became clear when they rebelled against the Tang court in 679. Subsequently, they reestablished their empire on the steppes (sometimes referred to as the Second Turkish Empire) as China was going through a political crisis during the reign of Empress Wu Zetian (690–705). After a brief revival, most notably under the rule of Bilge *qaghan* (r. 716–734) the Turkish empire once again descended into civil war. By 744 the Uyghurs, a coalition of several Turkic tribes under a *qaghan* named Kutluk, assumed power on the steppes. Kutluk reportedly sent the head of the last Turkish *qaghan* to the Tang emperor.

The change from Turkish to Uyghur domination of the steppes was in itself of little importance, being a relatively minor event in steppe politics. However, the Uyghurs faced a changed situation in China, where a much-weakened Tang dynasty was virtually powerless in the face of internal rebellions. As a result a symbiotic relationship developed between the two sides, with the Uyghurs providing much-needed military power to quell rebellions in return for payment, or, as in the case of the An Lushan Rebellion of 755–57, in return for the right to loot cities captured from rebel forces. Uyghur *qaghans* also routinely received biological daughters of Tang emperors as wives. With the considerable influx of goods from China, the Uyghur empire prospered and the Uyghurs probably became the richest steppe nomads of all time. They could even afford to build a permanent capital at Karabalghasun. Their adoption of Manichaeism as a state religion was the result of increased contacts with Sogdians, who also introduced their writing system to the Uyghurs.

Just as the Uyghurs were well on the way to becoming the most "civilized barbarians" their fortunes took an abrupt turn for the worse when the Kirghiz attacked in 840. The Kirghiz were a Turkic-speaking people who had not been part of either the Turkish or Uyghur tribal confederation. They succeeded in destroying the Uyghur capital and permanently displacing the Uyghurs from the Mongolian steppes. The greater part of the Uyghurs moved southwest, eventually adopting a sedentary lifestyle in and around the city of Karakhoja (Chin. Gaoche) in the Turfan Basin, an important trading post of the Silk Road. More than three centuries would pass before a new confederacy of tribes emerged on the Mongolian steppe.

Unlike their Turkic predecessors, the Mongols, by far the most famous steppe nomads of all time, are already an integral part of courses on World, East Asian, Near Eastern, and Russian history. The narrative of their ascendancy and sudden, almost explosive expansion over much of Eurasia appears in all available textbooks. The scholarly literature on the Mongol empire is substantial as well, though there are plenty of popular treatments of questionable reliability.[18] Yet there are several issues that the basic textbook narratives overlook or gloss over.

The first is the nature of the Mongol *conquest*. Nomadic people like the Mongols were "predators" (to use Barfield's term) and thus were a lot more likely to raid and exploit a sedentary civilization from a distance than to actually conquer it. One possible answer to this conundrum is that the closest sedentary neighbor of the Mongols was the Jin dynasty (1115–1234) in northern China. This was a so-called conquest dynasty with a ruling elite of ethnic Jurchens, ancestors of the later Manchus. A state run by semi-nomadic horse riders such as the Jurchens was disinclined to agree to a tributary relationship with its pastoralist neighbors. In fact, the Jurchens were on the receiving end of such a relationship with the Southern Song dynasty (1127–1279), a native Chinese dynasty ruling the southern part of the country. We can thus call the initial conquest of northern China a series of very successful raids, rather than a planned conquest.

Another issue is the rise to power of Chinggis Khan (1159–1227). Some authors claim that his later success was partially attributable to his early life experiences as an orphaned outcast. Without an ancestry that could legitimize his claim to power he had to rely on his track record as a raider to attract followers and ended up creating the most successful raiding machine the world had ever seen. A good exercise for more advanced undergraduate students could be to compare this hypothesis to the rather more hagiographic treatment of Chinggis's personality in the *Secret History of the Mongols*.[19]

A third issue is that of the extent of Mongol violence. Their initial conquest of territory was invariably accompanied by the calculated use of excessive violence in order to terrorize the victims into surrender. The discussion about the actual scale of the slaughter and its significance is ongoing, and students should be aware of this debate. A remarkable example of a scholarly discussion is an exchange on the H-Asia list-serv under the heading "The Mongols in Power" that took place in February and March 2005. It is easily retrievable from www.H-Net. org, and makes for a marvelous introduction into the world of scholarly disputes. Perhaps the most important point to make is that the initial destruction of northern China might very well have been a historical accident, whereas the conquest of the Song under Khubilai Khan was indeed a planned affair.[20]

The legacy of Mongol destruction was, itself, mixed. The Mongols destroyed the Kievan Rus' as a political unit during their invasion in the late 1230s, but never actually occupied and incorporated it into the political structure of the Golden Horde. Russian historiography has traditionally claimed that Russia remained under a "Mongol-Tartar Yoke" for more than two and a half centuries, and that the subsequent development of the Muscovite state occurred *despite* the terrible setback that the Mongols had caused. However, a different model of explanation is also possible.[21] The Mongols did indeed exploit the Russian cities, but they did so from a distance. In essence, they employed the tried-and-true methods of a nomadic confederation by extracting resources from a neighboring sedentary civilization without actually ruling it. They established a close working relationship with the aristocratic rulers of Russian cities, comparable to that of the Uyghurs with the Tang dynasty centuries before. Arguably, the rise of Moscow was due to the fact that the local princes there enjoyed a special rapport with their Mongol overlords. It is thus possible to explain the emergence of Muscovy as a direct result of Mongol influence in Russia. In other words, Moscow became the dominant city in Russia *because* of the Mongols, rather than *despite* them. While the "shaking off of the Mongol-Tartar Yoke" made for a useful patriotic narrative in early modern times, in reality a strong connection to the steppes remained an integral part of the Muscovite state. The yoke might have been gone, but the nomads were still there. The subsequent conquest of the steppes, starting with the capture of Kazan on the Volga by Ivan IV in 1551 and lasting effectively into the nineteenth century was a long and drawn-out process that transformed a volatile frontier into a secure borderland. Steppe nomads were gradually incorporated into an imperial administration and thus ceased to be a threat.

At the same time, a similar development was under way in the Chinese empire, ruled after 1644 by the greatest of the conquest dynasties, the Manchu Qing. The Manchus had incorporated some Mongolian tribes into their state since before their conquest of China and had thus divided the Mongolian steppes into an "inner" and an "outer" part. After establishing themselves in China, the Manchus sought to transform their northern frontier into a borderland as well. While most of the Eastern Mongols willingly joined the imperial elite as "Mongol sons-in-law," their Western brethren created the last major independent nomadic empire in Eurasia, the Zunghar empire. The Qing dynasty managed to destroy this state in 1757, thus eliminating the last serious nomadic contender for power in Eurasia. Russia and China, the two largest Eurasian overland empires, finally shared a common border.

For millennia, people living in sedentary civilizations have tended to see the steppes as barren and inhospitable and their inhabitants as wild and savage barbarians. The steppe was the home of the "other," that which separated "us" from "them," the civilized world from the rest. Yet no civilization can be entirely autarkic. The steppes and their nomadic pastoralist inhabitants provided the occasional link, be it through trade, technological exchange, or warfare. Sedentary "civilized" people ignored this fact at their own risk. Consequently, steppe frontiers figured prominently in the strategic decisions that sedentary civilizations made. In order to present a balanced view not only of world history, but also of the history of individual civilizations, the focus on core areas alone is insufficient. Steppe nomads should be an integral part of our courses on East and South Asia, Eastern Europe, and the Middle East, because their presence on the frontier and beyond indeed helped define these very civilizations.

Suggested Readings

Barfield, Thomas. *The Perilous Frontier: Nomadic Empires and China, 221 BC to AD 1757.* Cambridge: Blackwell, 1989.

Di Cosmo, Nicola. *Ancient China and Its Enemies: The Rise of Nomadic Power in East Asian History.* Cambridge: Cambridge University Press, 2002.

Grousset, René. *Empire of the Steppes: A History of Central Asia.* New Brunswick: Rutgers University Press, 1970.

Khazanov, Anatoly. *Nomads and the Outside World.* Cambridge: Cambridge University Press, 1983.

Khodarkovsky, Michael. *Russia's Steppe Frontier: The Making of a Colonial Empire, 1500–1800.* Bloomington: Indiana University Press, 2002.

Ostrowski, Donald. *Muscovy and the Mongols: Cross-Cultural Influences on the Steppe Frontier, 1304–1589.* Cambridge: Cambridge University Press, 1998.

Perdue, Peter. *China Marches West: The Qing Conquest of Central Eurasia.* Cambridge: Harvard University Press, 2005.

Poppe, Nicholas. *Introduction to Altaic Linguistics.* Wiesbaden: Otto Harrassowitz, 1965.

Sinor, Denis. *Inner Asia. History-Civilization-Languages: A Syllabus.* Bloomington: Indiana University Press, 1969.

Soucek, Svat. *A History of Inner Asia.* Cambridge: Cambridge University Press, 2000.

Twitchett, Denis C., and Herbert Franke, eds. *The Cambridge History of China. Volume 6. Alien Regimes and Border States, 907–1368.* Cambridge: Cambridge University Press, 1994.

Notes

1. The conventional spelling "Genghis" is the reason that his name is usually mispronounced by English speakers. Alternative spellings, whether with an initial "J" or "Ch," provide a much closer approximation of the way his name is (correctly) pronounced in much of the world.

2. Compare for example, René Grousset, *Empire of the Steppes: A History of Central Asia* (New Brunswick: Rutgers University Press, 1970) and Cyril E. Black et al., eds., *The Modernization of Inner Asia* (Armonk: M. E. Sharpe, 1991). Both books deal largely with Mongolia. Denis Sinor uses "Inner Asia" as a synonym for "Central Eurasia"; see Denis Sinor, "Introduction: The Concept of Inner Asia," in *The Cambridge History of Early Inner Asia*, ed. Denis Sinor (Cambridge: Cambridge University Press, 1990). Peter Perdue's *China Marches West: The Qing Conquest of Central Eurasia* (Cambridge: Harvard University Press, 2005) equates "Central Eurasia" with Eastern (or Chinese) Turkestan, today commonly referred to as Xinjiang.

3. For more information on climatic conditions and the use of maps see Rebecca Wendelken's essay in this volume.

4. This point is made in Thomas Barfield, *The Perilous Frontier: Nomadic Empires and China, 221 BC to AD 1757* (Cambridge: Blackwell, 1989), 16.

5. See Andrii Danylenko, *Slavica et Islamica: Ukrainian in Context* (Munich: Verlag Otto Sagner, 2006), 4.

6. Still the most comprehensive treatment of language and writing on the steppes is Nicholas Poppe, *Introduction to Altaic Linguistics* (Wiesbaden: Otto Harrassowitz, 1965).

7. A recent work on the subject is Michael Khodarkovsky, *Russia's Steppe Frontier: The Making of a Colonial Empire, 1500–1800* (Bloomington: Indiana University Press, 2002). See also John P. LeDonne, *The Russian Empire and the World, 1700–1917: The Geopolitics of Expansion and Containment* (New York: Oxford University Press, 1997).

8. For an extensive discussion of the types of outsiders in early China see Nicola Di Cosmo, *Ancient China and Its Enemies: The Rise of Nomadic Power in East Asian History* (Cambridge: Cambridge University Press, 2002), 93–97.

9. For a detailed discussion of this development see Anatoly Khazanov, *Nomads and the Outside World* (Cambridge: Cambridge University Press, 1983), 19–25.

10. On bow-making technology see Erik Hildinger, *Warriors of the Steppe: A Military History of Central Asia, 500 B.C. to 1700 A.D.* (Cambridge: Da Capo Press, 1997), 21–23.

11. Herodotus, *The History*, trans. David Greene (Chicago: University of Chicago Press, 1987); Ahmad Ibn Fadlan, *Ibn Fadlan's Journey to Russia*, ed. Richard Frye (Princeton: Markus Wiener Publishers, 2005); Burton Watson, *Records of the Grand Historian of China*, 2 vols. (New York: Columbia University Press, 1961).

12. This account appears in chapter 110 of the *Shiji*. For an English translation see Watson, *Records*, vol. 2, 161.

13. For a summary of the different theories see Di Cosmo, *Ancient China*, 163–66.

14. Ibid., 161–205.

15. Barfield, *Perilous Frontier*, 16–60.

16. Ammianus Marcellinus, *The Later Roman Empire: AD 354–378* (Hallingsworth: Penguin Publishers, 1986), 410–44; Jordanes, *The Gothic History of Jordanes*, trans. Charles C. Mierow (Princeton: Princeton University Press, 1915) is available in numerous reprints, also as *Origins and Deeds of the Goths*.

17. See for example Dimitri Obolensky, *The Byzantine Commonwealth: Eastern Europe 500–1453* (London: Phoenix Press, 2000) 42–68. A primary source with useful readings on the Avars is George T. Dennis, trans., *Maurice's Strategikon: Handbook of Byzantine Military Strategy* (Philadelphia: University of Pennsylvania Press, 1984), especially Book 11, "Characteristics and Tactics of Various Peoples."

18. The best overall treatment of the Mongols in East Asia, including non-Chinese dynasties preceding the Mongol conquest, can be found in Denis C. Twitchett and Herbert Franke, eds., *The Cambridge History of China. Volume 6. Alien Regimes and Border States, 907–1368.* (Cambridge: Cambridge University Press, 1994).

19. The full translation is available as Francis Cleaves, trans., *The Secret History of the Mongols.* (Cambridge: Harvard University Press, 1982).

20. On the Mongols in China, see Morris Rossabi, *Khubilai Khan. His Life and Times* (Berkeley, University of California Press, 1988) and J. D. Langlois, *China Under Mongol Rule.* (Princeton: Princeton University Press, 1981).

21. For a detailed analysis of Mongol-Russian relations see Charles J. Halperin, *Russia and the Golden Horde: The Mongol Impact on Medieval Russian History.* (Bloomington: Indiana University Press, 1987) and Donald Ostrowski, *Muscovy and the Mongols: Cross-Cultural Influences on the Steppe Frontier, 1304–1589.* (Cambridge: Cambridge University Press, 1998).

Chapter 8

Philosophical Reflections on National Identity

Tongdong Bai

Although there has been continuous migration and ethnic intermingling in the region, and despite enormous diversity within ethnicities, peoples along the Silk Roads still claim to belong to distinct nationalities. In recent years, these identities have served as the basis of independence for a few former Soviet Republics, and they are at the root of ethnic conflicts. But how do these peoples determine their identity? More generally, what is national identity and what role does it play? The Silk Roads provide us with a unique opportunity to study how national identities persist despite long-term cross-cultural contact, and to examine the nature of identity itself. In this chapter I will first address the question of identity on a philosophical level and then use the case study of Chinese identity to illustrate my points. Through this discussion I hope to challenge scholars' recent emphasis on globalization and "imagined" identities, and suggest the potential benefits of competing nationalities.

Identity: Imaginary or Real?

In the age of globalization, one might believe that national identity is disappearing and postnationalism will arise, and we are anticipating an age of "thinking beyond the nation." The Berlin Wall has come down, and even the Earth, according to some, is "flattened" by Internet and other global connections. One only needs to take a look at the popularity of the columnist Thomas L. Friedman's book, *The World is Flat*, both in this country and in the rest of the world, to see the power of this belief. But some scholars, including anthropologist Dru C. Gladney and sociologist Liah Greenfield, find this idea wishful thinking and argue instead that as long as people perceive nationalism to be the road to modernity it will not disappear.[1] The resurgent nationalism in today's world seems to confirm this evaluation, and scholars try to locate this nationalism "in core, primordial essentialized identities, now portrayed as 'tribes with flags.' "[2] Images of Sunni and Shiite Iraqis slaughtering each other offer a very convenient and convincing example of the strength and reality of nationalism. Gladney argues, however, that ethnic nationalism is not just tribalism and not just limited to the third world. In short, nationalism is here to stay for an indefinitely long time, and we must take it seriously.

Then, what is nationality or ethnicity, the basis of nationalism? Max Weber, a founding father of modern sociology, gave one definition of national identity that has influenced scholars for many years. According to Weber, ethnic groups are

> those human groups that entertain a subjective belief in their common descent because of similarities of physical type or of customs or both, or because of memories of colonization and migration; this belief must be important for the propagation of group formation; conversely, it does not matter whether or not an objective blood relationship exists.[3]

In other words, national identity is based on values, not objective facts.

Other scholars have built on this distinction. Benedict Anderson said that national identity was a social creation of "imagined communities" who believe they have common identities and histories.[4] Poststructuralists have argued that identity is artificial and constructed, and others have argued that nationalism creates its own traditions and becomes the history of people despite its artificiality.[5] In short, all these theorists consider national identity "imagined," "constructed," "invented," etc.

But then what is unimagined, "naturalized," "primordial," or real? What some social scientists consider real and objective are things such as "blood relationships," or, in biological terms, "genetic relationships." For the economist, what is real is self-(material) interest; for the Marxist, certain material conditions. In spite of the differences among schools of thought, what is common is that only the material or factual things are real. In contrast, national identity is a mere value or ideology to them, subjective and nonfactual.

This contrast is based upon the fact-value distinction, a fundamental concept of modern social sciences and a distinction Weber played a significant role in promoting.[6] In the studies of human affairs, certain things are "objective," "real," and "hard," such as blood type, eye color, and income; while others are "subjective," "imagined," and "soft," like social status, values, and beliefs. Generally, in order to keep their method scientific, social scientists try to focus more on the objective, the "facts," and not the "subjective," the "values." One person might find blondes beautiful, another might not be able to resist brunettes, and yet another might be mad about redheads. These are values, and they change from person to person. In this case, however, the "fact," unchanging and independent of personal attitudes, is that genetic or other biological structure determines hair color. Hair color is the primary condition, giving rise to secondary, or imagined, values. Of course, a social scientist can choose to study the preferences for certain hair or skin colors among peoples, but he or she has to describe them in a factual manner, or reduce them to material conditions that we can see, touch, hear, smell, or taste. Such a way of doing social sciences is an imitation of the project of modern physics. In the latter discipline, various physical phenomena are reduced to a few primary properties: space, time, and matter. Other physical properties are secondary in that they can be reduced to the primary ones. For example, colors we see are not real, but are small material points moving in a certain way in space over time. Since modern physics is such a success, why should we not expect the same in social sciences?

The problem is that, unlike physical forces, biological or social "facts" do not necessarily determine human actions, nor do they justify them. Suppose that a boy has been raised as a white American by a loving American family for twenty-five years. One day, he discovers that he was adopted and by blood relationship, he is Arabic. Does this "fact" mean that he *must* give up the "imagined" Anglo-American identity, abandon his adopted family, move to Saudi Arabia, and even join the jihad against the United States? People make different choices in such situations. It is true that blood relationship seems to be objective in the sense that it does not depend upon a person's choice, but to say that one's national identity *should* be based upon it is a matter of choice, a value. Generally speaking, the claim that only the factual should be the basis of human actions and one should go beyond subjective values is itself a value. Otherwise put, the fact-value distinction itself is often an implicit value judgment.

Therefore, if there is no clear distinction between fact and value, the anthropologist's and sociologist's descriptions of national identity as "imagined," "constructed," "invented," etc. are highly misleading, to say the least, in that there is also a subjective element in what they consider unimagined, "naturalized," "primordial," objective, or real. Deeming national identities to be imaginary, the anthropologist may think common people who believe in them are acting blindly, but he or she may also be blind. Moreover, as we see from the above discussion, the choice of which fact to take into account is itself a value judgment, and in dealing with human affairs, we have to make such a choice. In the case of national identities, the crucial questions—perhaps more important than discovering the "objective" foundation of national identities—are whether national identities are good or not, which set of identities are good, or how they can serve the human good. To take the anthropologist's deconstruction of "imagined" identities for granted may prevent us from asking this crucial value question, and from looking for the possible beneficial effects of such identities.

Nonetheless, it seems to me that this does not mean that we ought to jettison the question of "what" completely. In his attempt to deconstruct the traditional understanding of national identity, Gladney argues that national identities are often relative, and they depend upon the context in which they are constructed. He says the "when" question should replace the "what" question in our attempt to understand identities. That is, there are no unchangeable essences of identities, and so-called essential characteristics actually emerge and disappear throughout history. In my view, however, we ought also to try to see if the contextualized "what" has and should have a life of its own, beyond the context in which it is brought about.

The Chinese Identity

With these considerations in mind, I now turn to an examination of the Chinese identity to illustrate the points I have made so far. Scholars often claim that today's nationalism comes from the modern (European) concept of "nation-state," that is, a state is organized around one "nation," or one dominant group that allegedly belongs to the same ethnicity. There are apparently clear boundaries, physical and cultural, between states. This understanding of nationality can be partly traced back to ancient Greece, in which the friend-enemy distinction was drawn along the boundary of the city-state and patriotism or nationalism meant that citizens were expected to love their own state and their fellow citizens. An important expression of patriotism was the military duty of each citizen. This included not only fighting for their city during war, but also exercising in the gymnasium in peaceful times. The "gym" was not merely a place to build one's muscles or lose cholesterol, but a place to hone one's skill for battle.

Each city-state formed as an individual state based upon geo-graphical, political, and other factors. They waged wars against each other. But in spite of the wars between the Greek city-states, Greeks as a group would band together against the "barbarians" or non-Greeks. The term *barbarian* did not originally have a derogatory meaning, but meant people whose language sounded to the Greeks like "bar-bar-bar," that is, some random noise no one could understand. So, "barbarians" for the Greeks were non-Greek speakers. Thus, the distinction between the Greeks (Greek nations) and non-Greeks was based upon perceived blood relationship, military training, the friend-enemy distinction, and language. Aside from a crucial difference between Greek city-states and today's nation-states (different Greek city-states did not consist of different "nations" or peoples), many features of Greek city-states are quite close to how we understand nations today.

The ancient Chinese had a different understanding of nation. The Zhou dynasty (roughly from the eleventh century BCE to 250 BCE) was organized in a feudalistic, pyramid-like system, in which the king ruled over princes, princes over lesser lords, and these lords over people in their fiefs. The territory a prince ruled was a "state," and an individual was identified by his state of birth. During the later Zhou dynasty (from 722 BCE on), in the so-called Spring and Autumn and early Warring States periods, the king of Zhou only had a nominal rule over these states, and the latter became de facto independent political entities. The educated elite worked in administrative capacities for these states. But generally, they did not have a sense of "patriotism" comparable to that of the ancient Greeks, and they moved from one state to another with the sole intention of finding a place to realize their ambitions or political ideals. Their employment was based upon merit, and even if they were not originally from the state that employed them they did not experience differing treatment. This poses a sharp contrast to the situation of the *metics* in ancient Greece: the resident aliens who, under most circumstances, could not gain citizenship no matter how long and for how many generations they had stayed in their city-state of residence.

Of course, the fact that a citizen of a Greek city-state enjoyed many more benefits than a Chinese subject did in his state was a crucial reason that the ancient Greeks were so serious about citizenship. In ancient China there was no gymnastic system similar to the Greek one, and there were no Olympic games that celebrated nationalistic competition. There were Chinese schools of thought that took the art of war seriously, and the nobility had military training, but it never played a role as central as that in the life of a Greek citizen.

To sum up, in ancient China, the senses of citizenship (nationality) and patriotism (nationalism) were far weaker than in ancient Greece, and in spite of the constant warfare during the Spring and Autumn and Warring States periods, the ancient Chinese were far less openly militaristic. However, this does not mean that the Chinese identity was only constructed later, either by the Mongolian rulers of the Yuan dynasty (1271–1368) or the Manchurian rulers of the Qing dynasty (1644–1912), or as a response to the modern idea of nation-state. Rather, even during ancient times, the distinction between the Xia or Hua (the majority of the people of the states under the Zhou court) and the Yi (the barbarians) was already clear. What is peculiar about the Chinese identity or "nationality" is its emphasis on culture, rather than ethnicity in the sense of perceived blood relationship. A passage in a Confucian classic, *The Book of Mencius* beautifully illustrates this understanding of nationality. In 3A4 of *Mencius*, Mencius (Mengzi) praises Chen Liang, a native of the state of Chu, a state that the Chinese looked down upon as almost barbaric and not as a bona fide "Xia" (Chinese) state. He points out that, in spite of his "barbaric" origin, Chen Liang managed to grasp the Chinese culture (teachings of Confucius) better than the scholars from the Chinese states. In contrast, some disciples of Chen Liang, although likely from a "Xia" state, failed to follow the Chinese culture and thus degraded themselves to the level of barbarians. This passage clearly implies that "Chinese-ness" does not depend upon his or her state of birth or ethnicity, but on mastery of Chinese culture, including the Six Classics, customs, spoken and written languages, etc. While the distinction between the Greeks and the non-Greeks was also somewhat based upon language (those who speak Greek and those who speak "bar-bar-bar"), the adoption of the Greek language and way of life would not make someone a Greek citizen, whereas the assimilation into Chinese culture makes one Chinese.

Therefore, in ancient China, identity was partly based upon which Chinese state (at the time of unification, which county, province, or region) he or she was from, but it was not as strong as national identity in modern nation-states, or even as strong as citizenship in a Greek city-state. There was a sharp distinction between Chinese and "barbarians," but it was a cultural one, which was easier to overcome than ethnicity. This does not mean there were no boundaries. Central to Confucianism is the idea that one's love of others starts from what is close to him or her. That is, usually, one has to love one's family first. Only after learning how to love one's family, can one have a foothold to expand this love to neighbors, compatriots, aliens, animals, plants, rocks, and everything in the world. The ideal is to love everything, but it begins with family. One who does not even love the people close to him or her, but claims to love everyone, either makes an empty claim or is lying. Even if one achieves the highest stage of loving everyone and everything, it is only natural that there is still a hierarchy. That is, it is natural and humane that we still love our family members (or whoever is close to us) more than strangers. Just imagine: if both your mother (assuming you have a good relationship with her) and a stranger are drowning, and you can only save one of them, it is only natural for you to save your mother. Therefore, it is natural that citizens from one county, province, or state would put the welfare of neighbors higher than that of aliens. However, in Confucian terms, this natural predisposition does not justify a total disregard of strangers either. The Confucian idea of "nationalism" takes the middle ground between strong nationalism in the Greek or modern sense and universalism (equal love to everyone). For a Confucian, the former is too narrow, the latter is hopelessly naïve. If you try to love everyone equally, even if sincere, you will end up loving no one. To sum up, Confucianists justified distinctions among themselves, and with non-Chinese, but the difference was not insurmountable.

These features of Chinese identity have had profound historical implications. The understanding that Chinese identity is based upon culture helped the assimilation of different peoples and the growth of the Chinese people from its core of the Xia or Hua people of ancient times. Many nomadic conquerors and "resident aliens" of China embraced Chinese culture, and were completely assimilated into the Chinese people. One interesting example is that of the Jews who settled in Kaifeng (the capital of the Northern Song dynasty and a city in today's Henan province) China in the twelfth century and were assimilated, serving as perhaps a rare example of peaceful assimilation in ancient Jewish history.[7] This peculiar sense of identity also helped to reduce the violence against "foreign" rulers, as long as they adopted Chinese culture. Such an adoption partly explained the longevity of the Manchurian Qing dynasty (1644–1912), and the failure to do so adequately was a reason that the Mongolian Yuan dynasty was short-lived (1271–1368). Moreover, the relative lack of militaristic and evangelical elements in the Chinese identity was also partly responsible for the relatively voluntary and peaceful nature of acceptance and spread of Chinese culture among different peoples through tributary system and diplomatic marriages. To understand these characteristics of traditional Chinese identity—for example, the lack of expansionist ambition in spite of cultural pride—may also help us to understand today's China. More importantly, in global national conflicts of the post–cold war era, this cultural and non-crusading understanding of nationality may offer us a new and beneficiary perspective.

Here, I must clarify a few points. First, one should not ignore the historical conditions that helped to form the culture-based feature of

Chinese identity. The ancient Greeks, at least some well-educated ones, knew that some "barbarians" or aliens had superior cultures. For example, prominent philosophers from Thales to Pythagoras to Plato traveled to "barbarian" lands, in particular Egypt, for their studies. The ancient Chinese were, or considered themselves to be, culturally far superior to the "barbarians" surrounding them. This might partly explain why the ancient Chinese could adopt a cultural understanding of identity with confidence, and it is questionable that Mencius would still stick to this line of thinking if he recognized superior cultures surrounding China. After all, it took quite an effort for the proud Chinese to accept the fact that non-Chinese could invent such a sophisticated system of thought such as Buddhism.

Second, many people may find the claim that ancient China lacked expansionist tendencies peculiar. After all, the ancient Chinese empire was an empire, and it seems that an empire, by definition, is expansionist. Those who are sympathetic to the apparent sufferings of the Tibetans from the invasion by the Chinese would even find this claim outrageous. On the first objection, I have to point out that the term *empire* is misleading, especially to those who are familiar with past empires in the West and modern empires. Every ethnic group tends to expand, but this does not make it expansionist. An expansionist nation is one that actively seeks territorial gains that are beyond the need of outward migration as a result of natural population growth, such as the Roman, British, Russian, and Japanese empires. But the Chinese "empire" was very different from these empires. For one thing, most of the non-Chinese empires consisted of an ethnic minority ruling over diverse peoples. However, both the rulers and the majority population of most Chinese "empires" have been Han Chinese.

But we should also not be naïve about the peacefulness of Chinese identity, and should take geographical conditions into account. The nomads with access to good horses were usually militarily superior to the Chinese. They did not have a base the agrarian Chinese could attack and destroy, while the Chinese did. The steppe grassland was unsuitable for agriculture and therefore was useless to the agrarian Chinese, while the riches of the Chinese were an item of envy for the nomads, especially during a bad year in the grassland. Therefore, for the Chinese, the nomads were difficult to fight against, and the gain was little. It is, then, only natural that the Chinese in general had little interest in expanding to the land of the nomads, the only land they could expand into in the past.

My view is that culture and geopolitics influenced each other, and together molded the Chinese into what they are. There were a few exceptions to the nonexpansionist norm. Some Chinese emperors aggressively pursued the nomads (Emperor Wu of the Han dynasty, for example). But they did so as a more effective defense strategy to keep the nomads out, and they were usually criticized by Confucian officials for this strategy. For example, official scholars used the eulogized name "Wu" for Emperor Wu, which means "martial," a bad name for an emperor in Confucian terms. In contrast, scholars often reserved the eulogized name "Wen"—meaning "cultured" or "civilized"—for the best emperors who did not appeal to force to maintain peace.

Regarding the second objection, which concerns the fate of the Tibetans, historically Chinese "empires" never conquered, or intended to conquer, them. Rather, like many other nomadic peoples in Chinese history, the Tibetans were once a threat to the Chinese empire. At one time, they even invaded the capital of the Tang dynasty. Tibet became a tributary state to China only under the Mongolian Yuan dynasty, and this relation was strengthened in the Manchurian Qing dynasty. Even in the Qing dynasty, Tibet only needed to pay nominal homage to the central Qing government, and was not a colony in the sense that India was a colony of the Great Britain. The territorial issue only became significant when the English and the Russians were fighting over Tibet, trying to pull it away from China to use as a post to protect their own interests. In other words, Tibet became a problem only through the cultural and military invasion of the Western nation-states. The communists were the first Chinese to put Tibet completely under China's control. But their actions in this case were not entirely the result of ethnic or cultural Chinese nationalism, but of larger political considerations. Thus, in the case of Tibet, we should be very cautious attributing political phenomena to Chinese identity. There are many factors other than historical identity that determine a nation's actions.

Although Chinese identity is partly based upon culture, something not as "hard" as blood relationship, it nevertheless has stood the test of time. Culturally, the idea that peoples of different states of the Zhou court belong together supposedly comes from the Duke of Zhou, who introduced the idea that "there is one common lord of the whole empire" (天下共主). The Zhou court later lost control over its vassal states during the Spring and Autumn and Warring States periods, partly because many states expanded way beyond their original territories and became very powerful, even more than the Zhou court. But the much-expanded Chinese territories were eventually unified by the Qin state, and the sense that the Chinese people belong together may have played a role in this unification. In the following centuries, in spite of the frequent divisions and dynastic transitions, the Chinese continue to regard unification as the desirable norm. This poses an interesting contrast to the nomadic societies along the Silk Roads. Nomadic tribes, at certain times in history, have quickly unified and risen to incredible dominance. But they could not sustain their empires for long, and the unified groups split apart as quickly as they came into being.

One cause of such a quick demise is the succession problem. Ancient Greece, Rome, Europe, and the Near and Middle East seemed also to be plagued by the failure to maintain a unified empire. In contrast, despite frequent succession issues and dynastic transitions, ancient China often stayed unified or strove to do so. Of course, again, physical conditions may have played an important role here. The ancient Greek city-states were separated by geographical barriers that made unification of all Greek states difficult, and the Roman Empire and other trans-Eurasian empires had to control far more diverse populations and a more open area than those the Chinese empire controlled. Still, one has to wonder how much role culture plays in this contrast, and what makes the Chinese identity such a long-standing idea. Today, one may find it a good thing that an empire does not last for long. But as historians such as Niall Ferguson point out, contrary to the belief of contemporary liberal thinkers, empires in the past often played a benign role.[8]

That the Chinese identity is long-standing does not mean that it never changes. As we have already seen, this identity must have experienced numerous changes through expansion and assimilation. A persistent challenge to ancient Chinese empires was how to deal with the nomads. The Chinese generally had one of two responses, both of which provide different models of Chinese identity. The Tang dynasty (618–907 CE) demonstrated the first model. Faced with attacks, the Tang absorbed the military techniques and culture of the nomads, such as the extensive training in horse riding, into the traditional Chinese agrarian culture and Confucian society. As a result, they managed to occupy a territory larger than many dynasties, before or after, and they were very open to outside influences. The Tang capital, Chang'an, became a cultural and economic center not only of China, but also of the world far beyond. However, it did not last long. Eventually the nomads they let in drove them out of their own capital.

Following the collapse of the Tang, the founding rulers of the Song dynasty (960–1279 CE), as well as the later Ming dynasty, adopted a different model. They yielded the grassland to the nomads. In fact, the Southern Song dynasty even gave up the part of the Northern territory that traditionally belonged to the Chinese and retreated to the south of Yangzi River, a region that is not suitable for using horses in warfare.

Since the horse was a crucial part of the nomads' military superiority, this strategy helped to bring peace and prosperity to the Song, especially the Southern Song dynasty. In this isolationist model, Chinese identity revolved around the traditional agrarian and commercial culture and Confucianism. Despite this isolation (or perhaps because of it), even the Southern Song dynasty was eventually defeated by the invading Mongolians.

Again, the crucial question is: Which identity is better? I prefer the identity adopted by the Tang rulers. Many people today hope that all we need is love, but ruefully realize that we live in the fear caused by terrorism, a byproduct of extreme nationalism. The diverse, complex, and brutal struggles on the Silk Roads, past and present, have made this contrast between ideal and reality even sharper. A desire to downplay reality might have been a motive for some anthropologists to emphasize the imaginary nature of national identity. It also might have motivated teachers and students who teach and learn about Silk Roads to denounce national identities. But as I argued in the first section, the judgment that national identity is an imaginary and subjective value is itself a value judgment.

In human affairs, a crucial question we have to answer is: Which value is better? Upon close examination, one might discover that the abolition of national identity and the act of "disenchantment"—a term Max Weber often used—are not necessarily good, and the role of national identity is not necessarily bad. A retreat to one's customary self and seclusion from the other may lead to the deterioration of the self, of identity. Rather, a challenging presence of the other may help the awakening and deepening of the self. For example, my attempt, as a resident alien, to fit into American society may have helped me to understand my Chinese-ness, much more so than if I had stayed in China. I face various contrasts everyday, and I am constantly forced to answer the question "Who am I?" Instead of dreaming of a post-national identity and postmodern world, deploring the fact that it will not be coming soon, or becoming disenchanted, I would prefer to see a world of fighting identities. Of course, a world of fighting identities can be a world of brutal ideological and religious conflicts, a world of the Jihadists. But the solution should not lie in the abolition of national identities because it may lead to the superficiality of human existence due to lack of tension. Rather, the solution should lie in finding a way to guide the fighting identities in a fruitful and benign direction. Tension between the self and the other, properly conducted, is the condition for the perfection of the human race, and the possibility to perfect our existence is what makes our lives worth living.

Suggested Readings

Bell, Daniel A. "Just War and Confucianism: Implications for the Contemporary World" and "What's Wrong with Active Citizenship? A Comparison of Physical Education in Ancient Greece and Ancient China," in *Beyond Liberal Democracy: Political Thinking for an East Asian Context*, 22–51. Princeton: Princeton University Press, 2006.

Gladney, Dru C. "Relational Alterity: Constructing Dungan (Hui), Uyghur, and Kazakh Identities across China, Central Asia, and Turkey," *History and Anthropology* 9, no. 2 (1996): 445–77.

Weber, Max. "Ethnic Groups," in *Economy and Society*, vol. 2, ed. Guenther Roth and Claus Wittich, trans. Ephraim Fischof, 385–98. Berkeley: University of California Press, 1978.

———. "Science as a Vocation," in *The Vocation Lectures*, ed. David Owen and Tracy B. Strong, trans. Rodney Livingstone, 1–31. Indianapolis: Hackett, 2004.

Notes

1. Dru C. Gladney, "Relational Alterity: Constructing Dungan (Hui), Uyghur, and Kazakh Identities across China, Central Asia, and Turkey," originally published in *History and Anthropology* 9, no. 2 (1996): 445–77; Liah Greenfeld (1992), *Nationalism: Five Roads to Modernity* (Cambridge: Harvard University Press. In my essay, the page numbers for quotations from Gladney 1996 are from its Internet version: http://www.drugladney.com/articles/relational_alterity. pdf (accessed July 21, 2007).

2. Gladney, "Relational Alterity," 1–2.

3. Max Weber, *Economy and Society*, ed. Guenther Roth and Claus Wittich, trans. Ephraim Fischof, vol. 2 (Berkeley: University of California Press, 1978), 389.

4. Benedict Anderson, *Imagined Communities: Reflections on the Origin and Spread of Nationalism* (London: Verso, 1983).

5. See Gladney, "Relational Alterity," 3, for a discussion of these works.

6. See, for example, his two "vocation" articles. Max Weber (2004), *The Vocation Lectures: "Science as a Vocation"; "Politics as a Vocation,"* ed. David Owen and Tracy B. Strong, trans. Rodney Livingstone (Indianapolis: Hackett, 2004).

7. See, for example, Sidney Shapiro, ed. and trans., *Jews in Old China, Studies by Chinese Scholars* (New York: Hippocrene Books, 1984); Michael Pollak, *Mandarins, Jews, and Missionaries: the Jewish experience in the Chinese Empire* (New York: Weatherhill, 1998); and Xu Xin, *The Jews of Kaifeng, China* (Jersey City: KTAV, 2003).

8. Niall Ferguson, *Empire: The Rise and Demise of the British World Order*, paperback edition (New York, Basic Books, 2004).

Part III

Practicalities

Chapter 9

Silk Roads, Service Learning, and Mythmaking

Hirsh Diamant

In the past two years I have been developing courses on Silk Roads studies with my colleagues at The Evergreen State College. This area of study has a unique potential for interdisciplinary liberal arts curriculum that can promote global awareness for students in institutions of higher education and in K-12 schools, especially through service learning activities.

Evergreen is a liberal arts college that gives its faculty and students the freedom to design a unique interdisciplinary curriculum. Students attending Evergreen are not required to take prescribed classes to fulfill specific requirements for a Bachelor of Arts or Science degree. This freedom allows both teachers and students to learn and develop areas of study that they feel passionate about. My colleague Char Simons and I developed the Silk Roads as a yearlong interdisciplinary program. Each quarter the program was open to new and continuing students. In the fall quarter we concentrated on developing a foundation in historical and geographic understanding of the Silk Roads. In the winter quarter we focused on diffusion of religion, arts, and culture on historic and contemporary Silk Roads. The focus of spring quarter was on travel as a peacemaking activity. In spring quarter students had an opportunity to travel abroad and study in China, Turkey, and/or Jordan for three weeks. Students who could not travel abroad could travel locally within the United States.[1]

Service Learning was an important aspect of the program that allowed us to bridge theory and practice. Each quarter our students could earn up to twelve credits. The credits were allocated in history, education, arts, and community service. Although this program was developed at Evergreen where faculty and students have a greater freedom in designing curriculum, I believe that the Service Learning projects that we have developed with our students in the Silk Roads program could be easily adapted in other colleges and K-12 schools.

As early as the fifth century BCE, Confucius expressed the importance of experiential learning in his famous aphorism: "I hear and I forget. I see and I remember. I do and I understand." More recently, John Dewey articulated the importance of experience in learning in his vision of progressive education. Education becomes meaningful for students when they can bridge theory and practice. Also, something very important happens when students volunteer their service in the community and contribute toward greater common good. Robert Coles, in his book *The Call Of Service*, speaks passionately about the importance of "doing and learning" as a way of learning that "makes things better in the world."[2]

In the Silk Roads program we asked each student to devote forty-nine hours to projects and community service each quarter (calculated as seven hours per week for seven out of the ten weeks of each quarter). We defined projects as a sustained activity undertaken by individuals or groups of students to achieve a clearly perceived goal, for example, a community event, an exhibit, a performance, a new curriculum, a children's book, etc. The benefits of working on educational service learning projects included passionate and sustained educational inquiry, collegial work, community building, practical applications of theoretical study, and bridging significant differences.

In teaching the Silk Roads program at Evergreen we defined the Silk Roads not as a specific geographic location, or a place in time, but as a metaphor for cultural transfusion and a network of trade routes from early history to present day. From as early as the second century BCE, the Silk Roads facilitated cultural interactions, exchanges of material and intellectual goods, and the development of new economic institutions and technologies between China, Central Asia, the Middle East, and Europe. We envisioned that by understanding early globalization, we could embrace and deepen our understanding of global interconnectedness in today's economy, culture, and politics.

In our Silk Roads program we envisioned ourselves as mercurial agents connecting people and cultures and facilitating projects leading toward peace, understanding, healing, and renewal. By defining Silk Roads as a metaphor for peaceful cultural transfusions and economic development toward greater common good we were able to develop academic inquiries into the nature of peace and the possibility of a better world. In seminars and community art workshops we asked questions about whether or not peace can be defined without reference to war.

Our program's Web site allocated for each student a virtual space where they could blog their service learning projects, post their reflections of learning, and share their designs for development of lesson plans inspired by Silk Roads curriculum. The Silk Roads program allowed students to develop their own service learning projects and to participate in projects that we as faculty initiated in the community.[3]

As we were working with our students, it became apparent that travel and geography would be an important component of our program, allowing us to connect physically and intellectually with the regions we were studying. The other important component that evolved as our program developed was our investigation of the identities of the peoples who traveled and traded on both the historical and contemporary Silk Roads. We wondered, Who were the Sogdians, Persians, and Abbasids? How did political ideology, religion, ethnicity, gender, physical landscape, and culture influence and form national and individual identities of Chinese, Arabs, Mongols, and Indo-Europeans, and how do these factors influence and form our own identities?

To explore these questions, students and faculty of the Silk Roads program organized and facilitated at Evergreen three liberal arts academic forums that focused on identity. The first forum, in October 2006, brought together students from five academic programs to discuss issues of identity. The main questions included:

Does education inform and define identity? If yes, how?

What practices can help facilitate an understanding of various identities in areas of conflict or war?

What is the link between language and identity? How does the language people use affect and reflect their identities? How does the language others use about them affect and reflect identity?

How fixed is identity? If it can change; why, how and when?

To what degree do genes define our identity?

How is individual identity affected by culture and by shifts in culture?

What is the difference, or overlap, between public and private identities?

The first identity forum introduced us to the complexity and multilayered quality of identity issues and definitions. Five academic programs met for a seminar on Defining Identity. At the seminar students talked in small groups and shared the perspectives they had on identity from readings in their programs. Although the readings were from different disciplines, the common theme of identity allowed the students to connect in a meaningful discussion. Later, students wrote about their reflections and new learning from this forum.

We constructed our second forum, in January 2007, around Amin Maalouf's book *In The Name of Identity: Violence and the Need to Belong*, a philosophical exploration of cultural, political, and religious identities. We asked faculty members from participating programs to make short presentations about how they approached identity issues from their specific disciplines. Many students commented on how inspiring it was to hear faculty speak about identity from the perspective of gender, philosophy, language, culture, and the natural environment.

Once we got a better understanding of how identities are formed, we wanted to consider how identities could be transformed. All great cultural traditions can inspire us for self-cultivation, exploration, development, and nurturing of ourselves and one another. For our third forum on identity, in March 2007, we focused on the cultural traditions of the regions that we studied in the Silk Roads program. We invited to the forum world-renowned scholars and asked them to speak about identity, gender, and self-cultivation in Taoist, Confucius, Buddhist, and Islamic traditions. Silk Roads students transcribed and edited the presentations of Chungliang Al Huang, Roger Ames, Peter Hershock, and Mohja Kahf, which they included in the *Silk Roads Anthology*, a sixty-page publication that we produced in Spring quarter.[4]

Figure 9.1. Silk Roads Anthology. Book cover by Chrystal Sheppard.

As my teaching colleague Char Simons wrote in her introduction to the anthology: "A final component of our year-long study of the Silk Roads was to go 'on the road.' " We took thirty-six students and community members, ranging in age from twelve to seventy-nine, to China, Turkey, and Jordan. Those Silk Roads students who could not go with us found ways to explore the program themes closer to home. "In our journeys, we met with students, educators, writers, artists, musicians, community activists, environmentalists, religious and tribal leaders, journalists and politicians. We also experienced valuable meandering time where serendipity lead us to enlightening people and conversations that helped deepen our understanding of identity and culture." We have included the results of some of those experiences in our anthology.

In our study of the Silk Roads we discovered that peaceful traders and marauding invaders used the same roads and mountain passes. The idea to facilitate a New Year Peace art exhibit came from a question of whether peace can be understood and defined on its own terms and not as an alternative to war. We facilitated several workshops in the community asking the participants how they understood "peace." Silk Roads students contacted organizations for senior citizens, children's after school centers, and shelters for homeless in our community. We brought art materials and provided safe space and inspiration for making art, thinking, and talking about peace. We also contacted schools and facilitated Peace art workshops in K-12 classes. At the end of each workshop we spent time with the participants talking about art that they created. We took pictures of the artwork and invited the participants to submit them to our virtual Web-based art show dedicated to Peace. It was very exciting to see all the artwork that was submitted into our virtual show from all over the world. The virtual exhibit connected artists in our community with artists as far away as Ghana, Romania, and China, and helped us understand that the Internet is an important part of contemporary Silk Roads.

To create the physical Peace exhibit at the Evergreen Library a curating group of Silk Roads students selected art works from the virtual art show and invited artists to physically submit them to the show. The exhibit was a very successful project, allowing students to produce a meaningful event and to connect with local community. Marsha, a student in our program, commented how moved she was when in the peace art workshop with the homeless she understood that peace for them meant land of their own and housing.

The response to the Peace art exhibit was very positive both from the college and from the greater outside community. Local newspapers published several articles about the show, the art workshops and Silk Roads student involvement in producing the show. The show opened

PEACE PROJECT DRAWS COMMUNITY TOGETHER

Kylee Huebschman, 6, a first-grader at Madison Elementary School, adds her artistic touch Friday to a peace mural being created during the 12-hour "Draw for Peace" at SideDoor Studio in downtown Olympia. The event involved the studio and the Silk Roads Lunar New Year celebration at The Evergreen State College. "We thought it would be great to open it up to the whole community," studio owner Lori Vermillion said. "This is what it's all about. Exploring peace through art." The school will play host to a Lunar New Year festival March 9-11.

Figure 9.2. Photo and caption in *The Olympian* newspaper. January 20, 2007. Photo by Tony Overman, reprinted with permission of *The Olympian*.

during a winter storm that produced a power outage in the college. Since the opening was already announced, students thought that it would be best to continue as planned. The college and library were pitch black and the show opened with candlelight and flashlights. This unusual lighting added to the spiritual dimension of the show dedicated to Peace in the world.

Another important theme of our Silk Roads program was the understanding of culture and cultural traditions. To better understand Chinese culture our program facilitated a co-production with the neighboring South Puget Sound Community College of the Lunar New Year Spring Festival. We were able to invite the Seattle Chinese Orchestra and a traditional Lion Dance group for an exuberant cultural celebration. In the rehearsals for the concert and in the performance our students were able to see and hear musical instruments that were transmitted along the Silk Roads. By producing the festival we connected with local Chinese community and gained an understanding about Lunar New Year, the most important holiday that is celebrated throughout Asia.

Individual Service Learning projects allowed our students to share their learning about the Silk Roads with others and to develop Silk Roads curriculum in local K-12 schools. When looking for places to volunteer for

Figure 9.3. Silk Roads Poster for the Lunar Spring Festival 2007.

community service we asked students to connect with elementary schools in their immediate neighborhoods. For students who were new to the area, finding a school was sometimes a difficult task and we, as faculty, helped by connecting them with K-12 teachers that we knew personally from earlier projects. We also developed a simple contract form that helped students to speak with teachers and report on their service hours on their blog Web page. Students could continue working in the same school for all three quarters of the program, or work each quarter in a different school. The most difficult part in student projects and community service was connecting our students with K-12 schools. When we plan this program again in the future we will allow more time for our students to find a K-12 class and to spend more time in observing the classroom.

The variety of projects and lesson plans that our students developed was inspiring. Here are some examples:

Shapes and colors in Islamic art (K-1)
Origami and felt cutouts of animals on the Silk Roads: camels, horses, yaks, sheep, etc. (9–12 grade, YMCA)
Dance, drumming, and costumes on the Silk Roads (6 grade)
Feng Shui and a field trip to a local Japanese garden (K-5, YMCA)

Portrait and landscape in Renaissance, China, and Islamic
   art (9–12 grade)
Pottery in China and on the Silk Roads (9–12 grade)
Masks and puppets on the Silk Roads, in China, and Turkey
   (4–5 grade)
Drawing lessons on dragons and dragonflies (4 grade)
Puppets and Silk Roads stories (10–12 grade)
Japanese calligraphy and Haiku (4 grade)
Tai Ji and Chinese calligraphy (10–12 grade)

The themes for these projects came from collaborations between our
students and classroom teachers. We asked our students to spend several
days observing their classrooms and working as teachers' assistants before
they approached the teachers with ideas for possible lesson plans inspired
by their Silk Roads studies. The lesson plans had to be developmentally
appropriate and address particular needs of children and teachers. For
example, the teacher in Capitol High School wanted her students to
have experiences with sumi-e paintings. Our student, Matt, not only
developed several lessons in sumi-e painting for the Peace show but
also developed a lesson comparing portrait and landscape painting in
Italian Renaissance, China, and Islamic art. Matt had enough information from the lectures he had in Silk Roads program to further research
perspective and spatial representation characteristic of Western and Asian
painting. Travis, another student who worked in the same high school,
had a prior interest and skill in ceramics. He developed lessons about
ceramics on the Silk Roads, teaching about the importance of Chinese
porcelain. These community service projects were very satisfying for our
students and for the teachers and classes they worked with.
   One student in the Silk Roads program, Sue, worked with high
school students and developed lesson plans for puppet theater. Sue
reported in her Web blog:

> The importance of story telling in cultural diffusion along
> Silk Roads inspired a puppet theater activity that led students
> to study and analyze literature, write scripts with engaging
> dialogue, and create puppets. Ultimately students shared their
> puppet theater with daycare students emulating the Silk Roads
> program ideal of sharing with community.

Dorothea, another student in Silk Roads program, volunteered
at a juvenile detention center. Together with Carol, the director of
the Gateways Program for Incarcerated Youth at Green Hill center,
Dorothea brainstormed with her students how to create a project about

peace that all students could participate in. The incarcerated students conceived peace and the artwork about peace as a puzzle. Dorothea recorded comments that were made by incarcerated youth artists about what working on the Peace project meant to them:

> Peace to me is everyone coming together. The world is full of gangs, war and a lot of conflicts between one on one or one and everyone. This piece shows a lot of things of different natures, colors, shapes and sizes all coming together as one. I thought of this by thinking of all the problems we have today and how I wish we could all come together—kind of like a puzzle.
>
> This means to "give." A friendly way to make friends. I enjoyed seeing the pieces form individually, then form a whole. I had a good amount of fun making this piece of art. The whole experience was a peaceful time for me and I really enjoyed having the opportunity to do something constructive as a group.
>
> Peace to me is love, joy, family and new life. Also when people come together as one to accomplish something that will benefit everyone in a positive way.

Several students in the Silk Roads program were inspired to design children's books and to use them in their work in K-12 schools. Lecion and Sakura wrote and illustrated the book "An Oasis for Omar," a story about a baby camel that is born in a caravanserai on Silk Road.

Ken and Corine designed a children's book with a silk ribbon that wove through the pages of their book like a silken path. Silk Roads students also created children's books about Ramadan, Chinese Lunar New Year, and the Monkey King. Our students worked with these books in elementary schools where they did their community service projects. Elementary school children read the books in Reading Buddies programs where older children read to children in kindergarten and first grade.

Another very successful model of a service project was designed by Ken and Corine who worked with fourth and fifth grade students at Blake Lake Elementary school. For their lessons on geography and cultures of the Silk Roads, Ken and Corine invited international students to make presentations to the class. This was a great opportunity for college ESL students from China, Korea, Japan, and Saudi Arabia to practice English while sharing their cultures and traditional costumes with younger students.

The success of Community Service Projects was in direct relationship to the personal engagement of the students. Some of the projects lasted longer than one quarter; other students did several projects in one quarter. Students reported all of the hours of Project work and Community Service on their Web blogs. As the supervising faculty member it was important to me to see that students were engaged in this work and were internally motivated by their own inspiration and initiative. The community service work gave students a grounding in their local community. For students such as Lecion it created a connection and involvement with an international community as well. When we visited an orphanage in Beijing, China, Lecion was moved by the struggle of teachers and administration to provide quality living conditions and education for their students. Helping the orphanage with donations of unwanted school supplies from college students and seeking financial support from grants and local businesses became the focus of Lecion's project work. She is planning to continue her connection with orphanage even after our Silk Roads program is finished.

Just like the student projects and community service, the international study and travel allowed us to connect our Silk Roads program to the real world, which I believe gives education real meaning and value. Students wrote in their reflection papers how transformative and life changing their experiences in the Silk Roads program were and how important it was to connect their academic work with real experiences. When at the end of the program our students reported about their work, the wide variety of projects and the sense of accomplishment that our students exuded was empowering. In retrospect, looking at our program and the work that our students did in the community I am excited about the opportunities that Silk Roads studies can offer in curriculum development and in bringing students to active involvement in the community. Although developed at an alternative college, the themes and projects that I wrote about could be easily adapted in conventional colleges and K-12 classrooms. Silk Roads studies allow an inspiring metaphor for global education. The connection of this education to the local and international communities will make the study meaningful and transformative.

In my own work as a volunteer in schools I often share with students my love of and fascination with Chinese culture. One time I told second grade students a story about what a dragon looks like.[5] Children drew pictures of how they imagined dragons.

One boy, considered a slow learner, showed to me with pride his picture of a dragon and asked, "Do you know what it is?" He was pointing at a yellow shape by the dragon's mouth so I answered: "Is it dragon's breath?" "No," he said, and with eyes gleaming in glee of sharing important information he said, "Every evening the dragon swallows the sun and the every morning she releases the new sun out."

To me this story is an example of how one can become connected through drawing and art with a deeper layer of mythological imagination. By creating opportunities for our students for a passionate engagement with cultures of the world we helped create myths of our own time.

Suggested Readings

Coles, Robert. *The Call of Service: A Witness to Idealism.* New York, Houghton Mifflin, 1993.

Dewey, John. *Experience And Education.* New York: Free Press, 1997.

Foltz, Richard. *Religions of the Silk Road: Overland Trade and Cultural Exchange from Antiquity to the Fifteenth Century.* New York: St. Martins's Griffin, 1999.

Hanh, Thich Nhat. *Peace Is Every Step: The Path of Mindfulness in Everyday Life.* New York: Bantam, 1992.

Hopkirk, Peter. *Foreign Devils on the Silk Road: The Search for the Lost Cities and Treasures of Chinese Central Asia.* Amherst: University of Massachusetts Press, 1984.

Lewis, Bernard, trans. *Music of a Distant Drum: Classical Arabic, Persian, Turkish, and Hebrew Poems.* Princeton: Princeton University Press, 2001.

Maalouf, Amin. *In The Name of Identity: Violence and the Need to Belong.* New York: Penguin Paperbacks; Reprint ed, 2003.

Munif, Abdelrahman. *Cities of Salt.* New York: Vintage International, 1989.

Pamuk, Orhan. *Istanbul: Memories and the City.* New York: Vintage, 2006.

———. *My Name Is Red.* New York: Vintage, 2002.

Rodinson, Maxine. *Muhammad.* New York: New Press, 2002.

Williams, Jay, and Mercer Mayer. *Everyone Knows What a Dragon Looks Like.* New York: Aladdin Books, 1984.

Wood, Frances. *The Silk Road: Two Thousand Years in the Heart of Asia.* Berkeley: University of California Press, 2004.

Appendix A: Detailed Course Description

Program, Course or Contract Title:
Silk Roads: China, the Middle East, and the New World

Quarter and Academic Year
Fall 2006, Winter and Spring 2007

Credits
Up to twelve credits each quarter are awarded in History, Art, Cultural studies, Writing, Community Service, and Education

Description:

Faculty: Hirsh Diamant, PhD, and Char Simons, MA

Fall quarter, students enrolled for eight credits explored the historical diffusion of culture, art and religion along the ancient Silk Roads. The main texts were *The Silk Road* by Frances Wood and *Muhammad* by Maxine Rodison. Students wrote a series of response papers to the texts, engaged in seminar discussions, and wrote a research paper on the Silk Road-related topic of their choice. Students participated in 50 hours of service learning projects, including designing and implementing a mini Silk Roads curriculum in a K-12 classroom. They also worked on community projects, such as the New Years Peace Art show in which they helped coordinate the work of artists from the local community and other countries, and developed and implemented an interactive workshop on a photography and poetry exhibit workshop, "What Are You Afraid Of? Images of Iran and Jordan." Students shared their community and K-12 work through blogs and final presentations. Students enrolled in the program for 12 credits in addition to the work described previously also designed a more in-depth project, such as art or a research paper.

Winter quarter continued with the main Silk Roads themes and focused on historical and contemporary goodwill connections in the arts, including visual arts, music, poetry, literature, and film along the Silk Roads, culminating with a three-week study tour of China for some students. Central questions for the quarter included: How are cultures transmitted? How are people transformed by manifestations of culture that they encounter through art, poetry, music, etc.? How can transmission and transformation of culture promote peace and contribute to the common good? Student outcomes included developing a basic understanding of the geography, purposes, activities, and timeframe of the historical Silk Roads; exploring the formation of identity on multiple levels (religious, spiritual, gender, educational, historical, geographical); examining contemporary arts (calligraphy, poetry, music) of a variety of East and West Asian cultures; reading and reflection on the literature and folklore of other cultures; integrating their learning into service projects in K-12 schools and in the community. Texts included *Monkey*, Arthur Waley, translator; *Peace Is Every Step: The Path of Mindfulness in Everyday Life*, by Thich Nhat Hahn; *Istanbul: Memories and the City*, by Orhan Pamuk; *Music from a Distant Drum: Classical Arabic, Persian, Turkish and Hebrew Poems*, by Bernard Lewis, ed.; and *Cities of Salt*, by Abdelrahman Munif.

This four-credit winter course focused on International Travel and Study in China. The itinerary of our travel in China included visits to the three ancient and modern capitals of China: Beijing, Xi'an, and Hangzhou. Students visited historical sites, connected with students in Chinese universities, and dialogued on culture and cultural transfusions along the contemporary and historical Silk Roads. The preparatory, pre-travel study included readings, Internet research, and participation in classes and community events of the eight-credit Interdisciplinary program Silk Roads: China, the Middle East, and the New World.

Spring quarter, students had the option of traveling with faculty to Turkey and Jordan, or to do their travel pilgrimage independently in the United States. Regardless of country, an overall goal of the study tours was to experience travel as pilgrimage and a peacemaking activity through informal and formal meetings with students, educators, artists, musicians, writers, journalists, environmentalists, religious and political leaders. In writing, art workshops, and further work in K-12 schools and community organizations, students had the opportunity to integrate their travels with the Silk Roads program themes of identity, and the transmission and transformation of culture. A major product of the quarter was the Silk Roads identity and travel anthology, a 60-page publication that students planned and produced that included student, faculty, and guest scholars' writing, art, and photography.

Appendix B: Classroom Observation/Participation Contract

Silk Roads: China, The Middle East, and The New World
The Evergreen State College, Fall 2006

Each student enrolled in the program, Arts, Environment & the Child, is required to carry out 49 hours of project work during fall quarter. As a portion of this project work, students are expected to initiate contact with a school and classroom teacher in order to 1) observe students on a weekly basis for four weeks, 2) participate and help as appropriate, and 3) develop and carry out a lesson plan/activity that is age appropriate and that links with the other aspects of their work in this program. Contracts signed by both the student and classroom teacher need to be returned to faculty by Wednesday, 25 January.

The classroom teacher will be asked to orient the student to his/her classroom, give the student guidelines for observation and interaction, assess the student's lesson/activity plan, enable the student to carry out the lesson/activity, and write a one-paragraph evaluation of the student's work that must be received by the faculty no later than Wednesday, 8 March. Evaluations may be sent to:

Hirsh Diamant, diamanth@evergreen.edu or TESC, Sem II
  B3115, Olympia, WA 98505
Char Simons, simonsc@evergreen.edu or TESC, Sem II B3116,
  Olympia, WA 98505

To the classroom teacher:
We thank you for providing the opportunity for students to contribute
to the good work your school is doing and to learn from this experience. If you have questions about the program or what is expected of
students, feel free to contact Hirsh Diamant at xxxx, or Char Simons
at the above e-mail address or by phone at xxxxx.
Thank you.

****

Contract

I, _____, agree to carry out observations
for four weeks (Weeks 3–6, academic weeks of October 5-November
30) as well as plan and carry out a lesson or activity ideally in Week 7
(academic week of   )

_____ agree to participate as described
                Student's name

above on _____ at _____
              Day of the week/time   Name of school

My classroom teacher, _____ _____
                            Print name   Phone#

Agrees to provide supervision and a one-paragraph written evaluation to

be received by the appropriate faculty by December 5, 2006.

_____ _____
      Student's signature   Classroom teacher

Date _____

Notes

1. Program Web site is at http://academic.evergreen.edu/curricular/silkroads/06/.

2. Robert Coles, *The Call of Service: A Witness to Idealism* (New York: Houghton Mifflin, 1993).

3. For an example of students' blog pages see http://academic.evergreen.edu/curricular/silkroads/06/studentprojects.htm.

4. The *Anthology* is available as a PDF at http://www2.evergreen.edu/silkroads/final-version-of-anthology.

5. Jay Williams and Mercer Mayer, *Everyone Knows What a Dragon Looks Like*, (Aladdin Books, 1984).

Chapter 10

Taking Students along China's Silk Road

Marcia J. Frost

The Silk Road is many things: a romantic term evoking images of camel caravans, lost oases, and luxury goods; a metaphor for the historic exchanges between the peoples inhabiting the major steppe lands and civilizations of Eurasia; the actual places where such exchanges took place; and a useful device to explore the contemporary interactions and exchanges between China and her Western neighbors or between the Han and non-Han along the western periphery. This chapter will discuss a month-long summer study abroad/field experience program along China's Silk Road during the summer of 2007. *Wittenberg in China: On the Silk Road* is a multidisciplinary, experiential learning program designed to immerse students in the rich resources of China's northwestern regions and to explore both past and present cultural and economic interactions of the Silk Road. The discussion of this program in the following pages is exhaustive in its coverage of neither the exercises our students completed, nor our itinerary, but it should be a useful template for faculty taking students on the Silk Road for shorter tours and longer study programs, exploring experiential learning in general, teaching Silk Road studies, or integrating them into other courses.

Interest in the Silk Road, academic and popular, revived at the end of the twentieth century as travel across China and Central Asia became possible, and as new paradigms of world history developed. At my university, Wittenberg, in Springfield, Ohio, interest in the Silk Road was directly related to the generous funding from the Freeman Foundation through its undergraduate initiative to expand awareness of East Asia. Our grant proposal included funding for a faculty development trip along China's Silk Road with the expectation that participating faculty would develop a course about the Silk Road for the East Asian Studies program and/or integrate Silk Road materials into other courses across the curriculum. Although my own training is as an economic historian of South Asia and my contributions to the East Asian Studies program were courses on Economies in Transition, Economic Development, and a first-year interdisciplinary seminar on Mongolia, I was delegated the responsibility of developing the faculty trip. In July 2004, eight faculty from six departments (economics, English, geography, philosophy, religion, and anthropology) traveled China's Silk Road from Xi'an to Kashgar via Jiayuguan, Dunhuang, Turfan, Urumqi, and Khotan (Hotan, Hetian). Only two of the eight were trained in East Asian Studies and regularly contributed to the core courses in the program.

To say this trip broadened our horizons is an understatement. For those of us who had lived in or visited China, China was Beijing, Shanghai, and Hangzhou. Xi'an and Chengdu were the farthest west anyone had previously gone. But as we traveled west from Xi'an through Gansu's Hexi Corridor, across the Gobi, and into and around the Tarim Basin, our perceptions of China—her people, culture, history, art, daily life—changed, day by day, stop by stop. As a South Asianist, I felt right at home among the Uyghurs of Khotan and Kashgar, where the smells, the food, the dress, the faces were all closer to those of Delhi than Beijing, while my colleagues who were familiar with China felt they were in a foreign land. As we moved along our Silk Road route, we began to appreciate the tremendous diversity of peoples who had shared their material goods, religions, arts, technologies, and genes with each other over millennia, and we began to rethink the answers to basic questions: What is China? Who is Chinese? What is Chinese culture?

The initial results of this faculty trip were the development of two new courses, a team-taught interdisciplinary introductory course "The Silk Road" for our East Asian Studies program, and a 200-level topical course "Geography of East Asia." In addition, participating faculty made major revisions and introduced new foci to our course offerings in non–East Asian specific courses in economics, religion, and philosophy, as well as changes to our core introductory and capstone East Asian Studies 100 and 400 courses.

As we worked toward developing "The Silk Road" course (a joint effort by faculty teaching in departments of economics, religion, and sociology), we continued to share with our Silk Road fellow travelers, and colleagues on other campuses our fascination and new perspectives. We discussed what it means to be Chinese; how we define Chinese history; how Chinese culture assimilated and adapted new peoples and ideas; how Chinese society is divided into the haves and have-nots, and her peoples into the model Han and the non-Han ethnic minorities; and how to design our presentation of China to our students. Out of these discussions came the germ of an idea to actually take students along China's Silk Road. Over the next two years, including a return trip to travel the Silk Road in the summer of 2006, we developed a month-long field studies program "Wittenberg in China: On the Silk Road."[1] We inaugurated the course in May 2007 when my colleague, Stephen R. Smith (Professor of Anthropology and East Asian Studies), and I along with twelve Wittenberg students studied and traveled from Xi'an to Khotan.

We developed the program to appeal to a wide range of student interests and to allow students to pursue those topics of greatest importance to them. It is a six-credit program (the equivalent of 67.5 class contact hours) meeting Wittenberg's general educational requirements for either (1) Social Institutions, Processes and Behavior, or (2) Non-Western Cultures, reflecting our disciplinary training in economics and anthropology. As other colleagues share directing and teaching responsibilities in future summers, we will modify the program to meet their areas of expertise and interest, and students might meet general education requirements for (1) Fine, Performing, and Literary Arts, (2) Religious and Philosophical Inquiry, and/or (3) The Natural World.[2] The twelve students we selected (four rising sophomores, three rising juniors, and five rising seniors, and, surprisingly, four women and eight men) have or plan to declare majors and minors in art, biology, Chinese language, computer science, economics, history, management, math, political science, and East Asian studies. Most of the students had no previous courses on China or East Asia, only two had traveled to coastal China as tourists, and one was a native of Vietnam. Only four of our students had any Chinese language skills, and two of those had just completed their first year of study.

The program is interdisciplinary and designed to help students learn about both China's past and present through assigned readings, site visits, experiential learning activities, classroom lectures and discussions, and reflection. In 2007, one of the main themes of the course was the historic development of China through its interactions with the ancient civilizations of India, Persia, and the Mediterranean states, and the nomadic peoples and empires of Central and Inner Asia. Because the nomadic peoples of the eastern steppe and taiga, and Inner Asia (today's 'stans) played critical roles throughout the history of the Silk Road, sharing their technologies, arts, gene pools, and mercantile skills with the more widely known and celebrated settled populations, we took the program on the road, into Xinjiang among their descendants. Since one theme of our course was how the modern Chinese state is attempting to create a multiethnic nation from its diverse peoples and cultures, it was crucial that our students understood the history of periodic conquests by nomadic peoples and tributary relations between China and central Eurasia.

During the spring semester we met the students once a month for a class period to discuss (1) the program, our expectations, and their responsibilities, (2) administrative issues, what to pack, paperwork for visas and the University administration, etc., and (3) study-abroad issues from culture shock and adaptation to good Chinese dining etiquette. We had the students read Peter Hessler's *River Town* as the basis for a discussion of what it is like to be a stranger in a strange land, the surprising ways one finds cultural differences difficult to understand and accept, and how to live through and survive the myriad manifestations of culture shock with good humor. Between the end of finals and graduation we met them for two days of concentrated coursework, including introductions to (1) Chinese language, (2) China's geography, history, political system, civilization, and cultural values, and (3) our two main themes: the historic Silk Road and integrating minority peoples into the modern state. We assigned readings from a range of sources, including Judy Bonavia's *The Silk Road*, newspaper articles, standard anthologies on China, and excerpts from Pal Nyiris's *Scenic Spots*.

We explicitly designed the program around pedagogies of experiential learning. That choice had several ramifications. First, once we completed the initial class meetings on the Wittenberg campus during spring semester (a total of ten contact hours), the program would literally be on the Silk Road. We felt it was important that students understand the expanse of China, if only to imagine the expanse of Eurasia, and to experience, albeit in some comfort, the great range of diverse landforms, climates, and natural environments that Silk Road travelers crossed. We took the train or bus from Beijing to Urumqi, some 3,700 kilometers (2,500 miles), with stopovers of from one to five nights in Xi'an, Jiayuguan, Dunhuang, and Turfan. From Urumqi we then flew across the Taklamakan to Khotan, and back to Beijing. Traveling by train allowed us to (marginally) reduce the cost of the program, but more importantly allowed the students to observe the steady change in the landscape, the size and shape of villages and houses, the kinds of industry and crops, and the stature and dress of the people from the plains to the mountains to the deserts. While we traveled westward in the luxury of modern sleepers and air-conditioned buses, a journey that cumulatively totaled about sixty hours, it was a lot easier to imagine crossing that vast space in a camel caravan or on horseback than had we flown.

Second, we structured the program largely around a variety of experiential learning activities that got our students out of a classroom, away from their desks, and actively engaging with China and Chinese. In part, this design was out of necessity. With the exception of our stays at the foreign student hostels at Northwest University in Xi'an and the Xinjiang Normal University in Urumqi, we were unable to arrange for traditional classroom space. We lectured, more frequently in the first weeks than the later, met with students to reflect on their learning activities almost daily, and had students give formal presentations. When we did not meet in classrooms, we met in public gardens, hotel conference rooms, restaurants, in the bus, and anywhere else we could all fit. Nonetheless, we believe that traveling along the Silk Road, using China's diverse archeological and cultural sites, bazaars and night markets, even KTVs (China's ubiquitous karaoke hangouts), allows students to explore both past and present cultural and economic phenomena and interactions in ways more meaningful than reading a book or listening to a lecture. Students had a number of activities to complete during one or more of the train rides. One assignment all students completed was to walk the length of the train through soft and hard sleeper, soft and hard seat compartments, to observe the numbers of people, their dress and luggage, and their behavior. From this exercise students speculated, discussed, and came to some consensus on who these different people were, why they were traveling, how far, and for what purposes.

Third, students took a proactive role in their learning. While we believed there were some activities all students should engage in, we wanted to allow students the flexibility to explore their own interests while still achieving our learning goals. We identified nine different foci of learning activities: religion, markets, neighborhoods, museums, parks and squares, archeological sites and tombs, play, culture, and handicrafts and cottage industries. While there were usually one or two activities under each category every student was required to complete, each student had a wide range of alternative activities to meet the program requirements. Some required activities were group activities; these were most often dictated by the nature of the activity or by the difficulties (and expense) of organization or transportation. Other activities could be completed individually or in pairs or threes, with or without the assistance of program staff.

For example, to meet the religion requirement every student was required to visit the Big Wild Goose Pagoda and the Great Mosque in Xi'an, and to visit at least one additional site each relating to Buddhism, Christianity, and Islam. Students met these requirements by visiting other famous temple and mosque sites (i.e., Great Xingshan and Xiangji Temples outside Xi'an, the Emin Mosque in Turfan and the White Horse Pagoda in Dunhuang) and local, neighborhood (i.e., non-tourist) Bud-

dhist temples and mosques, attending Sunday mass services, exploring
the Museum of Steles, and participating in observances of Buddha's
birthday at Dunhuang's Mogao Caves. In addition to assigned readings
and formal lectures on Buddhism, Islam, and Nestorian Christianity, we
provided students with background material on each site (often including a site map), funds to hire a guide or rent an audio guide if they
so chose, and the option of bringing along (or tagging along with)
one of the program staff. At each site we required students to report
their observations in a daily reflection journal, answering the following
questions:

> What is the site? When was it constructed or developed?
>   For what purpose? Are there distinctive architectural traits
>   (i.e., religious, ethnic, regional)? How is it used now?
> Who is there (i.e., local or tourist, men, women, families)?
>   How many people are there? Where are they (i.e.,
>   inside, outside)?
> Why are they there? What are they doing?
> Are there religious instructions? If so, what kind? By
>   whom? To whom?
> What is the atmosphere (i.e., solemn, social)?

To meet the market requirement we required every student to
explore the night market in Xi'an's Muslim quarter, to find their dinner
at the night market in Jiayuguan, to shop for food and warm clothes
for an overnight in the Nanshan (Southern Mountains) and gifts for
host families in Urumqi's international bazaar, and to map Khotan's
Sunday bazaar. We also required them to visit at least one additional
night market, bazaar, or shopping area. Students explored modern, mul-
tistoried shopping malls in Xi'an, night markets in Dunhuang, Turfan
and Khotan, and tourist markets at Beijing's Wangfujing Street, Hong
Qiao, and Xiuhui (the Pearl and Silk markets respectively). In addition,
they made daily visits to small shops to purchase water and other drinks,
cigarettes, snacks, batteries, and the like. We asked students to observe,
record and reflect on the following questions:

> Who is at this market? Who are the buyers? The sellers?
>   (i.e., local, out of town, tourist? men? women? Han,
>   minority?)
> What is being sold? Is there a market specialty?
> How is the market organized?

How are transactions carried out? (i.e., fixed price or
  negotiated? silently [hand signals], quietly, loudly for all
  to hear? cash, credit, in kind?)

We purposely included activities that on the surface appear to be
pure play, entertainment, or fun as one of our requirements. These
activities, however, had just as much educational value as any lecture,
text, or other experiential learning activity. Among the play activities we
recommended were circumambulating Xi'an's city wall (on foot, tandem
bicycle, or electric cart), sliding down Dunhuang's Singing Sands dunes,
horseback riding in the Nanshan grasslands at three thousand meters
elevation, and camel trekking into the Taklamakan. By getting up on
the city wall, which enclosed just the area of the Emperor's palace
(Forbidden City), students were able to imagine the tremendous size
of Tang era Chang'an (Xi'an), then perhaps the most populous city
in the world, in a way not possible at ground level. They could also
recognize that walls and gates did not just protect the city from attack,
but allowed the state to control the movement of people and goods
into and within the city gates.

The camel trek into the desert north of Khotan was perhaps the
highlight of the entire trip for each of us. After being postponed for a
half-day due to a sandstorm, we headed into the desert in a long line
with legs hanging straight down (there were no stirrups). The sun was
incredibly strong; there was sand everywhere—not just at our feet but
in our hair and eyes. One minute we could see trees and fields in the
oasis; the next we were in an unending expanse of undulating hills of
yellow sand in all directions. One camel was barely controllable, threw
three riders in fairly quick succession, and then ran off out of sight. While
we waited for one of the camel drivers to find and return the camel,
the others dismounted, faced west, and said their afternoon prayers. It
was a profoundly moving moment, and there was not one of us who
did not imagine a merchant caravan crossing that same desert, dealing
with that same sun and sand, shifting weight to get some relief from
"camel butt and camel legs," listening to recited prayers—not for four
hours as we did, but day after day, week after week.

One of the great difficulties of learning about China and her people
while in China is gaining access to Chinese people. The Chinese, whether
by cultural norms or half a century of political repression, are far less
open with foreigners than one finds, for example, in India or Turkey.
As Stephen Smith and I worked our way across China in the summer of
2006, we explored every possible way we could have our students meet

and interact with the Chinese. Some of our plans came to fruition, others failed to materialize at the last minute, and some opportunities just came to us like manna from heaven. In terms of living arrangements, we had hoped to set up home stays and, as a second choice, to stay on university campuses. We could not get police approval for home stays except in Xi'an, and then only for a weekend overnight. Unfortunately just as we were due to arrive, the local district officials, with whom we had met and made arrangements, decided there were too many risks for them to host our students. We were unable to get either local police or tourist office approvals for alternative home stay arrangements. We also could not get approval to stay on university campuses, except in Xi'an and Urumqi. While foreign students are not permitted in dorms housing Chinese students, we still found our housing on these campuses served our goal of enhancing opportunities for students to learn about contemporary China.

At Northwest University our students sometimes chose to eat in one of the student cafeterias, giving them an opportunity to observe, if not communicate with, students their own age, and enjoy a wide range of dishes not available in the United States or local restaurants. For two days we held class outdoors, having lost our classroom to a conference of Communist Party officials; one day our students were giving presentations, the other we had a class discussion. A large number of students, faculty, and staff passing by observed us, and some later engaged our students in conversation. We were housed on two floors with Pakistani students (all male) taking an intensive year-long course in Chinese language before beginning their medical studies. Five times a day one end of the hall was blocked off as most of the Pakistani students observed their daily prayers. Since non-Muslims (and almost always) women were prohibited from entering the main prayer halls of the mosques we visited along the Silk Road during prayers, our living arrangements gave us all repeated opportunities to hear the beauty of the prayers, to recognize that they differed across the day, and to gain a very different perspective on the practice of Islam. Several of our students played sports and had conversations with the Pakistani students in the evenings.

One of the most unexpected changes in our program was a meeting with the Imam of the Great Mosque. We had tried, unsuccessfully, to set this up during our preparatory trip in the summer of 2006, and were delighted to be invited to a restaurant in the Muslim Quarter to meet the Imam between afternoon prayers. He gave us a fascinating lecture on Islam, the local Hui community, and Xi'an's mosques, and then took student questions. He left for prayers, and then returned to share dinner with us. We were also joined by three Hui students, all women, who befriended several of our students and met with them daily until our departure. After dinner, the Imam's translator arranged for our students (male and female) to meet his son and some of his friends who attend a sports school for a pick-up game of basketball. Through these contacts our students learned about the history of Xi'an (while walking along its City Wall), explored the Great Mosque, and were introduced to some Chinese people.

In addition to the meeting with Hui students, our students visited a middle school in Xi'an, where they had the opportunity to observe the Monday morning flag-raising ceremony followed by the students' military exercises; sit in on a tenth grade English class; and spend an hour talking in small groups with somewhat larger groups of Chinese upper middle school students. The noise level was incredibly high as some three dozen sixteen- to twenty-two-year-olds asked and answered each others' questions about their lives, educations, interests, and ambitions with great enthusiasm and excitement. Subsequent meetings with ethnic minority students working on master's degrees in Urumqi and Uyghur traditional medical students in Khotan, were less successful, especially the latter who neither asked our students any questions, despite the presence of translators, nor were particularly responsive to questions our students asked. As our students reflected on these experiences, they recognized how different life is in China for the relatively privileged and the relatively less privileged. Those who live in the heartland, learning English as a second language, have reasonable expectations to study or live abroad, or work in Beijing or Shanghai. Those who live in the far west, learning English as a third or fourth language (or not at all), are just hopeful they will be one of the 40 percent of graduates who could find jobs somewhere in Xinjiang, and have no expectation they could find jobs in the more economically developed east.

Of all the places we visited on our Silk Road travels, Khotan was the most likely place where our students, despite the language issues, could have experiences that would help them understand what life might have been like before the modernization of the twentieth century. In Khotan city and its nearby villages you can still find a few families making articles of everyday and special use that were common items of trade along the Silk Road. Khotan jade is the most valuable of all the nephrites mined in and around China, and was a major item of trade from the west into the Chinese heartland at least as far back as the Shang dynasty (second millennium BCE). No one chose the option to go into the river bed to mine for jade; the huge earth movers lined along the river bank dissuaded anyone from thinking they might be lucky. Instead, most of our students chose to visit a local jade carving workshop, where they could observe the entire production process from design to cutting to polishing. They also were able to appreciate the sophisticated technology and skill required to cut a stone which itself can cut glass and until recently could only be cut by abrading one jade stone with the jade grit from another. A fairly sizeable group of our male students spent half a day with a family that makes knives that are sold throughout Xinjiang's markets and across China. They observed each step of the process from stoking the coal fire to forging the steel blade to engraving the trademark brand and decorations to assembling the final product. They visited the family shop and home, and shared a long lunch with the male proprietors.

We required each student to spend a day with an artisan family. We sent four groups of three students, each accompanied by a translator (and unknown to us at the time, a police officer who had us under surveillance), to families we had met in 2004 and/or 2006. We instructed the students to learn what they could about the family and their home life, their artisan activity and its market, and the village where they lived. We asked the families to provide the students with lunch (tea, nan bread, and yoghurt), to teach the students what skills the family was willing to teach, and to take them into the village to see the shops, schools, etc., if any. Our local coordinator confirmed the arrangements with the families, and we paid for the students' meals from their daily food allowance. One family works with silk, and our students learned how to draw off the silk from cocoons, twist them into silk threads for dyeing (a process the family does but not the day our students were there), and hand weave the Uyghur *ikat* pattern. They sell the silk cloth in local markets, primarily for women's dresses. Another family, the last in the area, makes paper from mulberry bark. Our students had the opportunity to try to learn (they found it extremely challenging) to separate the inner bark from the outer bark of mulberry branches, then pound the inner bark into a paste, mix it with water and ash, and lastly screen the liquefied bark pulp and leave it to dry into paper. Most of the paper is purchased by the government in order to sustain this artisan activity; they sell the rest in local markets and to local hat makers as a stiffening material. The students learned that paper making is a soon to be lost art for two reasons: first, farmers are replacing their mulberry trees with more profitable walnuts, and second, demand for the caramel-colored, somewhat coarse paper has shrunk with the availability of cheaper alternative materials.

A third group visited a wooden bowl maker. In 2004, there were several families in this village making wooden bowls, using simple electric lathes to smooth the hand-hewn interior and exterior walls. But this past summer there was just one left, as the cost of wood, primarily poplar and walnut, had risen, making wood bowl production less profitable than other activities. This is a large nuclear family with five children, the oldest of which, now sixteen, is the bowl maker. These students learned a lot about village education in south Xinjiang: the limited resources available for rural education, the willingness of Uyghur families to send their girls to school, and the failure of government officials to implement and enforce China's free, universal, and compulsory school attendance (through lower middle school) laws. This family shared with our students their experiences with China's two-child policy for ethnic minority and rural inhabitants, showed them their farmland, and then took them by donkey cart to the local weekly market to sell their bowls.

The last group of students visited a family of felt rug makers. This was the only household where the students were not invited to explore the entire house or to meet, or work with, any of the women. The students learned each step in the process of felt making: carding the wool, laying it, making patterns from colored wool, wetting the wool, and rolling it. The felt pieces fabricated by these families are widely sold in local markets for use as saddle blankets and to cover the beds of carts used for transport of people and their goods. Our students noted that as motorized vehicles replace donkeys, camels, and horses, demand for this commodity, known to have been produced in Xinjiang at least back into the second millennium BCE, will also diminish and the number of households earning an income from felt making will decline.

We resolved relatively early in our program development process to spend at least half our time in China in the far west. There the most numerous and famous Silk Road oases are located, and the local peoples—their faces, dress, food, and housing—make it impossible to ignore the many diverse influences coming from north, south, east, and west. Thirteen of China's fifty-six ethnic groups reside in the Xinjiang Uyghur Autonomous Region: Uyghur, Kazakh, Hui, Xibo, Mongol, Kirghiz, Uzbek, Manchu, Russian, Tartar, Daur, Tajik, and Han. All can trace their movement into the region over the past two thousand years, and many to more recent centuries. However, none can claim to be the "original" inhabitants of the region, except to the extent that they intermarried with the earlier Indo-European, Indo-Persians who were living settled lives as cultivator-herders in the oases and northern grasslands as long ago as the third millennium BCE. The Hui practice Islam and are the descendents of Central Asians brought to the region during the Tang and Mongol dynasties (seventh-thirteenth centuries). The Uyghur, Kazakh, Kirghiz, Uzbek, and Tartars speak Turkic languages, while the Mongols and Daur speak Mongolian languages; all their ancestors came out of the steppes of southern Siberia and Mongolia. The Xibo and Manchu came from the eastern steppes of Manchuria during the Qing dynasty; Russians and Tajiks from the northwest. A few Han trace their lineages in Xinjiang back to the settlements of soldiers and peasants from central China under the Han, Tang and Qing dynasties, but most have been "migrated" by the government since the founding of the People's Republic of China.

Our students were able to recognize the complex mix of peoples living in Xinjiang through a number of activities in addition to their daily observation of life around them. One of the observational activities we required of all students everywhere we stayed was to note the clothing of young and old, male and female. By the time we arrived in Turfan, even the most unobservant of our students recognized that dress for all had become more conservative (longer over both arms and legs), less idiosyncratic, and somewhat less colorful (blacks and browns were more common). By the time we reached Turfan students also observed that nan and meat sticks were everywhere, not just in the night markets, but on every street and many formal restaurants, and many of the people we saw and met had longer noses, higher cheekbones, lighter hair, and sometimes even hazel eyes, unlike the predominantly Han people in Xi'an, Jiayuguan, and Dunhuang. In Urumqi we invited Prof. Tsui Yenhu, deputy director of Xinjiang Normal University's Institute of Social-Cultural Anthropology, to give us a lecture on Xinjiang's ethnic minority peoples; then we sent our students to the Xinjiang UAR Museum.

One-half of the ground floor of this relatively new museum is dedicated to the presentation of each of the Uyghur Autonomous Region's ethnic minorities. Each presentation includes a replica of their housing, male and female mannequins showing facial features, body type, relative stature, coloring and "native" dress, jewelry and clothes, and other items of daily and cultural life. Students had already had interactions with Manchu, Uyghur, Kazakhs, Kirghiz, Hui, and Han, and this exhibit allowed them to see similarities and differences among the ethnic minority groups, to classify them by various categories (i.e., nomadic, European-related), and compare what multiethnic means in China and the United States. The other half of the ground floor is the regional history section of the museum, a larger version of the standard Chinese presentation of local material culture from tools to fine art dating from Paleolithic times to the present. The role of Silk Road exchanges and influences is evident here more than in any other museum in China. The exhibits include wolf designs, chessboards, Buddhist reliquaries, wool and silk textiles, felts, pearl roundels, lapis lazuli, silver Persian and gold Byzantium coins, and a wide range of documents (including religious texts, contracts, census records, passports, merchant letters) on wood and paper written in a variety of languages and scripts. About one-half of the second floor holds the display of a very small part of the Department of Archeology's holdings from the excavated sites around and in the Taklamakan, including the desiccated corpses known as the Loulan Beauty and Cherchen Man. Students had already read selections from Wang Binghua's *The Ancient Corpses of Xinjiang*, and made presentations on the likely living standards and trade relations of the different settlements excavated around and in the Taklamakan based on the descriptions of the bodies and the artifacts found with them. Most students had also previously explored the exhibit of desiccated corpses in the Turfan Museum.

Three explicit statements—in one form or another, one display after another—tie these exhibits together. First, China has always been home to many different peoples of different ethnic origins, physical appearance, technical sophistication, and artistic aptitudes. Second, China is a nation of ethnic nationalities, all of whom collectively and each of whom individually are Chinese. Third, China, the political entity, has always included the territories currently claimed by the People's Republic of China. While students saw these same messages at various cultural and historic sites from Xi'an westward, it was in Urumqi, capital of the Xinjiang Uyghur Autonomous Republic, where students most clearly understood the depth and breadth of the government's efforts to redefine identities and make its borders. And of course, it is in Xinjiang where the Chinese government currently perceives the greatest threat to its national integrity. For Americans, now nearly a century and a half after the Civil War, it is difficult to understand the issues related to forging a nation from disparate peoples who may have alternative ideas of nationhood; this experience in China helped our students better understand these issues.

As the discussion of our program indicates, taking our students along the Silk Road provided a wide range of opportunities for them to learn not only about China's past but contemporary China, and to appreciate the incredible diversity of China's land mass and her peoples. We tried to find ways to use the resources around us to replace traditional classroom presentations and reading assignments as the primary means by which we taught and our students learned. Providing students with background information on where we were going and what they might explore, coupled with very specific observational exercises and frequent reflection (both individually and as a group) proved to be very effective. The range of experiences we offered our students and the freedom they had to choose which activities they would complete to meet our learning objectives were extremely important to the success of this program.

Each of the twelve students participating in our Silk Road program had an experience that has altered their life and perspectives of the world. Some students were most struck by the expanse of Chinese history that they engaged with from the fifth millennium BCE Neolithic site at Banpo to contemporary KTV nightlife. Most were impressed by the immense breadth of the country and the diversity of her peoples and cultures. Their perception of what China is and who the Chinese are has been altered dramatically. Several were profoundly affected by the relative poverty of Xinjiang's people, with respect to both Beijing and the United States, and have begun to struggle with issues of equity and public policy in new ways. Most came to recognize and respect alternative ways of living from house construction to family relations to medical practices. All acquired a confidence in their ability to communicate, even when they shared no common language with the people they were encountering. Two of our students changed their fall registration to pick up Chinese language; one has already begun to make arrangements for an internship in China next summer and now anticipates his future career will be China-oriented. Our students unanimously found the program challenging, exciting and rewarding.

As we witnessed our students' travels along China's Silk Road, Stephen Smith and I came to recognize and appreciate myriad new ways we can use the Silk Road to introduce students to Chinese history, culture, and contemporary issues. Our students found the mix of customary academic and experiential learning activities to be an excellent way to learn about China, keeping them steadily engaged with new and meaningful experiences. As teachers, we are excited about the possibilities the Silk Road offers: to teach across a wide range of disciplines either through an interdisciplinary or more focused approach; to give pre-med, education, and management students, who on our campus are least likely to study abroad, an opportunity to do so; and to introduce students to a different way of perceiving China.

Appendix

Summary Course Outline

May 10–12, Wittenberg University campus

Lectures

Introduction to Chinese language
What is experiential learning
Background on China: geography & climate, history, contemporary
    political system, Chinese civilization & cultural values, ethnic
    identities, national identity issues

Background on the Silk Road: nexus of Eurasian interaction, geography & climate, history

May 13–14, travel to Xi'an via Beijing
May 14–22, Xi'an

Lectures

Introductions to Shaanxi Province and Xi'an: geography, history, walled cities in China
Education in China
Buddhism
Islam and Xi'an's Hui community
Tang dynasty culture
Local artifacts from the Silk Road
Rural life

Group activities

Map the Northwest University campus and the center of Xi'an within the city walls
Excursion to Qin Shihuang Mausoleum, Terracotta Warriors, cave village, vinegar factory
Meeting with Imam and Hui students
Middle school visit

Experiential learning sites

Xi'an city wall, Drum & Bell Tower
Banpo Neolithic village
Shaanxi Provincial Museum, Xi'an City Museum, Museum of Steles
Big Wild Goose Pagoda, Small Wild Goose pagoda, Xingshan Temples, Xiangji Temple, Xingjian Temple
Great Mosque
Muslim night market

May 23, Jiayuguan

Group activities

Great Wall Museum
Jiayuguan Fort
Climb Great Wall

Experiential learning sites

Jiayuguan night market

May 24–26, Dunhuang

Lectures

History & importance of Dunhuang
Buddhist patrons at Dunhuang

Experiential learning sites

Mogao caves
Dunhuang Academy History Museum
Farmers' village overnight stay
Singing Sands
White Horse Pagoda

May 27–30, Turfan

Lectures

Introductions to Xinjiang &Turfan: geography & climate, history,
   contemporary social structure & economy

Group activities

Map the town
Tuyugou village: lunch w/ Uyghur family, caves, mosques & Yemeni
   tomb
Astana graveyard
Gaochang
Uyghur Song & Dance performance

Experiential learning sites

Turfan Museum
Karez Museum
Emin Mosque
Turfan bazaar
Bezeklik
Jiaohe
Sand Therapy Center

May 31–June 2, Urumqi

Lectures

Ethnic minorities in Xinjiang
Jade
Han migration
Nomads

Group activities

Meeting, dinner & nightlife with Xinjiang Normal University ethnic minority students
Nanshan grasslands (overnight stay)

Experiential learning sites

Xinjiang Uyghur Autonomous Region Museum
International & Erdaoqiao bazaars
Grand Mosque

June 3 7, Khotan

Lectures

Introduction to southern Xinjiang & Khotan: history, economic transition
Traditional medical systems: Chinese, Ayurvedic, Unani
Uyghur traditional medicine (Uyghur Medical College)
Silk and paper
Student presentations

Group activities

Map the Sunday bazaar
Taklamakan camel trek
Day-long stay with artisan families
Dinner with Uyghur medical students

Experiential learning sites

Jade carving, silk, carpet weaving, knife factories
Silk & Mulberry Research Institute

June 8–11, Beijing

Group activities

Great Wall and Yuan Gate at Juyong Pass

Notes

1. Again, Freeman Foundation funding was crucial in allowing us to investigate experiential learning opportunities to pursue old and make new contacts, to identify appropriate housing and emergency facilities, and do all the other due diligence required to set up a program abroad. In the preparation and execution of all three trips to date we have been ably assisted by Mr.

Zhang Xu of Beijing whose long experience with American academics and Silk Road tours has proved invaluable.

2. Based on our experiences and student feedback, in summer 2008 we modified the program to expand our students' contact with Chinese and Uyghur traditional medicine practitioners and the range of experiential learning exercises relating to contemporary education and business activity to appeal to students in our pre-med, education, and management majors.

Chapter 11

Mapping the Silk Road

Rebecca Woodward Wendelken

The geography of the Silk Road is important but problematic, whether you are teaching world history, Asian history, or a course dedicated to the Silk Road itself. As one of those old-fashioned history professors who think geography and history are closely interlinked, it is important to me that my students have a familiarity with maps. A frightening number of students arrive at college with little or no geographic knowledge. Some cannot find their home state on a line map of the United States, so remedial map work is critical. As I tell my students, "It does me little good to talk about someplace if you don't know where they keep it."

The geography of the Silk Road is especially challenging to teach. It is, after all, mostly in the middle of nowhere. With the exception of Chinese nuclear testing at Lop Nor and stories on the war in Iraq or Afghanistan, most of the places are unlikely to make the evening news. Only a handful of Westerners went to Central Asia during the period when the Silk Road was a major overland trade route, and they did not leave credible maps, so Europeans learned about the geography of the region from narrative sources describing a particular journey. However, place names were inconsistent and each traveler could have a different name for the same location depending on whom they had asked and what language that person spoke. Until the nineteenth and early twentieth centuries, Central Asia was, at least to Europeans, largely uncharted territory. Today, it is still just as foreign to us. Social Studies classes seldom cover the region. Even students with a good grasp of geographic place names will falter at finding the location of the "Kunlun Mountains" or the "Tarim River."

The name "Silk Road" itself is misleading. It appeals to the romantics, but it gives the perception that silk was the most important trade item. In fact, it was only one of many products. It could just as easily have been called the "Horse Road," the "Jade Road," or even the "Rhubarb Road." A few of my students thought "silk" referred to the surface of the road—as in "smooth as silk." "Road" is even more of a problem. It sounds like one single route, as in I-95 or Route 66. Often students visualize a modern, paved road—probably a four- or six-lane highway because, after all, it is important enough to have made it into the history textbook!

My object is to give you some practical suggestions about how to use geography to provide a more factual image for your students that better illuminates this trans-Eurasian pipeline for goods, ideas, culture, and technology. With some variation these ideas could work equally well in introductory courses as in upper level ones. Bright college students can work directly with the primary sources to create their own maps, but less advanced students will require digested material and a more structured approach. For the most part my suggestions are low-tech, since many of us do not have ready access to, or proficiency with Global Information Systems (GIS) software. However, those with both skills and access to such programs could easily adapt these ideas to GIS technology, and I encourage you to do so.

When I began this chapter, I saw it as a discussion of physical geography and ways to introduce physical geography in the classroom. As I thought about "mapping" in broader terms, I began to see numerous ways to map the Silk Road region. For the purpose of this discussion I will focus on three of them—physical, political, and cultural geography—exploring their problematic nature, and suggesting some practical solutions and exercises. Each of these approaches allows us to answer different questions. What mountains, rivers, deserts, etc. did travelers along these routes have to cross and how did geography help determine those routes? What climactic conditions did travelers encounter and how did those conditions affect their journeys? What were the states in the region at a given time period, who were their allies, and where were their borders? How do you map peripheral or migratory groups, especially nomadic ones who did not have defined physical borders? Where did ideas and technologies begin and how did others adapt them? What is the process of artistic and technological transfer? These are but a few of the questions that geography can help to answer.

I must begin with two caveats. The first is the problem of names. Many places were known by multiple names—Turkic, Chinese, Persian, Latin, etc. Also, names changed over time—Alexander the Great knew Samarkand as Marakanda but later the Chinese called it Sa-mo-kien, the farthest province of the Chinese empire. One way of dealing with multiple names is to mark alternative names on a master map. For beginning students I would include only the most common. You could also create a database and key alternate names on the modern one, or give students a handout that contains alternate names as an easy reference. More advanced students could create their own handouts and lists.

Another problem with place names is their spelling and pronunciation. Most anglicized Turkic names are pronounced as they are spelled. But Chinese is a different story. To complicate the matter, there are two major ways of transliterating Chinese into English. Many older books (and even some more recent ones) use Wade-Giles. Modern works use the newer pinyin method. So Hsin-chiang (Wade-Giles) and Xinjiang (Pinyin) are the same place. You could add these different spellings to the master map or database as well. Either way it is helpful to hand out a basic pronunciation guide to your students (Chinese pinyin: "q" and Wade Giles "ch' " = "ch"; "x" and "Hs" = "sh," etc.).

The second caveat is that the routes, cities, states, nomadic groups, trade goods, and so on varied over time due to environmental factors, regional conflicts, and changing markets. The Silk Road was never static. Understanding this fact helps students to better grasp concepts such as the flexibility of the trans-Eurasian trade system and change as a process in history. For example, the routes for the Han dynasty (202 BCE-220 CE) are different from those of the Tang (618–907 CE). You might also note on your master map the period when a particular name came into usage, or a particular route came into use, helping students to see changes over time. Again, you will need to adjust the exercises to the level of your students, limiting beginning students to the basic routes, names, etc.

Physical Geography

In his classic study on physical geography and history, W. Gordon East said, "It is not so much by [geography's] more violent manifestations—its earthquakes and volcanic eruptions, and its hurricanes and its floods—as by the expression of its normal everyday personality that the physical environment left its mark on human history."[1] The "normal everyday personality" of Central Asia is diverse, dramatic, complicated, and mostly unfamiliar. The Gobi, the Djungarian, and the Taklamakan are high plateau deserts surrounded by chains of high mountains, which both isolate and protect the area, affecting the climate and channeling the traveler who wishes to cross them. In addition, Central Asia lies very far from any major bodies of water. This has a dramatic effect on the climate, producing a condition called "continentality." This effect creates large fluctuations in temperature, for example, in summer the days will be very hot while during the night the temperature may fall to near zero. The thirteenth-century Mongol envoy Wu-ku-sun Chang Tuan describes this phenomenon in his writings. "In the fourth or fifth month (May, June) there the grass dries up, as in our country in winter. The mountains are covered with snow even in the hottest season of the year. When the sun rises it becomes hot, but as soon as it sets it gets cold."[2] Rainfall is often less than ten inches a year and in some places, such as the Taklamakan, it is virtually nonexistent. The high mountains such as the Pamirs, the Kunlun, the Altai, and the Tianshan that surround the deserts are formidable obstacles in the paths of the travelers. But where there is a will, or more accurately a profit, there has always been a way.[3]

Map Resources

At this point, making sense of the physical geography of Central Asia may seem nearly as daunting as traveling the entire length of the Silk Road itself! Today, almost every World History text includes a map of the Silk Road, but some are so small as to be useless and many contain little in the way of physical geography—no mountains, rivers, or deserts, just lines across Eurasia. However, there are multiple sites on the Web that can provide wonderful maps for classroom use. For general maps take a look at Google Earth release 4 (2007) which has a number of new features and advanced functions that are available at a low cost.[4] Microsoft Virtual Earth has great images—bird's eye views of the land that allow you to zoom in and out.[5] For maps of the Silk Road itself, Daniel Waugh's "Silk Road—Seattle" site has excellent maps showing the terrain of eastern and western Asia.[6] He also offers some very humbling "test yourself" maps that cover the cities, physical geography, and modern states of Central Asia. *Encarta* has another good map that shows the main route, the Eurasian steppe route, and the connecting routes.[7] The "Silk Road Foundation" has a variety of maps including ones showing the routes of travelers such as Marco Polo, William of Rubruck, and Faxian, which are particularly good when paired with the actual texts.[8] If, like me, you need something big to hang on the wall that you can point to, the Stanford Program on International and Cross Cultural Education (SPICE) has a very nice 30 x 64" laminated map, which you can purchase as part of a curriculum package that includes games, maps, lesson plans, and a DVD with materials for classroom use.[9] There are other map selections at the Fordham Medieval History Sourcebook Web site, Odden's Cartographic

Bookmarks, USGS Geode, and the University of Texas.[10] You can also find good maps in many of the growing number of books on the Silk Road. For example, Jonathan Tucker's *The Silk Road: Art and History* has a two-page map showing many different land and sea routes, and each section of the book starts with a map. However, although the maps show lakes and rivers, they do not show mountains or deserts and lack a scale, a major drawback. Nonetheless, the book is a fantastic resource for mapping art, religion, and technology.[11] Francis Wood's work, *The Silk Road: Two Thousand Years in the Heart of Asia* has a nice set of maps of the Central Asian region (roughly the end of the Gansu corridor to Merv) and the Silk Road land routes on the end papers. It also has an elevation map from Tyre to Luoyang using the Northern Route around the Taklamakan.[12]

Applications for the Classroom

So now you have a map or maps, but how do you use them to give your students an understanding of physical, political and cultural geography? While simply looking at a map is helpful, maps have little value unless students use them actively. A good method of developing an understanding of the relationships of geographical features along the Silk Road is by having students create a strip map, or rather a series of strip maps. A strip map is very elementary and requires little or no skills in drawing. It is basically a strip of paper that shows the sequence of geographic features you pass through or by to reach your destination. Distance and direction are not important, and students can draw one by hand or with a word processing program.

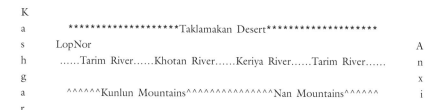

Figure 11.1. A simple geographic strip map of the southern route around the Taklamakan between Kashgar and Anxi. The asterisks around "Taklamakan" show that the travelers will have the Taklamakan to the north while the ^^^ represent mountains that hemmed travelers in from the south during their entire journey.

By adding the towns, cities, and for our purposes, oases, the strip map actually gives you more of an insight into how the route looked to the early travelers and merchants. Most roads were simply called the "road to xxx," "xxx" being the next city or town. The Chinese did not call the route "Silk Road" and neither did the Romans. The Chinese called the northern route around the Taklamakan the "*Tianshan bei lu*" or "the road north of the Celestial Mountains," and the Southern Silk Road "*Nan Shan Bei Lu*" or the "road north of the Southern Mountains." Such practices are still common today. Driving on I-40 near Raleigh, North Carolina, I pass "Fayetteville Road"—and if I take that road, I end up in Fayetteville. In Fayetteville, if I take "Cool Spring Street" I will pass what used to be a spring supplying water to the downtown area, hence the name. Developers looking for classy names for subdivisions have blurred the geography-based names of the past somewhat, but collecting such names from your town or area might help students better understand this type of mapping and gain insight into their own local area as well.

While a strip map gives you an idea about the relationship of cities and towns and major geographic features it lacks a lot of valuable information. It does not accurately portray distances, directions, or the size of physical features. So now it is important to transfer your information to a physical features map with an altitude chart. The elevation map I mentioned above in Wood's book is an excellent place to start and here is a short example of what this would look like.

If your goal is to produce a map with altitude chart for the entire Silk Road route or routes, you might want to use several charts (the northern route around the Tarim Basin, the southern route, the Kashgar-Bukhara-Merv route, the Kashgar-Balkh-Merv route, etc.) It would probably be a good idea to split the assignment up and allow individual

Kucha

Kashgar   Aksu   Karashahr   Turfan   Bezeklik   Hami   Anxi

Taklamakan Desert

Figure 11.2. A simple strip map showing towns for the northern route around the Taklamakan. After Matthew of Paris' "Itinerary from London," c. 1253 CE.

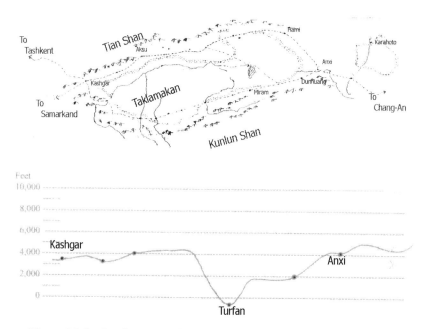

Figure 11.3. Combining a physical features map with an altitude chart.

groups to do particular sections. Other possibilities for charting and map combinations include temperatures for a particular time of the year—day/night temperature variations are particularly interesting—or rainfall. For many areas of Central Asia the graph for seasonal rainfall would be a virtually straight line hovering around zero.

One tried and true geographic exercise is to ask students to physically build a three-dimensional map using the information they have gathered. Even advanced students find this exercise not only fun, but also a genuine learning experience, especially if they are required to write a paper on what they have learned as part of the lesson. The advantage of three-dimensional maps is that they show concretely what students would not normally envision: for example, they really understand what it means when you say the Gobi Desert is a high desert. Several downloadable electronic three-dimensional maps are newly available on the Internet: Microsoft Visual Earth, mentioned above, has one that is in the developmental stage that you can download and try out.[13]

You are probably asking yourself, "Where do I get the data to produce an elevation chart?" Francis Wood's book is a good place to start. This gives you a baseline for part of the route. Then you can explore the Internet for more information. Jonathan Tucker's book also provides some important data. I use travel guides, such as *Lonely Planet* or *Cadogan*, which include data like distances and altitudes. You can also use the elevation map concept for other data such as rainfall. You often find average rainfall amounts in the same places you encounter altitude information, or you can check the various international weather sites on the Internet. But be advised that those Internet sites will give you today's figures. Things have changed somewhat since Silk Road times.

Films

Maps give us an understanding of space, but what does the actual terrain look like? Many books and Web sites contain pictures of terrain that you can combine with a map to better present the actual conditions, but there is nothing like a film to really get the point across. *The Silk Road*, a British- and Japanese-produced set of twelve films available in English, has wonderful scenes of *burans* (storms), salt flats, mountains, passes, deserts, and so on.[14] The DVD version is far superior to the original VHS, which had some sound problems. My students complain about the New Age background music of the film, so if yours do the same you can always do what I do—turn off the sound and provide your own music and narration. There are also Silk Road films available from China. One is a lengthier version of the Japanese/British set but is difficult to obtain in the United States. Another is called *New Silk Road* and is co-produced by CCTV and NHK.[15] Unfortunately, it does not have subtitles, but the pictures make up for it.

The above suggestions can help provide or increase your students' knowledge of the physical geography of the regions of the Silk Road. This provides them with a better background to understand the dynamics of the Silk Road and the challenges those who traveled along it faced. Written descriptions can convey only so much. They provide us with a limited point of view from a particular place and time, but they can only hint at the vastness of Central Asia. A three-day journey sounds like a long way, but maps can show us that over rough terrain it was often a very short distance indeed. Geography is to space what history is to time.[16] You need maps, and to an extent films, to supplement readings in order to convey the perils of geography and nature travelers faced along the Silk Road.

Political Geography

While physical obstacles were a problem for travelers and merchants along the Silk Road, human obstacles were even more important. Nomadic rivalries and the political divisions of states could delay or even destroy a trading party. Here, again, we are back in the realm of the totally unknown to our students. Most people have heard of the Romans, the Byzantines, and the Persians, but have no idea who the Sogdians, the Khotanese, the Tocharians, or the Yuezhi were. Even worse for mapping purposes, the states, borders, and groups changed dramatically over time. So how can we deal with shifting borders and still convey the idea of control over territory? Political mapping is a key part of the geography of the Silk Road.

The concept of precise borders is a relatively modern phenomenon. As a merchant on the Silk Road, you would be unlikely to see a sign that said, "You are now leaving Khotan. Come back soon!" In the more highly developed states you would be subject to taxes or tariffs when you entered or left their territory, but more likely you would only have to pay such fees at cities or towns along the route. What we normally find is that rather than borders, early states had "spheres of control" and "spheres of influence." Spheres of control are generally towns or cities and the areas immediately around them—areas that the military or policing forces can reach in a short amount of time. Spheres of influence are farther away from the urban areas, and usually only under indirect control. The situation in Afghanistan following the U.S. invasion in 2002 illustrates this concept clearly. The U.S. military had direct control in cities but only marginal influence in the countryside.

In terms of mapping, political entities present two problems. The first is knowing where the control ended and the influence began, and the second is portraying these differences. Most maps show definite borders for states of the Silk Road period, but you can use those to get a rough idea of areas of control versus areas of influence. Let's begin with the widest borders—those of influence. The borders on the maps in most history texts usually more accurately show where the *influence* of a group extended. But were they actually in control of the entire region within these borders? It is necessary to refine these political boundaries with your students. Look for cities and towns and military garrisons. These are definite areas of control. Roads connecting cities, towns, and garrisons are frequently areas of control. You can further refine these areas of control versus influence by examining period texts that discuss rebellions, tax collection, and other events. For example, during the mid-nineteenth century Muslim rebellions, the Chinese government had some influence in northwest China but little control.

Mapping alliances poses similar problems. There are often records of alliances with the larger states such as Persia or China, but immediately it becomes clear that there are many gaps in the information and that alliances could be temporary. If groups fought together in a battle they were probably allied, although it was not unknown for groups to change sides in the middle of a battle to support the victor and share in the spoils. Such was the case at the Battle of the Talas River in 751 CE, with the Turks, who, seeing their Chinese allies were losing or perhaps having been offered a better deal, switched sides, throwing the battle to the Arabs. It is important for students to understand that alliances then, as today, were fragile and shifting.

Primary sources provide the best detail for maps, borders, and alliances, and again the Waugh site comes to the rescue. Part VII of *Notes on the Western Regions* has information on population, distances, and administration. *The Western Regions according to the Hou Han Shu* is also useful. Section 4 of the *Weilue* describes the routes around the Tarim Basin and Section XXIII is on the "New Route to the North." The appendices of the *Weilue* are a fount of information on main caravan routes, and the names of peoples and places. Faxian (Fa-Hsien) discusses China's Uyghur allies and there is similar information in the *Han Narrative Histories*. Excellent secondary sources include Denis Sinor's *The Cambridge History of Early Inner Asia* and Chun-shu Chang's work *The Rise of the Chinese Empire*.[17]

Once you have determined control, influence, and alliances, the second problem remains of how to portray them. I am partial to the maps on Waugh's Web site, which have "fuzzy edges" to show the lack of concrete borders. A great student project would be to ask them to scan their maps (or download electronic versions) and then use a graphics program to shade areas of influence and control. But how do you show the same thing on those large laminated wall maps? A low-tech, easily reversible method is to use transparent plastic film such as colored plastic wrap. I take a section of plastic drop cloth and trace the areas of influence on it. Then I stick the cellophane or plastic wrap to the plastic and cut out the pieces. I repeat the process for the narrower areas of control. The plastic sheet serves two purposes. First it makes the cellophane easier to cut by adding thickness. Second, by drawing the outlines on the plastic you do not have to worry about marks on the edges of the cellophane. Next, I remove the cellophane and attach it to the map in layers with simple static cling. The layered cellophane is a lighter color on the areas of influence and a darker one on the areas of control because it is two layers thick there. When I am finished with it I just peel the cellophane off the map. You can also use the cellophane method (or computer graphics) to show alliances over time. If you do not want to deal with the cellophane, you can laminate your map and use dry erase markers, but test the markers to see how well they erase first—especially if you are planning to use the map again for something else.

Mapping Nomads

The conflict between steppe and sown, or nomadic and sedentary societies, is a main theme in Central Asian history, and thus in the history of
the Silk Road. Nomads need ample grasslands to feed their flocks and
a good supply of water. Traders like to travel over nice, flat land that
provides grass and water for their animals. It was inevitable that there
would be trouble. In fact, nomads played a key role in determining the
location of the Silk Road routes. Nomadic raids slowly forced merchants
who had been taking the easier northern steppe road to shift their routes
toward the south. They had to sacrifice time and ease for safety. The
southern route had fewer oases situated farther between and was longer
as well. But nomadic raiders were less likely to attack travelers along it
because the Taklamakan was a major barrier to them. It was possible
to make "deals" with the nomads by paying protection money, but one
could never be sure with nomadic groups, whose alliances and confedera-
tions were constantly shifting, whether everyone would honor that deal.
According to modern historian Liu Xinru, nomads were responsible for
the beginning of the Silk Road itself.[18] They collected booty and tribute
which they gradually traded west, alerting merchants there of the vast
profits to be made by trading with the East.

If states are hard to pin down in terms of territory, nomads are
far more so. They usually appear in history when they have an impact
on literate settled communities. The annals and histories of settled
societies such as China and Persia often report on nomads and other
peripheral groups that appeared on their borders, especially when there
was conflict. An example would be the Xiongnu, whose raids on the
Chinese border nearly destroyed Chinese control and led Han Wudi to
send Zhang Qian, the "father of the Silk Road" on his mission west to
seek allies. But nomads are constantly on the move and may only have
infrequent contact with settled societies. While most have set migratory
patterns, those patterns are subject to change due to climate, ecological
changes, and/or pressures from other groups. Although we do not have
complete information, primary sources again provide enough material
for us to make educated guesses.

So how do you show these mobile groups? One plan might be to
mark places on the map where conflict occurred between the nomads and
the settled peoples. The Han Dynasty did not extend the Great Wall all
the way to the Jade Gate just to keep Chinese soldiers busy![19] Again, the
computer would be optimal for mapping. You could show the groups as
arrows indicating the direction of movement and the relative size of the
group. You could show movement over time and the clashes between
groups as their areas of influence overlapped, ideally using animation to

show movement. But on wall maps, you can make use of the plastic wrap again. Layering the wrap would allow you to show where they were coming from and where they were headed and their varying strength over time. When you combine this information with the locations of major clashes, students can begin to see the whole picture.

The above exercises can help students gain a better understanding the interactions between states, as well as between states and peripheral groups such as nomads. It can also help them to understand how shifting political factors influenced trade and had dramatic impacts on those who traded along the Silk Road. Besides helping your visual learners, using maps can enable students to actually see how close political groups often were and how contested territories were created by overlapping areas of influence. Maps also provide clues to why some states failed to expand into or hold certain areas. Mountain ranges, rivers, and vast deserts are often missing from political maps. These barriers were limiting factors in the creation of early empires. On the other hand, huge areas of steppe lands with their relatively flat surfaces and their grass for herds can illustrate why many states such as China continually had difficulties with the nomads when steppe lands crossed territorial lines.

Cultural Geography

To me, cultural geography is especially compelling. The transmission of ideas, technologies, and goods across cultures shows how dynamic life was during the Silk Road period even in the most remote areas. Yet in some cases these intellectual goods leave even fewer traces than nomads. How do you determine where they began and how and in what direction they moved across the Silk Road? How fast did the ideas spread? As before, we must turn to those all-important primary sources. For the sake of brevity we will examine only a few of the many possibilities that you can explore.

Ideas

Perhaps one of the most influential ideas to travel the Silk Roads was Buddhism. Buddhism developed in India in the sixth century BCE. It moved through Gandhara (Afghanistan) by the third century BCE and arrived in China in the first century CE. From primary sources, we know that the kingdoms of Khotan and Kucha adopted Buddhism in the first century BCE. We can also look at the establishment of monasteries, religious cave complexes, and monuments and so on. Primary sources can provide information on the religious conversion of kings and queens. Also, the records of numerous religious travelers such as Xuanzang describe the presence or absence of Buddhist groups along their way.

To map these aspects it is probably best to concentrate on a few ideas. To continue the example of Buddhism, mark your map to show Buddhist sites and the earliest mention of them. In some cases the primary sources will provide you with exact dates of conversion or the establishment of a monastery. By examining the dates it is possible to determine the direction of the flow of such ideas. You can use the same type of mapping with overlapping colors that you used to show "control" and "influence" of political groups to map the spread of ideas. Use the map to show where Buddhism was actually the primary religion or in "control" and where it was just an "influence," one religion among many.

Technology

One of the more fascinating but least taught aspects of the Silk Road is the spread of technology. A good example is paper. There are several good works on the spread of paper, but the best is Jonathan Bloom's book *Paper before Print: The History and Impact of Paper on the Islamic World*.[20] The transmission of glass manufacture from west to east would make an interesting map and would involve examining art in Rome, the Middle East, Persia, and so on to China. The stirrup, which came from Central Asia, revolutionized horsemanship and made the nomads the formidable powers that they were. Images in art, archaeological finds, and primary sources can help provide information on the stirrup's spread. Other possible technologies to explore would be the spread of sericulture, types of weaving technology, and the use of various minerals in pottery. For example, the cobalt that the Chinese eventually used to produce blue and white Ming ware originated in Persia.

You can map the spread of technology in one of two ways: you can use the "influence" and "control" method or you can pinpoint places and dates in which the technology appeared. When did who use what and where? For example, you might map the spread of the use of paper. Beginning in China, mark its earliest mention there. Then mark the earliest mention of paper in India, in the Middle East, in Europe, etc. Then you can connect the points to show the direction of the movement of this technology. This allows you to see the speed of transmission as well.

Art Motifs

Art motifs, like ideas and technology, can provide examples of cultural transference. The tree of life motif, especially when paired with confronted, or facing, animals, found its way from the Middle East into Chinese weaving, and dragons, unicorns, and other animal motifs experienced similar transmissions. One of the most studied transferred art motif, the pearl-edged medallion or roundel, began in Sassanid Persia and moved eastward, going all the way to Japan.

Here the art and textiles are the primary sources themselves, and images of them are widely available on the Internet. Waugh's Web site provides several examples of motif transfer as well as a virtual museum tour. A good book is Ryoichi Hayashi's work on the Silk Road and the Shoso-in temple complex in Japan.[21] Liu Xinru and Lynda Norene Shaffer also provide good information as does Thomas Allsen's book *Culture and Conquest in Mongolian Eurasia*.[22] The University of Sidney has a particularly good site on the bone and ivory goods found in modern Afghanistan and how they show the mixing of motifs from Central Asia, China, India, and the West.[23] There are also many, many Web sites that show art objects from the Silk Road period. Choose the motifs or techniques you want to track. As you come across examples from your sources of art along the Silk Road, note them on your map along with the date when they were believed to have been made. As with the ideas and technology you will find that through mapping you can begin to see the direction and speed with which these motifs moved across Central Asia.

Figure 11.4. An example of a pearl-edged medallion motif.

Trade

Last, but not least, we need to map the types of trade goods that passed along the Silk Road. The wide variety of goods is truly remarkable. Rhubarb, for example, was grown in China, dried, and then shipped in large quantities to Europe where it was valued as a laxative! But "what" is only the first of many questions. Where did the goods originate and where did they go? Were they shipped as finished goods or as raw materials? How were they shipped—dried as rhubarb, in skeins like silk, or in powder form like cobalt? How much did they cost and what does that mean in today's terms?

Edward H. Schafer's classic *The Golden Peaches of Samarkand* is excellent for beginning a study of trade goods during the Tang dynasty and it has notations that give you information about earlier and later periods as well.[24] Luce Boulnois also provides sections on trade goods in *Silk Road: Monks, Warriors and Merchants on the Silk Road*.[25] Other sources include Thomas Allsen's *Commodity and Exchange in the Mongol Empire*, C. G. F. Simkin's *The Traditional Trade of Asia*, and Jonathan Tucker's *The Silk Road: Art and History*.[26]

Of course, it is relatively easy to have your students map the routes of various trade goods on the computer with a basic graphics program. But a low-tech way to map these goods in the classroom showing their origins and destinations is to simply mark the locations on the map and then connect the points. You might want to consider using

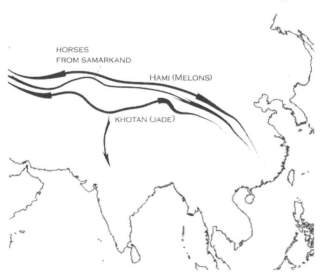

Figure 11.5. Map showing the "origin and destination" of trade goods.

specific colors for specific categories of goods—red for minerals, white for textiles, green for plants, and so on. You can show the direction of travel with arrows. You will find that for some items there is no specific destination, simply "Roman Empire" or "Europe." Depending on how thorough your research is, you might want to use two maps—one for east to west movement and the other for west to east to keep them from becoming tangled messes of points and lines.

The types of mapping I have described for tracking the spread of ideas, technologies, and art motifs and the movement of trade goods are just a few ways to provide students with a better understanding of the complex dynamics of the Silk Road. If you assign students the task of making these maps themselves, they can gain a more concrete sense of the interaction of cultures in this early example of globalization.

Conclusion

Central Asia contains an enormous variety of climates and landscapes that we can best see as a whole by examining a map. But the geography of the Silk Road need not be a boring memorization of difficult to pronounce place names. It can provide a way to excite students about this little-known area. Creating new ways to use maps in the classroom can not only give students more information about the physical geography of the Silk Road, it can instill in them a better understanding of global interconnectedness in general. The Silk Road provides rich teaching possibilities, allowing you to demonstrate a variety of concepts such as globalization, interethnic conflicts, imperialism, and cultural transference that were as important in the ancient world as they are today.

Maps are guides that show distances and directions, but they also model and can often clarify reality for our students. History analyzes events over time, geography analyzes them over space. By examining both time (primary sources) and space (maps) students develop an even better knowledge of the past and of the links between places and events. Through maps, students learn how and why the Silk Road shifted its route over time and how various peoples along the road were connected with their neighbors physically, politically, and intellectually. Maps clearly demonstrate the vast size of Central Asia and help develop students' spatial perspectives of this region. They also demonstrate man's relentless attempts to find the shortest route between two points to engage in trade and increase their profits. It is these spatial processes—trade, migration, the flow of technologies and ideas—that define and describe the Silk Road throughout history.

Suggested Readings

Chang, Chun-shu. *The Rise of the Chinese Empire: Nation, State, and Imperialism in Early China, ca 1600 BC-AD 08.* Ann Arbor: University of Michigan Press, 2007.

————. *The Rise of the Chinese Empire: Frontier, Immigration, and Empire in Han China, 130 BC-AD 157.* Ann Arbor: University of Michigan Press, 2007.

East, W. Gordon. *The Geography Behind History: How Physical Environment Affects Historical Events.* New York: W. W. Norton, 1999.

Liu, Xinru, and Lynda Norene Shaffer. *Connections across Eurasia: Transportation, Communication, and Cultural Exchange on the Silk Roads.* New York: McGraw-Hill, 2007.

Sinor, Denis, ed. *The Cambridge History of Early Inner Asia.* Cambridge: Cambridge University Press, 1990.

Tucker, Jonathan. *The Silk Road: Art and History.* Chicago: Art Media Resources, 2003.

Wood, Frances. *The Silk Road: Two Thousand Years In the Heart of Asia.* Berkeley: University of California Press, 2002.

Notes

1. W. Gordon East, *The Geography Behind History: How Physical Environment Affects Historical Events.* [1965] (Reprint. New York: W.W. Norton, 1999), 2.

2. *Travels of Wu-ku-sun Chung tuan to Central Asia*, 1219–1224. http://depts.washington,edu/silkroad/texts/pei-shi-ki.html

3. East, *The Geography Behind History*, 168.

4. Google Earth at <http://earth.google.com>.

5. Microsoft Virtual Earth at <www.microsoft.com/virtual earth>.

6. "Silk Road—Seattle," <http://depts.washington.edu/silkroad/maps/maps.html>.

7. "Encarta," <http://encarta.msn.com>.

8. "Silk Road Foundation," <http://www.silk-road.com>.

9. SPICE, "Along the Silk Road," <http://spice.stanford.edu/catalog/along_the_silk_road_2006/>.

10. Fordham Medieval Sourcebook at <http://www.fordham.edu/halsall/sbookmgr.html>; Odden's Cartographic Bookmarks at <http://odddens.geog.uu.nl>; USGS Geode at <http://dssl.er.usgslgov.geode>; University of Texas at <http://www.lib.utexas.edu/maps/historical/index.html>.

11. Jonathan Tucker, *The Silk Road: Art and History* (Chicago: Art Media Resources, 2003).

12. Francis Wood, *The Silk Road: Two Thousand Years in the Heart of Asia* (Berkeley: University of California Press, 2002).

13. Microsoft Virtual Earth at <www.microsoft.com/virtualearth>.

14. "The Silk Road," DVD, Central Park Films, 2002.

15. "New Silk Road," CCTV NHK. Distributed by China International TV Corporation. ISRC CN-A03-06-308-00/V.K.

16. George J. Demko, *Why in the World: Adventures in Geography.* (New York: Anchor Books, 1992), 5.

17. Denis Sinor, ed. *The Cambridge History of Early Inner Asia* (Cambridge: Cambridge University Press, 1990); Chang Chun-shu, *The Rise of the Chinese Empire: Nation, State, and Imperialism in Early China, ca 1600 BC-AD08.* (Ann Arbor: University of Michigan, 2007); Chang Chun-shu, *The Rise of the Chinese Empire: Frontier, Immigration, and Empire in Han China, 130 BC-AD 157.* (Ann Arbor: University of Michigan, 2007). See Jacqueline Moore's essay on using primary sources in this volume for more ideas.

18. Liu Xinru and Lynda Norene Shaffer, *Connections across Eurasia: Transportation, Communication, and Cultural Exchange on the Silk Roads* (New York: McGraw-Hill, 2007).

19. As a point of interest, textbooks usually state that the wall was built to keep the nomads out, but more recent research is showing that it served equally well to keep the Chinese in. See Liu and Shaffer, *Connections Across Eurasia.*

20. Jonathan Bloom, *Paper Before Print: The History and Impact of Paper on the Islamic World* (New Haven: Yale University Press, 2001).

21. Ryoichi Hayashi, *The Silk Road and the Shoso-in* (New York: Weatherhill/Heibonsha, 1975).

22. Liu and Shaffer, *Connections Across Eurasia*; Thomas T. Allsen, *Commodity and Exchange in the Mongol Empire: A Cultural History of Islamic Textiles* (Cambridge: Cambridge University Press, 2002).

23. <http://ecai.org/begramweb>.

24. Edward H. Schafer, *The Golden Peaches of Samarkand* (Berkeley: University of California Press, 1985).

25. Luce Boulnois, *Silk Road: Monks, Warriors, and Merchants on the Silk Road* (New York: W. W. Norton, 2004).

26. Allsen, *Commodity and Exchange*; C. G. F. Simkin, *The Traditional Trade of Asia* (Oxford: Oxford University Press, 1968); Tucker, *The Silk Road.*

Chapter 12

Using Primary Sources
to Teach the Silk Road

Jacqueline M. Moore

For historians, using primary sources is second nature to their own research, and most attempt to bring as many as possible into the classroom. But students often have a hard time understanding documents when they are not in contemporary or informal English. Teaching with primary sources can be rewarding, but time consuming, and usually we do not find much time to work with many of them in undergraduate classes. Thus, a plea to include more of them might seem impractical. Nonetheless, I would argue that the primary sources for the Silk Road are more than worth the effort, as they can provide insights your students would not otherwise arrive at as easily.[1] The problems with literal and cultural translation that the accounts raise can do more to reproduce the problems that the travelers themselves encountered than mere lectures or secondary readings can convey. Moreover, these accounts allow students to engage historic mentalities in an approachable way, while the concept that the past itself is a foreign country becomes patently clear. Thus, while the primary accounts may take time, at the end of it students can gain a holistic understanding of the period and the people they are learning about.

I first came to the task of using primary sources from the Silk Road in a freshman level team-taught interdisciplinary course called "Silk and Spices: East/West Encounters from the Ancient to the Early Modern World." Several of us on the Asian Studies committee had decided to hijack our required core sequence of Western Civilization courses and give them an East meets West focus. The Silk Road was an ideal topic to use in this regard as it involved interactions between both cultures. So I focused on this portion, and my colleague covered similar themes with the Spice Trade. In order to have courses count for the sequence, they needed to have a significant percentage of primary texts as part of the reading assignments. At first, this left my colleague and me somewhat stumped. We planned to use the *Travels of Marco Polo* and the *Lusiads* for one special focus unit, but we were unfamiliar with many texts beyond Western travel accounts. We were also concerned that our course would be too focused on Western exoticization of the East when we had hoped to emphasize that it was a two-way interaction.

As we investigated further we realized our fears were unfounded. Thanks to several great Web sites, including the *Medieval Sourcebook* and Daniel C. Waugh's incomparable *Silk Road Seattle*, there are a number of good texts or excerpts from them readily available to students online. There are also several collections of accounts such as Christopher Dawson's *Mission to Asia* that are still in print and relatively inexpensive. Lastly, thanks to Google Books, even the older massive translations such as Sir Henry Yule's *Cathay and the Way Thither* are accessible to students and faculty.[2] There are a number of accounts of Christian monks who traveled to the court of the Mongols in China and Mongolia either to look for the mythical king Prester John who would help fight the Muslims, or to set up formal diplomatic relations between the East and West. The most famous of these accounts include those of John Pian de Carpini (often called John of Plano Carpini) and William Rubruck, who traveled to the Mongol court from 1245–47 and 1253–55 respectively and whose accounts, first published together, give a vivid picture of Mongol life and the Mongol capitals. But there are also numerous accounts from French, English, and Spanish diplomats and merchants who traveled to Persia, India, and Central Asia.

Not only did I discover that these Western accounts were readily available, but there were a large number of translated nonwestern travel accounts too. I was especially pleased to find that the original accounts of the most famous Chinese pilgrims—Zhang Qian, Faxian, and Xuanzang—had been translated and printed in a variety of forms. Moroccan intellectual and Muslim pilgrim Ibn Battuta's account is the best known of the translated Arabic narratives. His narrative of his tour of the Muslim world between 1325 and 1349 is perhaps overall a better source for discussion of the Spice Trade, but he has a number of chapters on Persia and China that can be useful for Silk Road courses. *The Travels of Ch'ang Ch'un to the West* is an account of a Chinese Daoist monk who traveled to Chinggis Khan's court in the 1220s. Rabban bar Sauma, a Nestorian Christian Turk, also wrote an account of his trip from his home in Beijing to Jerusalem and then on to Europe, which is available in a much edited and translated form. Moreover, there are also official documents such as Chinese dynastic histories which include extensive descriptions of the lands and peoples of the West from a Chinese perspective, as there are official Greek and Roman accounts of Asia.

So far so good; there were counterparts to the Western narratives and official Chinese records. But I also knew that the vast majority of travelers along the Silk Road did not travel the whole distance and were not important merchants or officials, and I worried about teaching a top-down version of history. I was therefore very glad to find that there were large numbers of documents (and more discovered each year) of so-called ordinary travelers. Many of these documents came from caches discovered at the Mogao cave monasteries near Dunhuang, where explorer/archaeologist Aurel Stein found, among many other documents, a mail satchel sealed up that had been preserved since the fourth century CE by the desert aridity. These letters give insight as to Sogdian merchant activity as well as shed light on personal relationships. The Dunhuang caves have yielded a number of receipts, contracts, wills, and other documents that the Dunhuang Project is working to translate and make accessible, and there have been similar finds as well as material artifacts from around the Tarim Basin and across Eurasia that have allowed historians to piece together a more accurate picture of daily life on the Silk Road. One example is the translation of the inscription on a Nestorian stele from Chang'an, the Tang capital of China, which not only documents the existence of a thriving Chinese Christian community but also explains Nestorian doctrines using Asian style metaphors. In short, I found that there were abundant sources from a variety of geographic backgrounds and perspectives, all readily available for use in the classroom. (At the end of the chapter I list some of my favorite pre-1500 sources and their availability as of November 2008.)

The next question was how to use them in the course. While it might seem obvious to some, I would like to state a case for why these documents can be so useful as an introduction to the Silk Road. First of all they provide an immediacy to the students that no lecture and secondary scholarship can provide. In order to understand the eastern end of the Silk Road it is necessary to convey the geographical conditions, especially in the Taklamakan Desert. I can give statistics about average temperatures and rainfall which might impress the students, but I could not better convey the concepts than with the following excerpts:

From Faxian's account of the Taklamakan Desert (399–414 CE)

> The prefect of [Dunhuang] had supplied them with the means
> of crossing the desert . . . in which there are many evil demons

and hot winds. (Travelers) who encounter them perish all to a man. There is not a bird to be seen in the air above, nor an animal on the ground below. Though you look all round most earnestly to find where you can cross, you know not where to make your choice, the only mark and indication being the dry bones of the dead (left upon the sand).[3]

Swedish Explorer Sven Hedin (from an 1895 Expedition in the Taklamakan)

The height of the dunes was now one hundred and eighty feet. From the highest crest, I searched the horizon with a field glass. Nothing was to be seen but high, shifting dunes. A sea of yellow sand, without the slightest trace of a shore. . . . We had to get over them all, and over those beyond the horizon! Impossible! We had not the strength! Both men and animals grew weaker with every day that passed. The "Old Man" and "Big Blackie" were not able to follow us to that evening's camp. . . . I thought of those two camels, with horror, as I lay awake at night. First they had merely enjoyed the rest. Then the night had come, with its coolness. They would be expecting the men to return to fetch them. The blood flowing in their veins grew thicker and thicker. The "Old Man" probably died first. Then "Big Blackie" was alone. Finally, he too died, in the majestic stillness of the desert; and in due time the shifting sand-hillocks would bury the remains of the two martyrs.[4]

Such accounts not only show the dangers of travel in the region in a more descriptive and tangible fashion, but they also show the timelessness of these dangers, with about 1500 years between these descriptions. Indeed, Zhang He's narrative of her life in the Taklamakan desert near Khotan in the 1960s, which appears elsewhere in this volume, shows that these hazards persisted well into the twentieth century and still exist there today.

Primary sources can also draw students in through personal stories, and students often find that they have more in common with the people of Central Asia or Ancient China than they thought, a factor that helps them put themselves into the period we are discussing and become more interested in it as a result. A wonderful example of an all-too-contemporary sounding personal relationship comes in one of the Sogdian letters to Lord Nanai-dhat from his wife, then in Dunhuang:

Behold, I am living . . . badly, not well, wretchedly, and I consider myself dead. Again and again I send you a letter, (but) I do not receive a (single) letter from you, and I have become without hope towards you. My misfortune is this, (that) I have been in Dunhuang for three years thanks(?) to you, and there was a way out a first, a second, even a fifth time, (but) he(!) refused to bring me out. . . . In my paternal abode I did not have such a restricted [life] . . . as with(?) you. I obeyed your command (lit. took your command upon my head) and came to Dunhuang and I did not observe (my) mother's bidding nor (my) brothers'. Surely(?) the gods were angry with me on the day when I did your bidding! I would rather be a dog's or a pig's wife than yours![5]

These personal stories can also give a sense of adventure, and while it is important not to exoticize the Silk Road, nonetheless they help to pique the students' imaginations. The following excerpt gives a sense of how you might add a sense of plot to what students see as a parade of remote names and dates in an ancient history course:

Han History Account of Zhang Qian's Voyage (206–220 BCE)

At that time the Son of Heaven [the Emperor] made inquiries among those Xiongnu who had surrendered [as prisoners] and they all reported that the Xiongnu had overcome the king of the Yuezhi and made a drinking-vessel out of his skull. The Yuezhi had decamped and were hiding somewhere, all the time scheming how to take revenge on the Xiongnu, but had no ally to join them in striking a blow. The Chinese; wishing to declare war on and wipe out the Xiongnu, upon hearing this report, desired to communicate with the Yuezhi; but, the road having to pass through the territory of the Xiongnu, the Emperor sought out men whom he could send. Zhang Qian . . . responded to the call and enlisted in a mission to the Yuezhi; . . . The Xiongnu made him a prisoner and sent him to the Shan-yu [Great Khan or King], who detained him. . . . He held Zhang Qian for more than ten years, and gave him a wife, by whom he had a son.[6]

One lively and interesting medieval narrative is that of of Johann Schiltberger, a servant taken captive at the Battle of Nicopolis in 1396

by the Ottoman Sultan Bayezid I. He served the sultan for six years
and then was captured by Timur (Tamerlane) in whose service he
spent the next twenty-five years moving around Central Asia, escaping
in 1427. Part adventure, part observation, Schiltberger's *Reisebusch* or
Travels describes Armenian Christianity in detail, as well as how Indi-
ans grow pepper and the cities that produce silk. His narrative is also
a good source of information on medieval Islamic culture and Central
Asian history.[7] The modern accounts of the Great Game explorers Sven
Hedin, F. E. Younghusband, and Aurel Stein are especially replete with
exciting tales of derring-do, and would work extremely well in courses
on nineteenth-century European imperialism.

Many of the Western accounts come from church diplomats who
can highlight the political side of the Catholic Church for students. In
the thirteenth century as the Crusades faltered, the Mongols threatened
Eastern Europe, and the Pope and the Holy Roman Emperor struggled
for power, the Pope sent a series of envoys to the Mongols to negotiate an alliance against the Mamluks of Egypt. In 1245, Pope Innocent
IV sent Friar John of Plano Carpini to make contact with the Great
Khan in Mongolia. The sixty-five-year-old John, a rather portly monk,
was also an ideal diplomat, with a good eye for detail. His travel narrative, *History of the Mongols*, is thus full of good observations about
the Mongols, and how to deal with them. John, and his companion,
Benedict of Poland, (whose narrative is also available) traveled to Batu,
leader of the Kipchak Khanate (or Golden Horde) with letters from
the pope condemning him for the Mongols' brutal treatment of the
Hungarians and enjoining him to convert to Christianity. Batu demurred
at sending a response and sent the friar on to Karakorum, the Mongol
capital, in order to witness the installation of Guyuk as the next Great
Khan. Not surprisingly, Guyuk responded that he had no intention of
converting, and that the pope should show obeisance to him, or else.
John's narrative, therefore contains a chapter with the rather long title
"How to Wage War Against the Tartars; The Intentions of the Tartars;
Arms and Organisations, How to Meet their Cunning in Battle, The
Fortification of Camps and Cities, and What Should Be Done With
Tartar Prisoners," which gives detailed advice as to how to fight the
Mongols in terms of weapons, armor, and tactics.[8]

Friar William of Rubruck set out on his own, unofficial, mission in
this environment in 1253 to try to locate and save a group of German
slaves whom the Mongols had taken prisoner and had forced to work in
the mines in Central Asia—a group of whom he had read in an earlier
published narrative. He also hoped to make contact with a Mongol
leader who was rumored to be a Christian. A devout Franciscan monk,

William was another astute observer and with his companions—fellow monk Bartholomew of Cremona, servant and secretary Gosset, and an interpreter they named Homo Dei—he traveled the northern route across the Russian steppes.[9]

The issue of Christianity among the Mongols is one that these travel narratives can also shed light on. In addition to the split of the Catholic Church into Eastern and Western halves, a number of schismatic Christians deemed heretical after the Council of Nicaea, particularly Nestorian Christians, spread east along the trade routes converting new adherents as they went.[10] One of these groups was the Turkic Uyghurs, who, after they were conquered, provided the Mongols with a written script and much of their clerical support. The Mongols, like most Asian groups, were syncretic in their approach to religion, believing it better to support all religions than to suppress them. Thus, they patronized Nestorian Christians and brought priests to their court, seeking advice from them as well as from Buddhists, Daoists, and shamans. Nestorian Christians gained prominence in Central Asia, and as Mongol leaders often intermarried with those they had conquered, a surprisingly large number of wives and mothers of Khans were Nestorians. Indeed, some leading Mongols identified themselves as Christian, although by Roman Catholic standards they were not exactly exclusive in their religious practice, and still adhered to Mongolian shamanistic traditions.

Thus, Shatach, the Mongol ruler that Rubruck sought, was indeed a supporter of Christians. Moreover, he was the son of Batu, the leader of the Kipchak Khanate. But Rubruck realized that he was no Catholic, although he was very interested in the religious items Rubruck brought with him. In particular, he and the Nestorians he encountered were curious about the crosses he had with the image of Christ on them, as theirs did not. In general, Rubruck thought the Nestorians woefully ignorant of Christian doctrine and filled with superstition. At the court of Mongke in Karakorum, Rubruck, in tandem with the Nestorians, engaged in a debate with the Muslims and Buddhists as to the ideal religion, but thought the local Christians performed poorly. He deemed the Nestorian priest who represented the religion to be corrupt, especially in the matter of accepting gifts, which the Franciscans resolutely refused when offered. He also found that jealousy and rivalry the priest felt for him led to lack of proper interpreters and other difficulties.[11]

Yet despite Rubruck's and other missionaries' disdain for the Nestorians, at least in the thirteenth century there seemed to be far more tolerance for them than later. Perhaps it was simply that any Christianity was better than none in a faraway land, but another narrative, this time from a Nestorian himself, suggests that in fact this tolerance was in part diplomatic, and in part genuine. Rabban bar Sauma, a Nestorian monk from the region of Beijing, sought permission to leave on a pilgrimage to visit the Holy Land and other sacred sites in the Middle East around 1275. Khubilai Khan, like Mongol leaders before him, wanted to demonstrate his support of foreign religions, and gave Sauma and his companion Markos a pass for travel with his protection. As such the two became semi-official representatives of the Great Khan and so enjoyed a warm welcome when they arrived at the court of the Il-Khanate in Persia. Abakha, the Il-khan, was married to an Orthodox Christian, the daughter of a Byzantine Emperor, which also ensured a friendly reception. As a result of both their long journey from China, Khubilai's seal, and Abakha's friendship, the two monks quickly gained prestige among Nestorians in the region, and when the Nestorian patriarch, the Catholicus, died, they elected Markos as their new leader and appointed Sauma as the church's official representative in East Asia.[12]

In 1286, Arghun, the new Il-khan, sent Sauma to the pope and kings of Europe seeking an alliance. He had sent several envoys before but conditions had not been good for an alliance between the Mongols and the Christians. In the 1280s however, the Il-khan's biggest challenge came from the Mamluks of Egypt, who had resisted Mongolian invasion and who also controlled the Holy Lands. Thus, European Christians had a natural ally in the Mongols. Sauma visited the Vatican and toured the courts of Europe but could get no firm commitment for an alliance from any ruler. However, in the course of his visit to Rome, he had occasion to meet with the cardinals as they were electing a new pope. They questioned him in some detail about his religious beliefs, and unlike the Nestorians Rubruck encountered, Sauma was fully versed in the texts of his church. Moreover, they asked him to celebrate mass with them and to lead mass on several occasions. During his stay he had many opportunities to demonstrate his practices and appears to have been somewhat of a tourist attraction to the Roman Catholics. Yet they did not condemn him and allowed him to administer the sacraments in Catholic churches.[13] Sauma's narrative suggests that as a diplomat he had more leeway than most and as an educated man he earned the respect of his fellow Christians. His and other narratives show that the Catholic Church was not the only game in town in the Middle Ages and reinforce existing scholarship that the persistence of so-called heretical ideas was in fact a reflection of competing beliefs, and that the Church could enforce only partial orthodoxy.

The narratives and correspondence of John of Monte Corvino, Andrew Peregrine and Andrew of Perugia (the bishops of China) confirm the observations of earlier travelers about Nestorian presence, as does

Odoric of Pordenone, whose travels are a litany of Christian miracle tales. Odoric's narrative makes a brilliant contrast between William of Rubruck's and Marco Polo's accounts as, like the latter, he has numerous stories of wonders he assures us repeatedly he knows to be true, but like the former he has observations of life in China, including mention of bound feet and the friars at Zaiton, that give us glimpses of what life was like for Europeans in the East.[14]

All of these firsthand accounts have the detail, characters, plot, and humor that can draw in the students and raise their interest level more than a dry recitation of facts. Indeed, with a bit of discussion it is possible to cover a wide variety of material such as gender relations and religious practices that you might not get to in a normal lecture.

But having written such an (hopefully) elegant panegyric to using primary sources I have to admit that there are a large number of problems with using them. Most of the sources are not as pithy or exciting as the sections I have excerpted, and indeed often you have to wade through twenty pages of minutiae, unintelligible prose, and disjointed narratives to get to these nuggets. Florentine Merchant Francis Balducci Pegalotti's thirteenth-century *Handbook*, (excerpted on the Silk Road Seattle site and in Yule's *Cathay and the Way Thither*, Volume III) is particularly useful for its enumeration of the details of the trade with the East and the practicalities of both travel and trade. For example, he advises merchants to grow a beard to trade in Muslim countries, and says that while they can travel alone, they will receive better treatment if they pick up a woman in Tana to take with them. Whether that treatment was to come from those who showed them hospitality or from the woman herself is left to our imagination. However, most of his handbook, which he wrote while working for the Bardi Company, is more quantitative than qualitative.[15] The best way to work with it therefore is to ask students to either recreate the journey in map form, or to crunch a few statistics on profit and loss.

In the Chinese records, as in Marco Polo, each new town or country gets the same basic introduction. They record the location, size of population, regional products, type of money, and religious practices, so they read like almanacs, without the interesting detail, and one place sounds much the same as the next. The names that most of the sources use to refer to different cities and countries often seem completely unrelated to modern names. Marco Polo calls Dunhuang "Suchau," for example, which you can easily confuse with modern day Suzhou. The Chinese narratives generally refer to Syria as "Tacin" but use other names such as Li Kan and Fu Lin as well, which make it hard to keep the accounts straight.

Adding to these problems is the question of reliability of the sources themselves. Some of the information could simply be hearsay, for example, a Sogdian merchant could relate what he heard in Persia about the Syrians. Without clear and uniform maps it was very easy to confuse which country was which, and exactly which direction it was in; most travelers measured the trip in twenty to thirty mile stages from one town to the next. Marybeth Carlson addresses the issue of the accuracy of Marco Polo's account elsewhere in this volume. But the Chinese accounts are no better in this regard. They collected most of their facts from foreign visitors to the capital and tended to assume that once a fact was true it would not change. In an ironic twist on the West's view of China as a stagnant society, the Chinese assumed the West did not change, and saw nothing wrong with copying centuries-old accounts of the Western countries into the new dynastic histories. So while there are many accounts of China's views of the West from over the years, they often plagiarize directly from the old documents and repeat them almost word for word. Compare the following accounts:

Jiu Tang Shu ("Old History of the Tang Dynasty") circa 950 CE

> There are lambs which grow in the ground; the inhabitants wait till they are about to sprout, and then screen them off by building walls to prevent the beasts which are at large outside from eating them up. The navel of these lambs is connected with the ground; when it is forcibly cut the animal will die, but after the people have fixed the buds themselves' they frighten them by the steps of horses or the beating of drums, when the lambs will yield a sound of alarm, and the navel will be detached, and then the animal may be separated from the water-plant.

Ma Tuanlin's Ming Dynasty Account, Late Thirteenth Century

> In the northern possessions of this country there is a kind of sheep which grow naturally out of the ground. They wait till the germs are about to sprout, and then protect them by raising walls lest the beasts at large should eat them. Their navels are connected with the ground; if the navel is cut by force, the animal will die; but if by the sound of striking some object they are frightened, this will cause them to disconnect their navels, and they may be taken off the water-plants; they will not form flocks.[16]

The obvious copying and sometimes embellishment of these documents with their odd stories mean they are clearly not contemporary descriptions.

Even the document itself can be suspect. Again, *The Travels of Marco Polo* offers the most obvious example. Marco Polo made his journey between 1271 and 1292. Six years later, while a prisoner in Genoa, Polo met Rustichello of Pisa, a romance writer, who recorded his stories and published them. However, no original French version of the narrative exists, only six early versions in Venetian, Italian, Latin, and French that, combined, seem to make up the entire story. Nonetheless, it is clear that some of these versions have been embellished to meet the needs of the author (emphasizing the Christian aspects of Khubilai Khan in the version copied by a monk, for example), and others have been abridged. One can see the potential problems right away. How much of what Marco told Rustichello actually happened, and how much did he misremember? Did *Il Milione* (as Marco was nicknamed for his many stories) make up some of the stories to make himself seem more heroic? How much did Rustichello embellish the document to meet conventions of romantic writing? How much did later copyists make mistakes, edit, or add to the narrative for their own purposes?

The Chinese official documents are equally unreliable. It is not often clear what is an original document. Many of the older Han documents no longer exist except in copy form. Thus, when it seems that the description in a Han document is more complete than that in a Tang document, it does not mean it was always that way. The Han document might have been copied at a later date and incorporated information from the Tang document, or the Tang writer might have been writing based on a less complete version of the Han document and the later copyist had a more complete version. In at least one case the emperor who ordered a copy of an old document was not satisfied with its length and so asked his scholar to add more information to it.[17]

But a final and obvious problem with these primary accounts is one of translation. Xuanzang's explanation of the reason for his pilgrimage brings home the point quite clearly:

> Now Buddha having been born in the western region and his religion having spread eastwards, the sounds of the words translated have been often mistaken, the phrases of the different regions have been misunderstood on account of the wrong sounds, and thus the sense has been lost. The words being wrong, the idea has been perverted. Therefore, as it is said, "it is indispensable to have the right names, in order that there be no mistakes."[18]

Because most of the Silk Road documents are not in English, like Xuan-zang, we can only read translations of them. Even if modern translations are accurate, the travelers who wrote the accounts themselves may not have spoken the languages of the countries they were traveling to and might have misunderstood the facts. It is also possible that the people who told them these facts heard them only through a third-party trans-lation. A Gujarati sailor arriving at the Chinese court with stories of life in Rome, for example, might speak Malay but not Chinese, requiring a second Malay-Chinese interpreter. The stories travelers told could be like a game of "telephone" that children play at parties with a sentence becom-ing unintelligible as it travels from one person to the next. The "water sheep" in the Chinese accounts above is a shining example of mistransla-tion. It is possible that the water sheep were in fact some kind of bearded mussel from which Mediterranean peoples made a primitive type of silk. Unfortunately, we can never be sure; as it is clear the informants to the Chinese court could not come up with a Chinese equivalent term.

In addition to the issue of literal translation there is also the prob-lem of cultural translation. If you do not have a parallel for a cultural practice it is often difficult to explain it. Christian missionaries in China, for example, could not explain the concept of a monotheistic God, translating the term as "heaven," as there was no word for God. But "heaven" has a completely different sense in Chinese, and thus orthodox Christian theology was never very clear to many Chinese people. Ironi-cally, heretic Nestorian Christianity with its concept of a dual nature of Christ as human and divine found more resonance perhaps because it tied in with Buddhist ideas of *bodhisattvas*. Just as the missionaries had a hard time explaining their beliefs, travelers often did not accurately understand or explain the unusual cultural practices they witnessed. Marco Polo reports observing the following practice in Kamul:

> I give you my word that if a stranger comes to a house here to seek hospitality he receives a very warm welcome. The host bids his wife do everything that the guest wishes. Then he leaves the house and goes about his own business and stays away two or three days. Meanwhile the guest stays with his wife in the house and does what he will with her, lying with her in one bed just as if she were his own wife; and they lead a gay life together. All the men of this city and province are thus cuckolded by their wives; but they are not the least ashamed of it.[19]

My students and I have a long discussion of this episode as it appears early in the book and there are similar such stories throughout. I ask if they think it likely that it actually happened that way and if not, what other possibilities there are. We cover the following alternative scenarios:

> This practice is limited simply to the one household. Either the marriage is bad or the wife just felt like having a fling with the handsome young Italian who came to stay with them and the husband may not know about it.
>
> Marco misunderstood and the woman was in fact a prostitute, not a wife. (Or perhaps her husband thought there might be some profit in prostituting her to the passing European.)
>
> In fact the locals interpreted arrival of a party of Europeans with guns quite differently and let Marco stay with the wife out of fear of retaliation.

Once again, we can never know the accuracy of this account because of a possible cultural misunderstanding.

Lastly, there are the difficulties of translating ancient texts for a modern audience. In the words of British novelist L. P. Hartley: "The Past is a foreign country, they do things differently there."[20] As a result, some stories simply do not translate to modern sensibilities. Consider the following stories:

Xuanzang's Account of Dragon Lake

> To the north of a city on the eastern borders of the country, in front of a Dêva temple, there is a Great dragon lake. The dragons, changing their form, couple with mares. The offspring is a wild species of horse (dragon-horse), difficult to tame and of a fierce nature. The breed of these dragon-horses became docile: This country consequently became famous for its many excellent horses. Former records (of this country) say: "In late times there was a king called 'Gold Flower,' who exhibited rare intelligence in the doctrines (of religion). He was able to yoke the dragons to his chariot. When the king wished to dis-appear, he touched the ears of the dragons with his whip, and forthwith he became invisible." [21]

Benjamin of Tudela on Lot's Wife

> From the Mount of Olives one sees the Sea of Sodom, and at a distance of two parasangs from the Sea of Sodom is the

Pillar of Salt into which Lot's wife was turned; the sheep lick
it continually, but afterwards it regains its original shape.[22]

Marco Polo on the Miracle at Samarkand

[When Chaghadai became a Christian, they] built a big church
in the city. . . . And to make the base of the column which
stood in the centre of the church and supported the roof
they took a very beautiful stone belonging to the Saracens.
After Chagatai's death, the Saracens, who had always been
very resentful about this stone . . . resolved to take it by
force. . . . The government was now in the hands of the
Great Khan's nephew; and he ordered the Christians to
hand over the stone to the Saracens within two days. When
they received this order they were greatly perplexed and did
not know what to do. And then the miracle happened. You
must know that, when morning came on the day on which
the stone was to be handed over, the column that rested
on the stone rose up, by the will of our Lord Jesus Christ,
to a height of fully three palms and stayed there as firmly
supported as if the stone had still been underneath. And from
that day onwards the column has remained in this position,
and there it still is.[23]

When my students read these stories they are amused and incredu-
lous. I usually ask them what they think really happened. Were there really
dragons or just some great horses? Was the stone really supporting the
column in the church or did it just seem that way? The miracle that the
Travels of Marco Polo attributes to Samarkand is indeed a story repeated
about various locations, including Jerusalem, in other sources, and was
possibly added by Rustichello or another writer to boost the Christian
quotient of the narrative, a fact that also adds to the incredulity of the
students. But it is not just students who are skeptical. I tell my students
that my own first reaction on reading such stories is to come up with
a scientific explanation for them. The translator's note to the Benjamin
of Tudela narrative comments: "Pillars of salt are . . . caused by spouts
of water, in which so great a quantity of salt is contained as at times to
stop up the aperture of the spring. The latter, however, is again unsealed
through cattle licking off the salt near the aperture, and the same process of
filling up and unstopping goes on continually."[24] In a post-Enlightenment
world and the twenty-first century, we are trained to explain phenomena
rationally and we are cynical about magic and miracles.

But as I said before, the Past *is* a foreign country, and I repeatedly have to remind myself and my students of that fact. In ancient and medieval times magic was just a normal part of life, completely expected. In Christian tradition it was perfectly normal to believe that God could intervene in the world if He chose, and there was clear physical evidence of His intervention all around. In Ancient China dragons were not mythical beasts and in Daoist tradition court magicians and great sages had many ways to make themselves or their king invisible. The factual recounting of the impossible and the grotesque (or, in the case of John de' Marignolli, the explanation of these marvels) is a feature of almost all of the medieval travel narratives.[25] Whether or not these things actually happened is not the point. What *is* the point is that it is nearly impossible for us to understand what these travelers saw unless we recognize that they lived in a world where they believed these things were possible and common. If readers can accept that point they have a much better chance of understanding the writers in their own terms.

In the listing of the many problems with using Silk Road primary sources, I admit to an ulterior motive. What I hope has become clear is that in fact these problems are either easy to overcome, or they can be important teaching points in themselves. It is easy to solve the first problem of boring, confusing, or disjointed narratives with a little judicious editing and pointed reading questions, and for introductory courses I highly recommend taking the time to do these things and not assuming that students will read and understand what they are reading otherwise. I draw attention to the problems with my questions. I ask what sort of common information the Chinese accounts or Marco Polo give for each country/city. I ask why that information might be important and how they think the authors collected it. I draw attention to the more entertaining stories so their eyes do not glaze over, but ask them questions that tie them into their larger context. A discussion of the sexual patterns in Kamul or Tibet might reveal a lot about gender roles along the Silk Road (if nothing else, it is one of the few places you get to discuss women's actions), and it certainly can serve as a reminder not to take each story literally or as being truthful. An excellent resource for helping your students analyze travel narratives and ask the right sort of questions is Jerry Bentley's essay "Travel Narratives" currently available online.[27]

If the primary text is too long or too dense, do your own excerpting of it to focus on the bits you want them to read. The "Selections from the Han Narratives" are available online at Silk Road Seattle, for example, but the version uses the Wade-Giles romanization of Chinese which conflicts with my class use of pinyin. In addition, it refers to Rome and the West with a variety of names and uses odd names for places such as Ferghana or Bactria. While I wanted the students to get the idea and feel of the documents and to see what sort of story they told about Zhang Qian and early contact with the West, I was more worried they would be unnecessarily confused by the odd spelling and references when they were already contending with terms such as Xiongnu and Yuezhi and even Zhang Qian. So I edited the version for my students, putting it into pinyin as best as possible and simplifying place names to those we were using in class. I now post that version on my Web site (with much thanks to Dan Waugh at Silk Road Seattle who made the document available) and ask the students to read it there instead. Ironically, I am myself continuing the game of telephone by translating the translation, a fact which I point out to my students.[27]

The problems of reliability and translation are really opportunities to work on critical thinking skills with your students and to get them outside of themselves. Looking at different versions of any travel narrative or official document provides an opportunity for a historiographical discussion. What does it mean if the Chinese believed that facts did not change? How is that different from Western concepts of a stagnant China? How did people write history in the past and was historical accuracy one of the things they prized? Who wrote these histories and how might their own biases or agendas affect what they wrote? Students all too often assume that history is history and do not examine the process of its creation. But even for those students who believe history is all about opinions and not facts, this is a chance to examine the differences between contemporary and ancient historiography and methods.

The issue of linguistic and cultural translation is a metaphor for the Silk Road itself. After all, both ideas and goods were traded along the road through a continuous process of translation. Indeed, the metaphor of "telephone" is one I use continuously when I talk about the transmission of Buddhism, Christianity, or Islam throughout Eurasia. Making students aware of their own cultural biases in reading documents can help them better understand what it must have been like for the travelers themselves. And getting students to step out of their own experience, both geographically and chronologically, is key to understanding the Silk Road.

I firmly believe that using primary documents to explain the Silk Road in many ways is more effective than simple lecture and secondary readings. The detail, personal stories, and sense of adventure in these texts can draw students in and help them to place themselves within another person's experience. They can cry with Sven Hedin over his dying camels, wonder to stories of mythical beasts with Xuanzang, and tour the Mongol capital with William of Rubruck. More importantly, however, by engaging in critical thinking practices to analyze the problems with these documents, they can more deeply understand the material and absorb it. To be trite, they can make lemonade from lemons. After spending two weeks discussing the *Travels of Marco Polo*, my students not only understand just how alien his world is to ours but they are able to make a personal connection to it. They can discuss narrative, romantic writing, gender roles, religious syncretism, cross-cultural exoticization, Christian, Buddhist, Daoist, and Islamic mythology, Khubilai Khan and the Mongol Empire, Christian/Muslim tensions, and barriers to cultural understanding. By engaging in their own form of cultural translation they also experience what Marco himself might have undergone. In this way above all, primary sources are ideal teaching tools for courses on the Silk Road.

Jackie Moore's Top Ten Pre-1500 Favorites

1. Selections from the Han Narrative Histories Edited with Standardized Spellings and Place Names by J. Moore

http://artemis.austincollege.edu/acad/history/jmoore/Syllabi/
HWC22SilkSpices/SelectionFromTheHanNarrativeHistories.html

Good account of Zhang Qian's journey and foreign relations but a little like a catalogue sometimes. Assign with targeted questions to aid in reading.

2. Chinese Accounts of Byzantium and Rome

http://depts.washington.edu/silkroad/texts/romchin1.html

Slightly misleading title. Has a very lengthy introduction. Definitely catalogue of accounts of foreign regions but good to use for historio-graphical exercises to show how little the accounts changed over time. Assign with targeted questions.

3. Ancient Sogdian Letters

http://depts.washington.edu/silkroad/texts/sogdlet.html

Great for personalities and day-to-day life on the Silk Road. In addition, everyone loves the Sogdians.

4. Faxian's Account

http://depts.washington.edu/silkroad/texts/faxian.html

Nice eight pages of excerpts from his story. Shows some governing customs but also emphasizes the extent of Buddhist influence in the region. For the complete two hundred page version, see James Legge, trans. *Record of Buddhistic Kingdoms being an Account By the Chinese Monk Fa-Hien* [sic] *of His Travels in India and Ceylon in Search of the Buddhist Books of Discipline*. 1886. Reprint. Kessinger Publishing.

5. Xuanzang's Account

http://depts.washington.edu/silkroad/texts/xuanzang.html

Book 1 only with a cosmological description of the world and a catalog of countries mixed in with some stories. Nice description of Balkh, Bamiyan, and Kapisa but pick and choose excerpts otherwise. The full account is available as *The Great Tang Dynasty Record of Western Regions* by Xuanzang.

    Journey to the West is a fictionalized version of Xuanzang's travels with two versions available, one by Anthony Yu and another by W. J. F. Jenner. Yu's is supposed to be more faithful to the original language; Jenner's is more poetic from an English language standpoint. *Journey to the West* is itself four volumes long and many prefer to have an abridged version called *Monkey*, by Arthur Waley which is back in print. There are two other abbreviated versions: Aaron Shepard's *Monkey: A Superhero Tale of China*, which is a children's book, and David Sheridan's *Monkey: A Journey To the West*, which seems to have edited it down to the best action scenes.

6. Nestorian Stele

http://www.fordham.edu/halsall/eastasia/781nestorian.html

Skip the very biased Christian intro from the early 1900s and you get a nice record of the flourishing of Christianity (albeit Nestorian) in Asia and Tang China. It explains Christian doctrines with Asian-style metaphors and would make a nice companion piece with Faxian and Xuanzang.

7. Accounts of Mongols

Travels of Ch'ang Ch'un to the West

http://depts.washington.edu/silkroad/texts/changchun.html

Starts with really nice letter of invitation from Chinggis Khan and he is a *Daoist* monk! 21 pages. Really good descriptions of Mongol life, pairs well with

John Pian de Carpini's account

http://depts.washington.edu/silkroad/texts/carpini.html

10 pages, with a great storyline and good images.

William of Rubruck's account

http://depts.washington.edu/silkroad/texts/rubruck.html

Waugh has 63 pages, nicely bookmarked by topic. Really good descriptions of Mongol daily life and shows how cosmopolitan Karakorum was as well as the influence of Nestorians.

John Pian de Carpini's account was originally published with William of Rubruck's and you can get them inexpensively in a package deal as a digitized version of William Woodville Rockhill's translation *The Journey of William of Rubruck to the eastern parts of the world, 1253–55, as narrated by himself, with two accounts of the earlier journey of John of Pian de Carpine* [1900] (Reprint, Maryland, Rana Saad, 2005). The version by Peter Jackson, trans., *The Mission of Friar William of Rubruck*, which is supposed to be the definitive translation with the best annotations, is unfortunately out of print.

8. Rabban Bar Sauma's Account

http://depts.washington.edu/silkroad/texts/sauma.html

The full narrative title is E. A. Wallis Budge, trans and ed., *The Monks of Kúblái Khán Emperor of China. Or The History of the Life and Travels of Rabban Sawma, Envoy and Plenipotentiary of the Mongol Khans to the Kings of Europe, and Markos who as Mar Yahbh-Allaha III became Patriarch of the Nestorian Church in Asia*, and is out of print. Sauma was a Nestorian Christian Turk from Beijing and this account is less of a travelogue than a story of a Christian community and the deeds of

Sauma and his companion Markos who became the Catholicus of the Nestorian church. Sauma dies half way through this account. His narrative is best read alongside Morris Rossabi's *Voyager to Xanadu*, which contextualizes it.

9. Cathay and the Way Thither

Sir Henry Yule, trans. and ed., *Cathay and the Way Thither: Being A Collection of Medieval Notices of China*, 4 vols., (London: Hakluyt Society, 1916), available for download on Google Books. This massive set includes the narratives of all the missionary friars, as well as those of Pegolotti, Marignolli, Ibn Battuta, Benedict Goes, and Odoric of Pordenone. Volume I is Yule's essay on intercourse between China and the West. While the book is out of print, I was able to purchase a used set for only $89 through an online bookseller.

10. Ruy Gonzales di Cavilo's Account

http://depts.washington.edu/silkroad/texts/clavijo/cltxt1.html

The King of Castile sent him on an embassy to Timur's (Tamerlane's) court in Samarkand. He has great descriptions of Timur and the city and the account is easy to read with lush detail as well as good travel information. 31 pages on Dan Waugh's site.

Lastly, One Favorite Modern Account from the Great Game Period

Sven Hedin, *My Life as an Explorer*, 560 pages. Listed as one of *National Geographic*'s top travel adventures of all time. Thrill as Sven races through the desert, stealing artifacts, as one by one his men and a succession of horses, donkeys, and camels fall prey to the elements or bandits.

Notes

1. For the purpose of this chapter I use the term *Silk Road* to mean the many routes between Europe and Asia over which people carried out economic, social, religious, and political activity and interacted with each other. The Silk Road, in this sense, can imply a metaphor for cultural transmission as much as an actual trade route. This chapter is based in part on a presentation given at the Annual Meeting of ASIANetwork, April 20–22, 2007, and published in a *much* abbreviated form in ASIANetwork *Exchange* in 2008. I would like to thank the East-West Center and the NEH for the Summer Institute, which inspired this volume.

2. *Medieval Sourcebook*, <http://www.fordham.edu/halsall/Sbook.html>; *Silk Road Seattle*, <http://depts.washington.edu/silkroad/texts/texts.html >; Christopher Dawson, ed., *Mission to Asia* (Toronto: Medieval Academy Reprints for Teaching, University of Toronto Press, 1980); Sir Henry Yule, trans. and ed., *Cathay and the Way Thither: Being A Collection of Medieval Notices of China*, 4 vols., (London: Hakluyt Society, 1916), available on Google Books.

3. Faxian, *A Record of Buddhistic Kingdoms: Being an Account By the Chinese Monk Fâ-Hien of His Travels in India and Ceylon (A.D.399–414) in Search of the Buddhist Books of Discipline*, trans. James Legge (Oxford: Clarendon Press, 1886. Reprint. Kessinger Publishing), 12.

4. Sven Anders Hedin, *My Life as an Explorer* [1925] (Reprint. Washington, DC: National Geographic Adventure Classics, 2003), 117.

5. Nicholas Simms-Williams, trans. "Ancient Sogdian Letter No.3," published at *Silk Road Seattle*, Daniel Waugh, ed., <http://depts.washington.edu/silkroad/texts/sogdlet.html>. Accessed June 21, 2007.

6. "Selection from the Han Narrative Histories," originally taken from the *Silk Road Seattle* Web site, Daniel Waugh, ed., but edited and simplified by Jacqueline M. Moore for classroom use. At <http://artemis.austincollege.edu/acad/history/jmoore/Syllabi/HWC22SilkSpices/SelectionFromTheHan-NarrativeHistories.html>. Accessed November 2008.

7. J. Buchan Telfer, trans., *The Bondage and Travels of Johann Schiltberger, A Native of Bavaria* (London, The Hakluyt Society, 1878), available on Google Books.

8. John of Plano Carpini, "History of the Mongols," in Dawson, *Mission to Asia*, 43–50. The letters from the pope and the reply from Guyuk as well as Benedict's narrative follow this account as an appendix.

9. William of Rubruck's Account of the Mongols, digitized from William Woodville Rockhill, trans. *The Journey of William of Rubruck to the eastern parts of the world, 1253–55, as narrated by himself, with two accounts of the earlier journey of John of Pian de Carpine* [1900] (Reprint, Maryland, Rana Saad, 2005), 11.

10. Morris Rossabi, *Voyager from Xanadu: Rabban Sauma and the First Journey from China to the West* (Tokyo, New York, London: Kodansha International, 1992), 25–26.

11. *William of Rubruck*, 35, 53–81, 93–98.

12. Rossabi, *Voyager*, 43–47, 60, 72–75.

13. Ibid., 83–169.

14. For Monte Corvino, Peregrine and Perugia see Dawson, *Mission to Asia*; Sir Henry Yule, trans. *The Travels of Friar Odoric: Blessed Odoric of Pordenone*, [1866] (Reprint. Grand Rapids and Cambridge UK: William B. Eerdmans, 2002).

15. Yule, *Cathay and the Way Thither*, III, 138, 151, 152.

16. Both accounts are from "Chinese Accounts of Rome, Byzantium and the Middle East, c. 91 B.C.E–1643 C.E.," *East Asian History Sourcebook*, <http://www.fordham.edu/halsall/eastasia/romchin1.html>. Accessed June 21, 2007.

17. See introduction to "Chinese Accounts of Rome, Byzantium and the Middle East, c. 91 B.C.E.–1643 C.E."

18. Xuanzang, *Record of the Western Regions*, trans. Samuel Beal, digitized at *Silk Road Seattle*, Daniel Waugh, ed., <http://depts.washington.edu/silkroad/texts/xuanzang.html >. Accessed June 21, 2007.

19. Ronald Latham, trans., *The Travels of Marco Polo* (New York and London: Penguin Books, 1958), 88.

20. This is the much-quoted opening line of Hartley's 1953 novel *The Go Between*.

21. Xuanzang, *Record of the Western Regions*, <http://depts.washington.edu/silkroad/texts/xuanzang.html>. Accessed June 21, 2007.

22. Marcus Nathan Adler, *The Itinerary of Benjamin of Tudela: Critical Text, Translation, and Commentary,* digitized at *Silk Road Seattle*, <http://depts.washington.edu/silkroad/texts/tudela.html>. Accessed on July 21, 2007.

23. Latham, trans., *The Travels of Marco Polo*, 81–82.

24. Adler, *The Itinerary of Benjamin of Tudela*, <http://depts.washington.edu/silkroad/texts/tudela.html>. Accessed on July 21, 2007.

25. "Recollections of Travel in the East by John De' Marignolli," in *Cathay and the Way Thither*, III: 209–69.

26. Jerry Bentley, "Travel Narratives," on the George Mason University Center for History Web site *World History Sources* <http://chnm.gmu.edu/worldhistorysources/unpacking/travelmain.html> Accessed November 2008.

27. "Selection from the Han Narrative Histories," originally taken from the *Silk Road Seattle* Web site, Daniel Waugh, ed. but edited and simplified by Jacqueline M. Moore for classroom use. At <http://artemis.austincollege.edu/acad/history/jmoore/Syllabi/HWC22SilkSpices/SelectionFromTheHan-NarrativeHistories.html>. Accessed November 2008.

Part IV

A Personal Perspective

.

Chapter 13

Flashes at the End of the Sky— My Personal Khotan on the Silk Road

Zhang He

Coming to Khotan

Khotan is a far, far away little town on the edge of the world's second largest desert—the Taklamakan—in northwestern China. It is as far away as "the end of the sky" according to a Chinese expression, set in the Kunlun Mountains between the Tarim Basin and Tibetan plateau, in one of the fertile oases where there are water resources to grow grains and raise sheep and cows. The earliest traceable residents were probably Sakas, an Iranian language–speaking people, who later mixed with Qiang-Tibetans and Turkic peoples. In about the ninth century CE, a Turkic people called the Uyghur became the dominant population. They converted to the Muslim religion, and thus there is a strong Muslim presence in the region today. The Han Chinese people have founded small communities there since the Han dynasty. Geographically and historically, Khotan has been an important trade center for caravans, pilgrims, explorers, and even diplomats: a place to stop for a rest, to reload supplies, and to conduct trade. Early travelers who stayed in Khotan and left their remarks about the place include Zhang Qian, the envoy to the West Region during the Han dynasty; Xuanzang, the Tang dynasty Buddhist monk who traveled to India; and Marco Polo, the merchant of medieval Venice and ambassador of the pope to Cathay, to name the best known. And, of course, there was Aurel Stein, the Hungarian-British archaeologist, who made Khotan even better known to the world at the turn of the nineteenth and twentieth century with his famous rediscovery of ancient Khotan.

My parents, who were assigned to work for a local newspaper, the *Khotan Daily*, brought me to Khotan in the early 1960s, when I was five years old. Both of them had been artists and editors-in-fine-arts, my father for a publishing house and my mother for the only women's magazine in Xinjiang Autonomous Region. The Chinese Communist Party (CCP) had secretly labeled my father as "having Right Opportunist opinions," and supposedly sent him to Khotan to help with frontier development. Mother had to go with him. However, since there were so many things going on in the country at that time, my parents did not know the true reason they were chosen until some twenty years later. The Party had called on educated people to go to the remote and poor areas to work. The District of Khotan sent delegations to the big cities to recruit people with up-to-date knowledge and skills; and the government tried to relocate people from big famine-affected provinces to Xinjiang. My parents, young and idealistic (naïve, too), simply believed they had responded to the party's call for the noble cause of constructing a communist new China. Only a few years earlier, the CCP had called on them to help build the new Xinjiang and sent them from Xi'an, the ancient capital city in central China, to Urumqi, the largest city and the capital of Xinjiang Uyghur Autonomous Region. Now we were on the road again from Urumqi to Khotan.

We traveled on a military truck that had a grass-green-colored heavy canvas cover. We sat on our suitcases and luggage rolls and were tossed up and down on a poorly paved road along the edge of the desert. Three other families and a few young retired soldiers were packed in with us. All of them, including my parents, were so optimistic and enthusiastic that they ignored the length and boredom of the journey. As my mother recalls, the journey was not really so bad. It was early spring. Within a day or two of driving in the dull barren desert there were occasional areas with fruit trees full of blossoms and green fields, and these always caused great excitement. All I can remember is that when we stayed in Kashgar (another large oasis town) for two days, my father took me with him to a bazaar to look around, and I became obsessed with a small colorful doll the size of my hand carved out of rough wood. It took us twelve days to get to Khotan.

Khotan welcomed us with its cheerful blossoms. For new settlers, as for travelers throughout time, its abundance of fruits, grains, and lamb meat, make strong impressions. Thanks to the everlasting snowmelt of water in the Kunlun Mountains, the crops of the oasis are secure. Actually, at the time we got there, it had such surplus that the Khotan District was responsible for shipping its grain to Tianjin, the third largest city in China, to relieve the devastating famine there.

In the town, people who were Han Chinese like my family made up only 2 percent of the population. But to my surprise, I gradually learned that Han Chinese had lived there all along. These included the families of merchants from the central provinces, descendents of Qing dynasty's officials, and those who had helped the Russians to build railways in Siberia and fought for them during World War I, but became stuck in Khotan on their way back home. Many of these people had married local Uyghurs, Russians, and in a few cases, Jews. We called these Han Chinese "Old Khotanese."

Growing up in Khotan, I was happy, although to many people it was such a miserable and unlivable place. Sand was everywhere—in the air, on the ground, in and out of your houses, all the time. No matter if you sat in an outdoor movie theatre (there was no indoor one) with rough wood benches for two hours, or went out for a short time to shop for groceries, you needed to whisk off the dust and sand from your head, shoulders, and feet before you could go into your one- or two-room apartment. Every year in the spring there were sandstorms. Sometimes they could be so thick that the entire sky became dark like nighttime. One storm could last for an hour or two. When it passed, you would find sand at least an inch thick on everything in the room, no matter how well you had shut or even sealed the doors and windows. We called these storms a "black wind" if they were very bad, or a "yellow wind" if they were not so bad.

Water, obviously, was precious here. Each government agency or residential compound had a man-made reservoir called a *laoba* to store water for daily use. There was one *laoba* in the *Khotan Daily* compound. It was the size of a standard American swimming pool and held water for about one hundred residents (employees and their families). Twice a year canals would bring in water to refill the reservoir. Most of the time the water was brownish and opaque. And of course, we were not the only ones who needed water. There were other creatures: birds, toads, bugs, water-worms, and so forth that also shared the same water. It was my mother's strict rule that we must boil the water before drinking it. Even then, it would still take a couple of minutes for the dust particles to fall to the bottom of a cup before you could drink it. My father, and later on my brother, was responsible for fetching water for the family, with our two aluminum buckets. Occasionally there were bad years when we were very short of water. When that happened, the entire family would use one bowl of water to wash all our faces in the morning, and we saved it to wash our feet in the evening.

Because of the moisture around the *laoba*, willow trees and fruit trees grew nearby. They were the famous native fruit trees: apricots,

peaches, pears, and plums. A man who was publicly denounced as a
"Counter-Revolutionary" and therefore not given any other job but
janitorial work was in charge of taking care of the *laoba* area. He seemed
to put all his time and energy into planting many kinds of flowers, which
turned the field into a beautiful garden. It was this garden which we
called the "circle of the *laoba*" that became our kids' Eden. We children
spent most our off-school time playing there. Still today we remember
this place fondly.

The grape trellises all the way to the roofs in front of our apart-
ments and office buildings created another pleasant and common scene
in the compound. We could reach the grapes right outside the apartment door. But of course, we were not allowed to pick the grapes on
our own until the autumn time when the grapes were ripe and shared
by all members of the agency. All the fruits grown in Khotan were
extraordinarily sweet.

There were never any extra material goods other than the most
basic. I remember I had only one doll all my childhood. Four of us
lived in a two-room apartment without any appliances but some make-
shift furniture, including three beds made of plain wooden boards,
a small cabinet for clothes, a wooden shipping case used for storing
the kitchen utensils, a desk and a chair, a very small eating table with
four little stools, and a large bookshelf. There was neither kitchen nor
bathroom in the apartment. In the summer we cooked outside on an
adobe stove on the ground, and in the winter we had an iron stove set
in one room for both heating and cooking. The birthday treat was two
boiled eggs for the birthday child, and the other could have only one
egg. I did not receive any birthday present until my twelfth birthday
when my parents spent more than half of their monthly salary to buy
me a violin—the greatest luxury in all their lives and mine until then. It
was heyday of the "Cultural Revolution." My parents were criticized as
"black" (meaning bad) artists with bourgeois and revisionist ideas. They
had to burn or hide pictures of any Western art except for the Russian
socialist realistic art. They did not want us to follow in their footsteps
to become artists anymore, although they had dreamed of training me
to be a painter and my brother a sculptor. But Western musical instruments were all right if we played revolutionary music on them. So there
they were, my parents, with this beautiful violin, wishing I would grow
up artistic and elegant.

Some years later I brought my violin with me to Grandma's in
Shanxi Province, just to kill time there. I had played only some folk and
revolutionary songs. One day my first uncle asked me to follow him
to his room. He moved pillows from an old broken couch that had

a strong steel frame. He crawled down looking for something under the couch. Surprisingly, he tore the seat from underneath and took out some old records, and then a record player. It was like magic. He said he had had to hide these things when the Red Guards had come looking for anything feudal or bourgeois. I helped him carry the player and records to Grandma's room where my third uncle helped set up the record player. They played famous classical music for me, which I had never heard before. All Western music had been banned during the Cultural Revolution. It was the first time in my twenty-year-old life that I heard Beethoven, Mozart, Chopin, and many others. I was electrified the moment Beethoven's No. 5 Symphony started. I stood like wood by the record player for about an hour or so without noticing my uncles' gesture telling me to sit down. How could there be such beautiful music ever in the world! And why was it not allowed to be played? The world I had known became suddenly so small and so ridiculous. A hunger for more knowledge burst out inside me. I realized there was another much larger world out there. It was the darkest moment before dawn, to use a Chinese expression. My uncles and I played the music every day after that; but we played it with low volume and with all doors and windows closed, so nobody on the street could hear us. While I tried to suck in every note of the music, my uncles fell into their remote memories and dreams. I felt very sorry for them.

I am grateful to my parents for passing on to us their optimistic attitude toward hardships. Bad as our circumstances were, their artistic eyes always sought out beauty from this sandy, barren, harsh, difficult, and forgotten corner of the world. Father's landscape paintings were of the lofty Kunlun Mountains, of peaceful pastures with grazing horses and cows, of yellow diversiform-leaved poplar trees and Red Willow shrubs stubbornly growing in the desert, of farm workers riding on little donkeys going to markets. Mother's fine-line paintings of Uyghur girls with many little hair braids and beautiful dresses dancing on Khotan-style carpets under the grape trellis, or of Tajik children caring for their baby sheep, all made us love the place and feel fortunate to live here.

The Bounty of Khotan

Khotan has been famous for a variety of beautiful things since ancient times, especially jade and silk. In the Shang dynasties (sixteenth-eleventh century BCE), Khotan jade found its way to the royal courts in central China. According to *Shanhaijing* (*The Classic of Mountains and Seas*), a book from the second century BCE, in the tenth century BCE, a

Zhou dynasty ruler, King Mu, traveled to the Kunlun Mountains to find white jade. Khotan jade has been the privileged royal and national jewel for China ever since.

Jade caught my attention in an unlikely manner. On a street corner a small, deformed Uyghur man had a little vendor's stand. On Sundays, my father often took me to the bazaar (Uyghur people use the word for market) to buy our vegetables and fruits. The bazaar was a little down from the town center at the only intersection of two dusty roads. Uyghur vendors and farmers from far away sold vegetables, fruits, herbs, spices, meat, live chicken, eggs, crafts, firewood, and local food such as *kaoyangrou*, roasted mutton kabob; *zhuafan*, rice polo; *nang*, baked flatbread; and *lamian*, hand-pulled long noodles. At one corner of the intersection next to the bazaar, a man, shortened by polio, always kneeled or curled up beside a shawl about two feet square laid on the ground. On it were some pieces of jade: wine cups, tobacco pipes, rings, bracelets, cubes for seals, and raw pebbles. The beautiful shining colors of the jade—pale green, dark green, cream, white, and orange, etc. made a dramatic contrast against his always-blackened all-weather *chiapan* (a kind of long robe) and his sheepskin hat. Very often, he was pushed and even buried in the Sunday crowds. Few people paid attention to him. As if never noticing anything around him, the little man always faced his "jewels," never calling out to sell them, never moving. He sat like a black statue. My father and I were constant visitors to his two-foot stand. I remember over the years Father bought a few cubes of jade for carving seals to stamp on his paintings. I liked to hold the cups or play with the bracelets, but Father never bought any for me. We simply could not afford such luxury. I always felt, and still feel, guilty for not buying more jade from the poor man. He disappeared during the Cultural Revolution.

It was at this little jade stand that my father enthusiastically talked to his only audience, me, about Khotan jade. The Kunlun Mountains to the south of Khotan are home to the largest deposit of the best quality jade in the world. The two kinds of jade are both produced here: nephrite and jadeite. Jadeite is a hard stone, mostly in green colors, which exists in many places all over the world. Nephrite is softer and occurs mostly in white colors. There are only three or four places in the world where nephrite deposits are known, and Khotan happens to produce a very rare type, called "sheep-grease," which is creamy white and partially translucent. In the spring, when the snow in the mountains melts, the flood pours down with rocks, and jade pebbles appear on the riverbed. Interestingly, the two different jades are always found separately in two separate rivers, the two main rivers running through Khotan, one on the east side, the other the west. So it is not a surprise to find that one river is named *yurung kash* in Uyghur language, meaning white jade, the other is *kara kash*, black jade.

Since ancient times, specialists have made a living picking up the stones in the river. But almost every person living in Khotan has had the experience of looking for jade. Each winter the town government would organize people to go to the rivers to repair the banks and dams. School kids from the fourth grade up always went. We often heard that someone we knew had found a piece of jade while digging the riverbed. Or a farm worker heading to market had randomly picked up a stone from the river to put on one side of the load on his little donkey to balance the weight, and the rock only later was recognized by prospectors in the market to be a valuable chunk of jade. Everybody in Khotan can tell you one or two stories like that.

The two jade rivers, like two living dragons, yield their most precious treasures, water and jade, to Khotan's people. But sadly, for the last ten years, under the greed of the new commercial wave, the rivers have been turned upside-down as deep as several meters. The businessmen from developed areas brought in the most powerful modern machinery to dig, screen, and to destroy the riverbed for money.

Another famous product of the region is silk. Nobody is really sure exactly when sericulture reached Khotan. It seems it has been there all along. In the Tang dynasty, Xuanzang visited the town and recorded their legend of the Silk Princess who had first brought silk to Khotan. The princess from the East Kingdom married the prince of Khotan. Before leaving for her new home, she was advised to bring some silkworm eggs and to raise the worms and make silk of her own so she would not feel homesick. However, there were strict rules forbidding anyone to take the secret of silk making out of her home kingdom. So the princess hid the eggs in her fancy hairdo and carried out the eggs to Khotan. From then on, Khotan had its own silk. More than a thousand years after Xuanzang's visit, Aurel Stein excavated a wooden board from the Tang period with a painting identified as the Silk Princess.

The kids in Khotan were all completely familiar with silk and silk production. We almost all raised silkworms as pets. We normally started with some nearly invisible tiny black dots fixed on a slip of bark paper—one egg is smaller than a dot from a ballpoint pen. The kids would tear the piece of paper into even smaller pieces to share among themselves. When the weather gets warmer in the spring, the worms come out of their shells, as tiny as the tiniest ants in a brownish color. They have to be put on white paper for the first few days so people can see them, or they could be easily wiped off without being noticed at all. As they grow they become white and fat, and two inches long. It was fun to go out of town after school to pick mulberry tree leaves for the worms. It usually took us thirty minutes to an hour one way to get to the outskirts where poplar, sand-date, and mulberry trees lined the road on both sides. Imagine how happy we were to walk under the trees with friends after a long school day, not just picking the leaves but also eating the berries! The mulberries were always so irresistibly sweet and juicy, like all the other fruits grown there, that we could not resist eating and eating until we had no more room in our stomachs. We were experts on picking the right leaves and processing them. The leaves have to be young and tender and must be washed and dried before you feed the worms. The chewing noise of the creatures is pleasant like music, but could be annoying as well, especially when you tried to sleep at night. Some of us were also good at forcing the worms to spin their silk into cocoons of whatever shape we desired, either normal or into a neat flat sheet. Many of us used the flat sheets that came as stuffing in the containers for calligraphy ink. You could fold one into a small square and fit it back into the little brass box. Sometimes, we could get special worms that would produce colored silk. I once had silkworms that produced bright yellow and pale green silk. I never figured out how they could make colors out of their bodies.

There was a silk reeling factory in town. The local farm workers bred silkworms and grew mulberry trees on their own, and then sold silk cocoons to the factory to be processed. The master workers in the factory had come from "the capitals of silk," Suzhou and Hangzhou, near Shanghai. The factory recruited many Uyghur girls and sent them to Suzhou for training. The local factory helped revive the fame of the old silk town on the Silk Road, and the parents of many of my classmates worked in the factory. Once, a story came to my mother's attention at the *Khotan Daily*. A young man on a farm in Yutian County was looking for a Uyghur girl whom his mother had nursed almost fifteen years before in Suzhou while her mother was in training there. He hoped that newspaper reporters could help him find her. He had no address or names, but my mother asked a reporter friend to work with her to find the whole story. After going to many places and interviewing many people, they found out that the girl's mother had moved to Kashgar and left the daughter with a grandmother. It took my mother and her colleague more than a year to finally locate the girl. To my mother's surprise and delight, the girl happened to be my classmate sitting right next to me. Her name is Bahargul in Uyghur, meaning Spring Flower. My mother drew a picture book about the story and published it. From then on, we thought of Bahargul as a modern silk princess.

The Desert

To many people who have never been there or who have only tasted it a little, the desert can be romantic. To most people who live next to it, it can be annoying or dangerous. But if you truly understand it, and therefore deeply love it, it is beautiful and sublime. Classical Chinese poems about the western frontier always describe the desert as vast, barren, harsh and lonely, a place where Chinese soldiers fought against "barbarians," a place to which good guys were exiled. Only when heroism, loyalty, life, and death were involved with the vastness, extreme hardships, and loneliness did the poems raise the desert to the level of a tragic beauty and a manifestation of the sublime. I am sometimes disappointed to find so few poems about the desert that express something other than sad feelings or violent death. It is a pity we have not found poems written by people who lived in the desert all their lives or by caravan travelers who walked through the desert countless times.

I have traveled along the rim of the desert several times by bus, once—that first time—by truck, from Khotan to Urumqi, and then by train, from Urumqi to Xi'an to visit my grandparents. It took eight and a half days, one-way, by bus, and four days by train. I do not know if I was fortunate or not in never having traveled by riding a camel; that seems so romantic. So, I had passed through most portions of the Silk Road east of the Pamir mountain range. On these trips, perhaps because I had lived in the desert for too long, I was not really sensitive to it or inspired by it. When jolted in the bus with your stomach turning upside down for eight days, you cannot and do not enjoy the scenery. After all, there is only one scene—the endless, dull-colored sand, sand, and more sand. However, the desert's infinite space, the blurring of the sky and earth, and the mysterious mirages that follow one after the other on the horizon, did leave strong impressions on me that remain till today.

My real understanding of the desert only occurred when I had my "reeducation" years on a farm deep in the desert. Although it is as far away from metropolitan areas as it is, Khotan did not escape the "Great Cultural Revolution." Upon high school graduation, the government sent us all deeper into the countryside to be reeducated by farm workers. The idea was to let young people learn and share the feelings of poor farm workers by living and working with them, and, at the same time, help them to improve their fieldwork and living conditions, and ultimately to realize the Communist Ideal. The idea was noble. And it was the call from Chairman Mao and Party. Although no one knew it then, we were the last ones who had to go into the countryside. The Cultural Revolution was near its end. I did not have to go because my brother went down to a farm two years earlier and was still there, and by then there was a new policy that each family could keep one child in town. However, I felt it would be shameful if I did not go. I was so naïve and idealistic. In a public speech I gave at the farewell meeting in the town I vowed that I would "take root" in the countryside and do what farm workers do for the rest of my life. I declared that from bottom of my heart. So there we were, about thirty graduates from high school and middle school, sent to a small farm west of Khotan.

The place we settled in was called Happiness Farm within Happiness Commune in Pishan County, one of the seven counties in the Khotan District. The farm was located beside a little seasonal stream twenty kilometers from the headquarters of the commune. There were about twenty or so families of Han Chinese who some years earlier had fled from the big famine in Gansu Province and managed to settle here. We were given an adobe building with one single row of rooms. Six girls shared one room, with a single adobe bed that stretched from one end of the room to the other. It was just big enough for the six of us to lay down our bedding next to each other (each space was no more than a twin size). Each of us had a wooden chest for clothes and other belongings, and two basins for washing. Water was a thirty-minute walk away in the stream.

The first room on one end of the building was the kitchen. We took turns cooking for the whole group. Because of the scarcity of water, we did not grow vegetables and therefore did not have vegetables to eat. The meals were always the same: plain corn gruel and steamed corn bread for breakfast; steamed or pan baked corn bread for lunch; and thick, salty corn porridge and corn bread for supper. No meat, no vegetables, no main dishes at all. After a few days of eating that kind of food, most of us got a seriously sour stomach and stomachache. We could not complain because the farm workers were no better off than we were. Once every couple of months, one or two of our parents would manage to come for a visit, and bring salted veggies (something like pickles) bottled in jars. The bottled vegetables had to be very salty to preserve them. There were no paved roads and no public transportation to the farm, so it was very difficult for us to get out, and for our parents to get in. We had to budget the salty veggies so they could last until the next time some parents came.

For the first six months there, we only had wheat flour buns two or three times and boiled carrots once. Never having been in such a situation, you cannot imagine how delicious boiled carrots can be. It was the best dish I had ever had, and I could not believe it of myself who had been so particular about food and never liked cooked carrots

at all. I was, indeed, reeducated in that sense. We also had a rare chance
to have meat to eat. That was when the boys had caught a wild hog
and slaughtered it. With such irresistibly delicious meat, nobody could
ever be picky about food anymore. It was a big feast. We celebrated
it joyfully.

Our daily work on the farm was to hoe up weeds, loosen the soil,
carry the manure to the cornfields, and open up the new fields, etc.
In the spring we plowed and planted; in the autumn we harvested ears
of corn, shelled the kernels, cut the corn stalks, and so forth. To our
disappointment, all work was done in the most primitive way. We used
sacks to carry everything on our backs: manure, cornstalks, and anything
else that needed to be moved. To plow a field, which was the hardest
work, we used a kind of pickaxe (which looks like a hoe but much
bigger and heavier). I could not figure out why we, as Chinese, who
had been farmers for five thousand years, still used the same methods
our great-great grandfathers had used. Some of us students did try to
improve things by using a carrying stick with baskets on the two ends,
and even a one-wheel cart to carry things.

Winter work on the farm was either gathering grass and shrubs
from the desert to make compost, or cleaning and repairing irrigation
canals. Once we went to Sangzhu, a small village at the foot of the
Kunlun Mountains near the upper reaches of our water source to work
on the construction of a major canal and dam. Sangzhu (Sanju) village
was on a shortcut to Kashmir and India, near a pass in the mountains.
The trail to the pass was dangerously steep and narrow. Caravan travelers
commonly lost their camels and even their own lives falling off the trail
on the cliffs. In the March 1996 issue of *National Geographic*, there
is an old photo Owen Lattimore took in 1926 showing his group on
the pass. But back then none of us knew much about the place. For
almost ten years, schools had been paralyzed by the Cultural Revolution so that we had not had history or geography classes. There were
no regional maps, either; actually, no concept of regional maps existed
in our mind. You can imagine how surprised I was ten years later in
the United States when I saw satellite photos of Pishan County shot by
NASA and published in the February 1996 *Scientific American*, clearly
showing the mountains, villages, and even the streets in town.

We had been assigned to work there for two weeks, but instead,
we stayed for only two days because the farm workers really pitied us
and sent us back. At the construction site, there were mountains on
one side and desert on the other. There was no house or any kind of
shelter for us to stay in. We built a circle with rocks for cooking. At
night, we slept on the open ground. The experienced people taught us

how to find a good spot out of the wind for sleeping at night. This was usually behind sand dunes where the roots of a Red Willow bush were buried. There was always wind at night; it was just a matter of whether it would be big or small. But even the least wind could be very annoying, and the wind was sometimes dangerous. We soon learned that we had to cover our faces completely with wool scarves, or sand would fill our noses, mouths, eyes, and ears, and even choke us. Even covered, we still felt we were chewing sand all the time. At first it was such an exciting experience to sleep in the open desert. I thought I would look at the sky counting the stars or dreaming about romance all night. Oh! There was no way you could lie on your back with your face up. All your open orifices would fill up with sand. Reluctantly, I covered myself completely under the thick quilt, as it was very cold too. In the morning, we all laughed at each other, because we still looked like people made out of sand, no matter how well we had covered ourselves, but there was no water to wash ourselves with.

In the desert, any degree of a wind could make a sand twister. It was fun to look at the twisters dancing around. Sometimes I suspected that Wang Wei's famous line of poetry about desert might refer to a twister, although it is usually interpreted as a signal fire:

> In the vast desert, there's a lone smoke straight up;
> Above the long river, the setting sun appears so round.

Gathering shrubs for compost was another normal winter task. One cold winter day, very early in the morning, we got up, packed a little corn bread and water, and went into the desert. Our job that day was to cut, gather, and bring back shrubs for making compost. The air was chilly and fresh. The sky was dark blue and full of bright stars. I saw the entire sky like a huge upside-down bowl resting on the earth. It was beautiful and awesome. I wondered if there could be any better scene in the world. Nobody talked. We were simply quieted by the overwhelming cosmic silence.

There are only a few kinds of plants that grow in the area. Among them are the Red Willow (a kind of five-stamen tamarisk), a shrub tree whose thick, deep roots we commonly dug up for firewood, and Camel Thorn (*Alhagi maurorum*), a shrub with needle-sized thorns that had no use except to rot for compost to fertilize soil. I always felt sorry to cut them down. In the dull desert, they were the only colorful things that could cheer you up. Red Willows have small red-purple blossoms stuck along the branches, and Camel Thorns grow tiny purple flowers the size of your smallest fingernail. But Camel Thorns were the ones we wanted for this particular job.

The shrubs grew so widely scattered that we had to spread far apart in the desert. We reminded each other to keep close enough so that we would not get lost. Quite soon, we could only hear but not see each other. At one point I helped two girls put their bound loads on their backs ready to go. When the sun rose high, I saw the last one off. She actually insisted that we two go back together. But I did not feel I had enough. So I told her to go ahead, and I went farther into the desert to gather more shrubs. I did not notice how much time passed before I had gotten a big hill of thorns gathered in front of me. I pressed and tightened it with my whole body. I tramped and jumped on it so it could be bound into a bundle. I did my best to tighten and tie it. (Many years later, in the States, I could still feel one or two thorns poking out here and there from the sheep's wool trousers I had knit myself and had on that day.) But the bundle was still bigger than me, and it was so heavy that I had very hard time loading it up on my back.

From behind me, one would have been unable to see a person, only a hill of bushes moving slowly. It took several minutes before I suddenly realized that I should check the direction to make sure I was heading home. There were no roads, no trails, but only endless sand. I was afraid that I might not be able to put the bundle back on my back again by myself, so at first I hesitated whether I should drop the load and go up to a hill looking for some signs. But my instinct told me I should do it right away. So I dropped the load and climbed to the highest sand dune nearby.

When I got to the top of the hill and looked around, I was shocked. All directions looked exactly the same. There was not a single sign showing the way home. The farm with the little village was totally beyond the horizon. Instantly I collapsed, my heart beating wildly and my legs shaking. A great panic fell over me. At first my mind went blank and then I could not think rationally. I do not know how long I kneeled there before I realized I should do something. I managed to stand up and call out loudly, hoping somebody was still around. "Is there anybody here?" "Can somebody hear me?" But to my horror, no sooner had I begun to shout, than I realized that my voice was completely gone. I could not get a sound out. I had lost my strength. I pulled up myself and tried again. "Hello! Is anybody there?" This time the sounds came out of my throat but were immediately swallowed by the vast empty space. The power of the desert overwhelmed me. I looked up. It was cloudy. I could tell the sun was directly overhead; there is no way to use the sun to determine directions when it is noon. And I knew that since we came to the farm I had not paid attention to the directions anyway. I was totally lost. Desperate, I began to think about death.

Taklamakan, the name of the desert in Turkic language, simply means "a place one can go into, but will not come out of." All the stories about the desert poured into my memory. Some told how people lost their way in the desert and were only found mummified years later. Some described how the wind moved sand dunes from one side of the road to the other overnight but kept them in the same shape, so after a storm travelers did not notice the change and therefore went the wrong direction and got lost forever. There were even reports of well-prepared explorers vanishing in the desert. Furthermore, everybody knew that cargo truck drivers always went in a group carrying more than enough water and food in case there were unexpected situations.

Now, kneeling in the sand, alone, shaking all over, I found the stories became real. But I was only nineteen, too young to die. "I cannot die like this." I had to find a way out. The sun above me reminded me that it was noon, and I had several hours to try to find a way out before it got dark. I struggled to stand up. Still, every direction looked the same, all reached to the end of the earth. I slid down the hill, leaving the food bag behind as a sign, and looked around. Something caught my eyes. Goat droppings. And then, donkey droppings. My heart almost jumped out of my throat. I knew I might have a chance. Soon I found the animals' tracks. I crawled on the ground to study them. But, the more tracks I found, the less confidence I had. There were too many of them, and they pointed in all directions. I did not want to give up. I decided that I would go to the direction I felt right by instinct, and if I did not see any sign of a village within one or two hours of walking, I would come back and go in the opposite direction, but staying always within range of the animals' tracks. Having made this decision, I felt relieved a little, and went up the hilltop to eat my corn bread. The bread was already frozen, too hard to bite. I put it under my arms to warm up. I still had some water in the canteen, partially frozen. Luckily it was not summer, or I could have been fatally dehydrated already.

While eating, I began to think whether or not I should carry the big load—my whole purpose in life by this time. "Maybe it won't be too late to drop it if the plan goes really wrong," I persuaded myself. So again, I knelt down and leaned my back against the load, put my arms into the rope loops, straightened myself up, bent a little bit forward, crawled a few steps on my hands and knees, and then lifted the weight and stood up. Before I started to walk, I dug out a Red Willow stick from the sand hill, and dragged it on the ground while I walked in order to draw a line as a sign, in case I had to come back to the opposite direction. I actually changed directions several times. I did not know how long it took me to get out of the desert. I did not have a watch. When I suddenly saw the trees in the distance, I staggered and almost cried. I said to myself, "Don't fall. Hold up. Don't fall. You've survived." Several years later, when I sat in the university library reading Jack London, I felt like saying to him, "Hey, buddy, I've been there."

When I arrived at the village it was late afternoon. I was too exhausted to step up even the three inches off the ground to the scales, to record how heavy a load I had carried. Two guys had to pull me up. I had carried a load of about 130 pounds, twenty pounds heavier than myself. At supper that evening, one of my roommates said to me, "You stupid girl. Why are you so serious? Look at our Boss! He brought only twenty pounds. Do you want to die?" I only smiled wearily. I did not explain to anybody why I came back so late. I did not want to talk about my experience of life and death casually to those who had not had a similar experience or who would not understand such things. I needed time to myself to think and digest the meaning of it. It was like a sudden enlightenment that made me begin to think both philosophically and realistically about my life.

Before graduation, the school authorities and the Communist League had organized us to study Chairman Mao's theories and discuss the significance of the strategy of letting students go "up the mountains and down the countryside." At those meetings, we studied a case of "Regional Realization of Communism"—the Da Zhai Commune in Shanxi Province. There the farm workers had reached the goal of supplying enough food to the commune members and even achieved a surplus to contribute to the government as well. They could afford to send all the children to school and were able to provide medical care to all the members of the commune. All the villagers had become better off equally. The example was exciting and tangible. In the past, communism had looked so vague and abstract to me, but now it became concrete and something that could be accomplished. If people of Da Zhai could make it happen, we could too. So when I got to the farm, I calculated how much income I could possibly make, and then the total needed for all villagers to have sufficient food and other supplies. To my disappointment, I realized that at my best, by the end of each year I would be earning a share of 330–440 pounds of grain plus 100–200 yuan cash (about 10–20 dollars). This meant I would be able to have about one pound of grain for food and 0.40 yuan (or 4 cents) cash to spend per day. But I thought that was good enough.

Now, suddenly, I felt how ridiculous the Communist Ideal was and how foolish we were to believe in such nonsense. How could I have been so naïve and so stupid and so blind? How could we change people's life and change the world by using the most primitive production methods and by sacrificing young people's lives in the desert? How could such minimum basic survival conditions be the Communist Ideal?! What is communism anyway?

The Taklamakan desert transformed me. Not because I was scared by the desert, but because I experienced the overwhelming power of nature so closely and truly. If I had ever had a religious feeling, it was then, when I was overwhelmed in the desert, kneeling to pray to it to have pity on me. Even when I overcame it, it was with great awe and respect, and I saw my limits.

New Jersey
July 5, 2007

About the Authors

Tongdong Bai is an assistant professor of philosophy at Xavier University in Cincinnati. He has teaching and research interests in Chinese and comparative philosophy. In addition to a few articles on pre-Qin thought, he is finishing a book in Chinese that argues for the comparative and contemporary relevance of classical (pre-Qin) Confucian political philosophy. He would like to thank Daniel Bell, Jiang Qian, Morris Rossabi, and Jonathan Skaff, from whom he has benefited greatly in writing this essay. He would also like to thank Jacqueline Moore and Rebecca Wendelken for the excellent editing work.

Marybeth Carlson is an associate professor of history at the University of Dayton, in Dayton, Ohio, where she teaches courses on European and world history. In 2005 and 2006, she directed education abroad programs in China, and she taught at Shanghai Normal University in 2006. Her research projects examine poor relief and conditions for working women in the eighteenth-century Dutch Republic. She is currently at work on a book about revolutions in the colonial Atlantic world.

Hirsh Diamant teaches at the Evergreen State College in Olympia, Washington. In his teaching he develops interdisciplinary programs that reach across boundaries in the arts, culture, humanities, education, and human development. At Evergreen he has been developing the field of Silk Roads Studies. Hirsh was born and raised in Russia and educated in Israel and China. As an artist and educator he received several awards including a Ford Foundation award, an American Israel Cultural Foundation award, and most recently the Secretary of State Award for innovative teaching and community development.

Robert W. Foster is associate professor and chair of History at Berea College in Kentucky. He would like to thank the National Endowment for the Humanities and the East-West Center in Honolulu for allowing him to participate in the summer institute that inspired this piece. He would also like to thank the editors for encouraging his participation in the project.

Ronald K. Frank is associate professor of history at Pace University in New York. He teaches Japanese, Inner Asian, and Russian history, as well as general East Asian studies courses. He places a consistently heavy emphasis on Central Eurasia in his teaching and has conducted travel courses to Mongolia and the Silk Road. His research interests are in Japanese and comparative legal history in which he has published numerous articles and book chapters.

Marcia J. Frost is associate professor of economics and East Asian Studies at Wittenberg University in Springfield, Ohio. She teaches courses on economic development, economies in transition, and American economic history, as well as a first-year interdisciplinary seminar on Mongolia, team-teaches a course on the Silk Road, and co-directs a month-long program in China "Along the Silk Road." Her research is on early-nineteenth-century Indian demographic and agrarian history. She thanks her NEH colleagues for their inspiration and the editors for their diligence and drive.

Gang Guo is Croft Associate Professor of Political Science and International Studies at the University of Mississippi. He teaches graduate and undergraduate courses on comparative politics and on East Asian studies. His research interests revolve around the quantitative study of local politics and governance issues in mainland China. Since 2005 his articles have appeared in such journals as *Journal of Contemporary China*, *Journal of Chinese Political Science*, *Comparative Political Studies*, *Asian Survey*, *Political Research Quarterly*, and *Journal of East Asian Studies*. His current research projects investigate the relationship between local leadership turnover and policy performance in China. He can be reached online at www.olemiss.edu/~gg.

Jacqueline M. Moore is professor of history and former director of Asian Studies at Austin College in Sherman, Texas. She teaches American and Asian history, including courses on the Silk Road. She is the co-editor of the African American History Series and is the author of several books including *Booker T. Washington, W.E.B. Du Bois, and the Struggle for Racial Uplift*. She just completed a book on nineteenth-century cowboy masculinity, and is also planning an introductory history of the Silk Road for undergraduate use. She would like to thank the authors in this volume for their hard work.

Joan O'Mara teaches Asian art history and has directed the East Asian Studies Program at Washington and Lee University in Lexington, Virginia. Since first traveling the Silk Road in 2004, she has taught seminars on the subject and participated in the 2006 NEH Summer Institute that occasioned this volume. She has also chaired the Executive Board of ASIANetwork, a consortium of undergraduate liberal arts colleges with Asian Studies programs, and recently worked with a Luce Foundation–funded initiative to survey Asian art in collections of consortial member institutions. She is co-editor of *Reading Asian Art: Windows to Asia in College Collections*, forthcoming in 2009.

Rick Parrish earned his PhD in political science from the University of Wisconsin-Madison, and has taught at Loyola University New Orleans and West Texas A&M University. He is the author of *Violence Inevitable: The Play of Force and Respect in Derrida, Nietzsche, Hobbes, and Berlin* (Rowman and Littlefield, 2006), *The Anthology of Global Political Theory* (Prentice-Hall, forthcoming 2009), and several articles. Rick's current research focuses on contemporary interpretations of classical Chinese political thought. He now lives near Washington, D.C., where he advises on international politics.

Masako N. Racel is an instructor of history and the director of the AP World History Summer Institute at Kennesaw State University in Kennesaw, Georgia. She is also a member of the Executive Council of the Southeast World History Association (SEWHA). Her areas of interest include world history, East-Asian history, and intellectual history. She teaches world history survey courses at Kennesaw State University while pursuing a PhD at Georgia State University. She would like to thank Dr. Stephen Rapp of Georgia State University for contributing his valuable insight to this article as well as the National Endowment for Humanities, the East-West Center in Hawaii, and all the participants of the Institute for providing an opportunity to study the importance of the Silk Roads, and the inspiration to write this piece.

Morris Rossabi is a professor at Columbia University and City University of New York and a historian of China and Central Asia. He is the author of several books including *China and Inner Asia* (1975), *Khubilai Khan: His Life and Times* (1988), and *Modern Mongolia: From Khans to Commissars to Capitalists* (2005). He is the former chair of the Arts and Culture Board of the Soros Foundation and has helped organize exhibitions at several major museums including the Metropolitan Museum of Art and the Asian Art Museum of San Francisco. He is a contributor to the *Cambridge History of China* and travels frequently to China, the Middle East, Central Asia, and Mongolia.

Rebecca Woodward Wendelken is an associate professor and chair of history at Methodist University in Fayetteville, North Carolina. She teaches courses in Central Asia, Russia, and world history. In 2004 she spent the summer in Mongolia as part of a Fulbright-Hays program. She is currently working on a monograph on copper mining in Kazakhstan during the late tsarist and early Soviet period and is doing research on the transfer of pottery motifs and technology along the Silk Road.

He Zhang is an associate professor of art history at William Paterson University of New Jersey. She teaches Pre-Columbian art, Asian art, and other general art history courses. Her research interests include Olmec imagery and hieroglyphic writing, comparative study of ancient American and Asian cultures, and the art of the Silk Road in Central Asia. She has published scholarly articles on ancient American ritual arts and writing systems. She is currently working on two book projects: *Cosmological Expressions in the Arts of Ancient Mesoamerica and Asia* (in English), and *Maya Art and History* (in Chinese).

Index